Understanding Religious Ethics

A Complete Guide for OCR AS and A2

Richard Wright

OXFORD
UNIVERSITY PRESS

OXFORD
UNIVERSITY PRESS

Great Clarendon Street, Oxford OX2 6DP

Oxford University Press is a department of the University of Oxford.
It furthers the University's objective of excellence in research,
scholarship,and education by publishing worldwide in

Oxford   New York

Auckland Cape Town Dar es Salaam Hong Kong Karachi
Kuala Lumpur Madrid Melbourne Mexico City Nairobi
New Delhi Shanghai Taipei Toronto

With offices in

Argentina Austria Brazil Chile Czech Republic France Greece
Guatemala Hungary Italy Japan Poland Portugal Singapore
South Korea Switzerland Thailand Turkey Ukraine Vietnam

Oxford is a registered trade mark of Oxford University Press
in the UK and in certain other countries

© Richard Wright 2010

British Library Cataloguing in Publication Data

Data available

ISBN 978-1-85008-525-6

FD5256

10 9 8 7 6 5 4

Printed in Singapore by KHL Printing Co Pte Ltd

Paper used in the production of this book is a natural, recyclable product
made from wood grown in sustainable forests. The manufacturing
process conforms to the environmental regulations of the country of
origin.

Acknowledgements

Advisory Editor: Libby Ahluwalia
Editor: Hannah Lees
Page design: Clifford Hayes, www.hayesdesign.co.uk
Page layout: The Manila Typesetting Company (MTC),
www.mtcstm.com
Cover design: Rosa Capacchione

Front cover image: ©iStockphoto.com/GeorgeClerk
AS divider © Piccaya/Dreamstime.com; graphic elements on each page
(clouds etc.) © Photodisc; p.12 © Brigida Soriano/Fotolia; p.17 © FELoader.
Image from BigStockPhoto.com; p.21 © The Art Archive/Alamy; p.29 ©
jlgoodyear. Image from BigStockPhoto.com; p.31 © INTERFOTO/Alamy;
p.42 © geom. Image from BigStockPhoto.com; p.46 © iStockphoto.com/
Steven Wynn; p.53 © Joe Gough/Shutterstock; p.55 © iStockphoto.com/
nicoolay; p.65 © Jeff Blackler/Rex Features; p.70 © Rex Features; p.73
© Antonio V. Oquias/Shutterstock; p.81 © Dorio Diament/Shutterstock;
p.92 © Colin Underhill/Alamy; p.99 © Digital Stock; p.101 © iStockphoto.
com/hannahgleg; p.114 © hsandler. Image from BigStockPhoto.com;
p.128 © Bill Cross / Daily Mail /Rex Features; p. 132 © iStockphoto.com/
ktsimage; p.137 © nruboc. Image from BigStockPhoto.com; p.145 ©
newsteam.co.uk; p.147 © iStockphoto.com/syagci; p.150 © jgroup. Image
from BigStockPhoto.com; p.156 © iStockphoto.com/David Sucsy; p.162
© AP/Press Association Images; p. 165 © cameraman/Fotolia; p.170 ©
iStockphoto.com/Nikada; p.178 © iStockphoto.com/Craig DeBourbon;
p.182 © iStockphoto.com/Thomas Bendy; p.185 © NICK UT/AP/Press
Association Images; p.189 © vivalapenler/Fotolia; A2 divider © Tersina/
Dreamstime.com; p.201 © photodog. Image from BigStockPhoto.com;
p.204 © Ellende. Image from BigStockPhoto.com; p.208 © Pictorial Press
Ltd/Alamy; p.217 © David Fisher/Rex Features; p.219 © iStockphoto.com/
Catherine Yeulet; p.229 © iStockphoto.com/Georgios Kollidas; p.231 ©
iStockphoto.com/Duncan Walker; p.235 © Bettmann/Corbis; p.243 ©
iStockphoto.com/picture; p.248 © CSU Archives/Everett Collection/Rex
Features; p.253 © iStockphoto.com/Karen Ilagan; p.259 © Gardawind/
Shutterstock; p.265 © iStockphoto.com/Jan Rysavy; p.276 © iStockphoto.
com/jean frooms; p.285 © mark yuill/Fotolia; p.292 © Clare Kendall/Rex
Features; p.294 © Joe Gough/Fotolia; p. 307 © morane/Fotolia

Bible quotes are taken from *The Holy Bible: New Revised Standard Version
(Anglicized Edition)* (Oxford University Press, 1995)

p.13 Human Rights Act 1998, 1998, Chapter 42. Office of Public Sector
Information (OPSI) website: www.opsi.gov.uk Crown copyright material
is reproduced with the permission of the Controller Office of Public
Sector Information (OPSI). Reproduced under the terms of the Click-Use
Licence.; p.149 Medical Ethics: Select Committee Report HL Deb 09 May
1994 vol 554 cc1344-412 © Parliamentary copyright. Reproduced under
the terms of the Click-Use Parliamentary Licence.; p.151 Assisted Dying
for the Terminally Ill Bill [HL]: Volume II Evidence © Parliamentary
copyright. Reproduced under the terms of the Click-Use Parliamentary
Licence.; p.159 Committee HC Deb 21 April 1868 vol 191 cc1033-63 ©
Parliamentary copyright. Reproduced under the terms of the Click-Use
Parliamentary Licence.; p.236–237 © Norman Swartz
1997, 2004.

Although we have made every effort to trace and contact all copyright
holders before publication this has not been possible in all cases.
If notified, the publisher will rectify any errors or omissions at the
earliest opportunity.

Contents

Preface

This book looks at Christian ethics and the major secular alternatives to it. It contains everything that you will need for the examinations at AS and A2. It also has additional material that will allow you to understand Ethics better.

You will find that there are features throughout the book that are there to help. These include **key terms** that are clearly marked. These should be learnt, as using them appropriately will help you gain a good grade. **Key points** summarize essential information. **Extension notes** are designed to extend your knowledge and to help you understand better the background to the various topics examined. There are suggestions for further reading in the **Develop your knowledge** sections.

The **To think about** sections are designed to stimulate your thoughts. They are intended to provoke discussion, debate and, possibly, argument. Ethics is not an easy subject, but it is an important one as it affects the whole of your life. Ethical 'solutions' are often controversial. Relish this fact and try to be open to the ideas of others, both those in this book and those in your class.

Author's thanks

A few thanks are necessary. I am extremely grateful to Minh Ha Duong and Hannah Lees who have worked hard to keep me on track. I am particularly indebted, here in the West Midlands, to my long-suffering colleagues, especially Canon Andrew Hutchinson, Naina Cheetham and Geddes Cureton. Without their support this work would not have been possible. I also wish to thank my former colleagues down south, especially Viv Graveson and Dr Chris Pines. It was my great pleasure to work with them for many years.

I am also indebted to several other people. My late parents inspired me to look at human life in its entirety and to treat people equally. I owe a lot to two priests. Canon Charles Smith, who I have known my whole life, taught me to laugh at myself and to realize the value of every human being. My thanks also must go to Revd Dr John Thewlis and his wife Sarah. Friendship never dies; it only changes. To the thousands and thousands of students who have been taught by me, I will forever be grateful. Last, but not least, I dedicate this book to Ray and Honey. Life is not easy. It's not meant to be. Yet all things come right in the end!

AS

AS

What is ethics?

Introduction

The word ethics is derived from the ancient Greek work *ethike* meaning 'morals'. This term is itself derived from another Greek word, *ethos*, meaning 'nature' or 'disposition'. It can be understood as a trait, something that a person has that makes that individual a good citizen; an upright member of the *polis*, the city-state.

The ancient Greeks established city-states on the coastline of the Aegean Sea and in Sicily. From the beginning, these city-states created laws (legal codes) which citizens and slaves were obliged to obey. Soon, however, these regulations were shown to be of limited value. Laws were obeyed yet society did not improve. Increasingly, these states began to develop norms of behaviour, conventions, which were designed to establish peace and harmony. They were being civilized. For example, in most city-states it was lawful for an owner to beat his slave to death for a variety of offences but, at the same time, it was considered as socially unacceptable to do so. What was legal was not the same as what was right. What was legal was very different from what was ethical. It became clear that the people needed more than law to control the excesses of human nature. In this climate, ethical values began to replace the narrowly-focused laws that governed the city-states.

A second dimension was added to ethics around the time of Plato (428/427–348/347BCE). This was not the social norm that made the city-state civilized, peaceful and harmonious. It was instead the particular qualities that make the individual a good person. The **sophists** concentrated on humans and human society, they looked at creating social conventions which they believed were different from one society to another. Ethical principles were no more than social conventions, which differed from society to society. These sophists were, in modern terms, relativists. Plato, on the other hand, was not. His ideas opposed the sophist view of ethics in two ways. He argued that:

- Morality is universal and absolute. It does not change from one society to another.
- The pursuit of changeless ethical qualities such as virtue, justice, beauty and love makes the individual a good person.

Key term

relativism – the theory that there are no universal truths, truth is relative to the subject and can vary from person to person and society to society.

Key point

Ethics is concerned with good/bad and right/wrong. Do they exist? If they do, what are they? If they do, how are they applied to human life?

While all ancient societies created norms of behaviour to ensure peace and harmony, it was from ideas of ancient Greece that Western thought developed. Today modern ethics is concerned with four fundamental questions, which relate to the way in which an individual should live. These are:

1. Do good/bad and right/wrong exist?
2. What is meant by the moral terms good/bad and right/wrong?
3. Are there good/bad or right/wrong actions?
4. What ought the individual or society do in order to be morally good or to do right?

Moral philosophers, since the time of Plato, have disagreed about the answers to these questions. These arguments have resulted in the development of three different branches of ethics.

The three branches of ethics

Modern ethics is made up of three branches. They are:

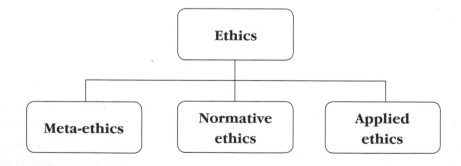

Meta-ethics

The word *meta* means 'beyond' or 'outside of'. Meta-ethics is not concerned with particular ethical theories or moral problems, such as abortion or euthanasia. It does not engage with practical issues of what to do and how to behave. Meta-ethics relates to ideas that are outside of the practical issues of how to behave. Essentially meta-ethics covers a variety of **epistemological** questions, including: Does moral good and right exist? What do good and right mean? It also addresses specific questions, such as: How do we know that a particular ethical argument is useful to answer moral questions?

Normative ethics

Normative ethics is concerned with practical or substantive issues of what constitutes morality. It is not only **descriptive**. It is also **prescriptive**. It seeks to influence the individual or society, by stating that there is a method by which the right moral action can be discovered.

However, since the time of Plato and Aristotle (384–322BCE), moral philosophers have disagreed over what this approach or method should be. These disagreements have created various types of ethical theories:

- **Consequentialism**, based on the consequences or results of an action (see Chapter 4 Utilitarianism).
- **Deontological** morality, based on a sense of duty or obligation towards others and to yourself (see Chapter 3 Kantian ethics).
- **Virtue Ethics**, based on improving the nature of the **moral agent** (see Chapter 11 Virtue Ethics).
- **Voluntarism**, based on the moral agent's obedience to a set of norms or values that are generally God-given (see Chapter 5 Christian ethics).

Key point

Normative ethics is concerned with moral theories that contain norms (ethical principles) that govern human behaviour.

Applied ethics

Applied ethics is concerned with the application of moral theories to particular issues. The issues examined in this book are abortion, the right to a child, euthanasia, genetic engineering and issues relating to war and peace at AS level. At A2 level the issues are business, environmental and sexual ethics.

Key terms

epistemology – the theory of knowledge including the origin of knowledge, the roles of experience and reason in generating knowledge and the validity of knowledge.

descriptive – describing how things are.

prescriptive – instructing how to act.

consequentialism – the consequences of an action solely determine whether it is the right thing to do.

deontology – a moral system based on duty. What is moral is what you have a duty to do.

We can apply any of the ethical theories studied in this book to any of these issues. For example, we can use theories of Utilitarianism to consider the morality of euthanasia and also to discuss whether it is right to produce genetically-modified crops.

Other ethical divisions

There are other divisions within ethics. The most important of these are the divisions between:

- absolutist and relativist approaches to morality
- objectivist and subjectivist approaches to morality
- deontological and teleological approaches to morality.

These three divisions are examined in the following sections.

Moral absolutism

Introduction

Moral absolutism covers a variety of ethical theories. Some have their origins in religion while the remainder are secular. Moral absolutism is also known as **moral** objectivism.

Moral absolutists believe that certain ethical norms or precepts exist independent of human experience. These moral principles are objective and universally applicable. **Objectivity** and universalizability are crucial; moral norms cannot differ between societies. The American philosopher Louis Pojman (1935–2005) makes the point that a moral absolutist does not have to believe that all moral laws are universally applicable. It only requires one moral principle to be non-negotiable for a particular ethical theory to be regarded as absolutist.

Moral absolutists not only assert that an ethical norm for one society is valid for all. They go further. They argue that it would be illogical if an ethical principle were morally right for one society yet ethically wrong for another. How can something be

Key terms

Virtue Ethics – morality based on the good an action produces for the moral agent.

moral agent – the person who makes an ethical decision or is primarily affected by one.

voluntarism – morality based on obedience to the will of God or a system of thought.

objectivism – the notion that certain things, especially moral truths, are independent of personal or communal opinions or values. Moral objectivists assert that the validity of ethical statements cannot be a matter of subjective personal choice.

both good and bad at the same time, just because you have crossed an international border? It seems to be common sense that, for example, the torture of prisoners is either morally right or wrong in all societies and places and at all times. As a result many of those opposed to torture argue that it seems intuitive that all human beings, all things being equal, should be treated in the same way. You would not wish to be tortured; by applying this principle universally it is clear that you would not want another person to be treated in this way either.

Ethical absolutists are divided over the grounds on which moral laws are universally applicable. These divisions are important. Take the example of torture. Most moral absolutists would agree that torture is morally wrong. But on what grounds is it wrong? Is it because torture is intuitively wrong as it degrades the fundamental value of human life? Is it because what is bad for one individual is ethically wrong for all? Is it because torture conflicts with the unchallengeable rights of an individual? Or is it because, for the religious Jewish or Christian person, 'God created humankind in his image' (Genesis 1:27) and 'breathed into his nostrils the breath of life' (Genesis 2:7)? To torture a human being therefore is equal to torturing God.

While moral absolutists agree that there are fundamental ethical laws they disagree over the **authority** behind these laws. Three distinct types of moral absolutism are examined here, any one of which may be used to illustrate an absolute ethical theory. They are:

- human rights
- Platonic idealism
- religious absolutism.

Key terms

universalizability – the principle that moral values are universal and therefore universally applicable.

form – in Plato an ideal that exists independent of human life, such as beauty, truth or virtue.

Key point

Absolutism asserts that at least one moral principle must be universally applicable

Plato

Plato put forward the first significant Western example of an absolutist ethical theory in the early years of the fourth century BCE. Plato gradually developed what is known as the theory of forms. The forms are concepts that are eternally constant. They give meaning and structure to the universe. These forms are eternal and unchangeable whereas the material world is in a constant state of flux.

Plato's moral philosophy based on forms was absolutist in character and opposed to the relativism of the sophists.

Key term

salvation history – the idea that the Bible documents God revealing himself in history as Saviour.

In Plato's later work these unending and unchanging **forms are reducible to a single unalterable ideal**, the **Form of the Good**. Indeed, Plato came to the conclusion that forms are only aspects of the Form of the Good. Therefore, beauty is the Form of the Good in aesthetics, justice the Form of the Good in politics and virtue the Form of the Good in ethics. The purpose of the Form of the Good is to link other forms together in harmonic unity and to give humanity an ethical wisdom that gives meaning and value to life.

All the forms are linked in harmonious unity with the Form of the Good.

Religious absolutism

Religious absolutism comes in a variety of forms, which are to be found in the sections on Natural Law (see Chapter 2 Natural Law) and the Divine Command theory (see Chapter 5 Christian ethics). Most world religions accept the premise that God created the universe. This belief led to the development of the **Natural Law theory**, which draws from both the biblical understanding of Creation and also from the work of the ancient Greek philosopher, Aristotle.

Many Christians also believe that the Bible is **the inspired Word of God**. In the Bible, God starts an historical process that will lead to the Incarnation, when God enters the world in human flesh as Jesus Christ. The Bible is therefore salvation history, which gradually unfolds the **divine nature** and God's moral teaching. The **Divine Command theory** was developed from this understanding of the Scriptures.

Human rights theory

An understanding of human rights theory is important for your course because:

- it is an example of moral absolutism
- it affects every practical ethical issue, from the right of a woman to have a child to euthanasia.

The basis of this theory is that the individual is endowed with certain fundamental rights. Jack Donnelly, in *Universal Human Rights in Theory and Practice,* argues that human beings have certain unchallengable rights, such as the entitlement to protection by the state. The Catholic Natural Law philosopher John Finnis gives several examples of what he considers as basic human rights. These include being able to have children and being free from the threat of murder. Elsewhere the *European Convention on Human Rights* states that 'Everyone has the right to freedom of thought, conscience and religion'.

Rights are a consequence of being human. They derive from the dignity or value placed on human life. Cristóbal Orrego, the Chilean human rights philosopher, defines a right as:

> . . .*that-what is-due-to-another because he has a title to that object. (Cristóbal Orrego, 2006,* Human Rights & Wrongs: Exceptionless Moral Principles, *Thomas More Institute available from www.thomasmoreinstitute.org.uk/node/36 [accessed 28/05/2010])*

Orrego gives the example of life itself. As he puts it:

> *'My life', for example, could be called a right in this sense, as it belongs to me. (Orrego,* Human Rights & Wrongs: Exceptionless Moral Principles*)*

Today human rights pervade every area of society. Human rights have an impact on moral and legal decision-making surrounding issues such as whether the terminally ill should have the right to take their own life. It affects the right to have a child and the right to an abortion.

Human rights theorists agree that individuals have certain intrinsic and unchallengeable rights. They differ over the extent of these rights. Some human rights theorists speak of **primary rights** and **secondary rights**. To help distinguish between the two, imagine human beings' lives before the creation of nations and governments. At this stage human beings had certain natural rights. They were free to work, to move from place to place, to express their opinions, to be happy or sad, and to raise families. Such rights (that are independent of the state) are known as **primary rights**. **Secondary rights**, on the other hand, presuppose the existence of a state and government. Such rights include the right to medical treatment, to education and to social welfare. Today many leading human rights scholars talk of **families of rights**. These include:

1. **Security rights**, such as the right to live peacefully in a community without the fear of being attacked, kidnapped or unlawfully killed.
2. **Legal rights**, such as the right to property, the right to protection in the workplace or the right to join a trade union.
3. **Political rights**, such as the right to vote or the right to freedom of speech.
4. **Welfare rights**, such as the right to education and the right to medical healthcare.
5. **Equality rights**, such as the right to be treated equally and fairly irrespective of ethnicity, disability or sexuality.

To think about

List five things you would consider to be human rights. Would these rights apply to anyone, wherever they lived and whatever their circumstances?

Strengths of absolutism

Absolutism has a number of strengths. The most significant of these are:

1. **Morality is not based on individual or group preferences** but rather on absolute and universal values.
2. It allows **different societies to share common values**, some of which are to be found in the Ten Commandments, for example, 'You shall not murder. You shall not commit adultery. You shall not steal.' (Exodus 20:13–15)
3. It allows for the possibility of **dialogue between and within different societies**, because they have shared values.
4. It **gives authority to human rights legislation**, which is designed to protect people. A relativist approach to ethics has, it is argued, no place for fundamental human rights.
5. It **allows one society to evaluate the morality of another society**. It is argued that, before the time of human rights conventions, it was possible for genocide to take place and not be punished.

6. It gives **clear moral judgements** in situations where there is a need for ethical guidance, for example, in a war or conflict situation.
7. It allows **quick ethical decisions** to be made.

Weaknesses of absolutism

Absolutist ethical theories have a number of weaknesses. Many of these are set out in the sections on particular absolutist moral theories. The most significant disadvantages of absolutism are:

1. It takes **no account of historical developments**. There is a static quality to an absolutist theory; what was moral in the past will be moral in the dim and distant future. Consequently, an absolutist ethical theory has no place for the evolutionary nature of humanity in general, and of moral theories in particular.
2. It takes **no account of cultural differences**. It is argued that moral laws differ from society to society but this is not recognized by absolutists.
3. It takes **no account of individual lifestyles**. There is no recognition that people may differ in their perception of morality due to lifestyle differences.
4. It takes **no account of the situation**. Moral decisions do not take place in a vacuum. Scholars argue that absolutist moral theories ignore the circumstances in which ethical judgements are made.
5. There is a big gap between absolutist theory and its implementation. How is it possible to move from an ethical theory to its application in the world without falling into subjectivism? It is argued that you may know a particular absolutist ethical theory but how you implement it will depend on your own personal values.
6. The application of absolutist ethical theories is often **condemnatory and harsh**. The moral law has to be obeyed no matter what the consequences to the individual.

Relativism

Introduction

Relativists believe that there are **no objective truths**; moral values are relative to societies and to individuals. The expression 'one man's terrorist is another man's freedom fighter' reveals the ideas behind moral relativism. Different societies and individuals view concepts such as goodness, justice and truth in a variety of ways. No particular view is the right one. The job of ethics, therefore, is not to create morality but rather to interpret and reflect on individual and social traditions. Relativists believe that moral statements are products of the interaction of the individual with the social values and customs of his or her society.

To think about

Explain what the phrase 'one man's terrorist is another man's freedom fighter' means, and how it relates to the idea of relativism.

According to relativism there are no absolute truths which are common to all human beings. However, relativists do argue that there is one philosophical absolute (although they do not use the word absolute to describe it). This is the foundation principle that **truth is relative**. This is not open to debate. The whole basis of relativism would be undermined if it were.

Some moral relativists assert that the individual should be free to develop his or her morality and then relate that free choice to a particular group of people who share that morality. An example is the idea put forward by the American philosopher Richard Rorty (1931–2007). This form of relativism is often called **subjective relativism**, since it involves the individual subject creating his or her moral framework for life.

Others argue that morality is constructed within social groups, for example a faith community. This form of relativism is known as **cultural relativism**. Fundamental to this idea is the principle that the **morality of one society is no better than that of any other; they are just different**. This type of freedom creates a multicultural society, which is a collection of minorities, equally valued and equally free.

Relativism is therefore divided between those who argue that morality is based on personal choice (known as **subjective relativism**) and those who see it as a cultural phenomenon (**cultural relativism**).

Types of cultural relativism

Cultural relativism can be divided into four distinct types. They are:

- **The diversity thesis**: This asserts that ethical rules differ from society to society as a result of unique historical developments. As a society develops in isolation from its neighbours it produces moral laws, often based on **social taboos**, which are unique to that society. This was the view held by the anthropologist Emile Durkheim (1858–1917). In his thesis *The Elementary Forms of Religious Life,* Durkheim supports this view by referring to Australian Aboriginal culture. Each group of the Aboriginal peoples has a unique moral code centred on a particular sacred spot. Morality stems from communal feelings of ownership.

Ayers Rock/Uluru, Australia. According to Durkheim each group of the indigenous peoples of Australia has a focal point that gives them a sense of identity. From these sacred places unique communal moral norms grow. It follows that moral norms will vary from community to community as the sacred places vary.

- **The dependency thesis**: William Graham Sumner (1840–1910) argued that the morality of a society is dependent on the aspirations, beliefs, environment and history of that society. Each person has a different set of beliefs arising from personal circumstances. Over time morality develops as a kind of common denominator; common laws and traditions that win social approval. There is nothing transcendent or mysterious about such moral laws or norms. Society's values change with time and it is possible for moral laws to alter radically over the years, for example, attitudes towards slavery. As a result, there are no moral absolutes either between societies or within them.

- **Conventionalism**: Conventionalists argue that moral rules (conventions) emerge on an ad hoc basis; based, not on a set of values, but on reactions to particular and often immediate circumstances. Conventionalism recognizes the importance of the social environment in generating moral customs and beliefs. This means that if you commit a murder in a country where the culture permits the execution of murderers, then it is morally acceptable to do so. If it is not the custom of that state, then it is ethically wrong to execute the murderer.

- **Pyramid relativism**: Pyramid relativism starts from the principle that all societies and individuals develop fundamental principles that govern their morality. These principles are either universal, such as the idea of charity or love, or they are specific to a particular society. These basic principles are the top of a pyramid, from which societies create a vast number of other moral norms that originate from these basic principles. A society therefore creates its moral pyramid not by accident but rather by logical deduction from first principles. Different societies have different first principles and therefore one society's pyramid will be different from its neighbours.

Key point

Moral relativism asserts that there are no universal moral principles. Morality is relative to particular societies or groups of individuals.

Subjective relativism

Some philosophers believe that morality depends not on the customs of a particular society but on the views of the individual alone. Morality is like taste or aesthetic judgement; it is a matter of personal preference or choice. Therefore you may feel no compulsion to help an impoverished neighbour, whereas another person may see it as his/her moral obligation. There can be no debate since both attitudes are right for the person concerned.

The sole basis for criticizing an individual's moral judgement is, in this form of relativism, over the matter of **hypocrisy**. If x does not follow his/her moral code then there is no internal consistency and a condemnatory judgement can be made. Yet hypocrisy is not a matter of being consistent over how you treat people. It is about self-consistency and the question, 'Am I being true to myself?'

Rorty is one of the chief exponents of this form of relativism. He maintains the need for a **relativist framework** for society in order to maximize the freedoms of the individual. People can have completely different beliefs and still live in harmony as long as they respect and tolerate each other.

Rorty goes further. He thinks it possible for an individual to live, at the same time, in different **micro-societies** (societies within society). This can easily be illustrated. You go to college or school and you meet your mates. Are your moral attitudes different when you are with them than when you are with your parents? Rorty argues that people vary their moral norms according to which micro-society they are with at the time. You may behave differently when you are playing sport or clubbing with friends than when you are visiting your grandparents. Is one set of values better than another? Rorty argues that they are just different. Individuals can live with different moral norms without being hypocrites, as long as they understand their customs vary from micro-society to micro-society. For subjective relativists, notions of good and bad have no interpersonal evaluative meaning or relevance.

To think about

'Criticizing the moral values of another society leads to moral imperialism and eventually to conflict.' Discuss.

Strengths of relativism

Relativists argue that there are a number of important strengths to their moral position. They are:

1. Relativists believe in **tolerance** and **respect** for other people's societies. Modern societies are by nature multicultural and multi-ethnic. Mass migration has caused a radical difference in societies all over the world. It is impossible to change this human development. Rather, it has to be embraced. Relativism is therefore the only practical moral philosophy for postmodern society. It is non-confrontational and rejects the idea that one group's moral norms are superior to any other. This respect for diversity produces a peaceful and harmonious society, which is a moral necessity. Caleb Rosado puts this idea in an interesting way:

   Cultural Relativism, as a new way of seeing, is a necessary optic to perceive the socio-cultural reality in today's multicultural, world society. (Caleb Rosado, 1994, Understanding Cultural Relativism in a Multicultural World (Or Teaching the Concept of Cultural Relativism to Ethnocentric Students), *available from www.rosado.net/pdf/Cultural_Relativism.pdf [accessed 28/05/2010])*

2. There is a **rejection of moral imperialism**. The twentieth century was beset by wars that killed hundreds of millions of people. These wars were largely fought for ideological and cultural reasons. Relativism rejects the unique truthfulness of any ideological position. It rejects the idea that, for example, Western liberal values should be imposed on other cultures. It is up to those societies themselves to develop by their own internal dynamics.

3. Relativists argue that language is not neutral, which seems to be common sense. **Culture determines language**. Relativists assert that it is self-evident that words

vary in their meaning from society to society, language to language. Therefore words like goodness or justice, truth or freedom, mean different things in different parts of the world and at different times in history.

Extension note

Patterns of discovery

Norwood Russell Hanson (1925–1967) was an eminent philosopher of science who was influenced by the linguistic philosophers of the twentieth century, such as Ludwig Wittgenstein (1889–1951). Hanson, in his book *Patterns of Discovery*, gave an example of the way differences of understanding can produce radically different ways of understanding elementary things. Let's suppose you are looking at the sun rising in the east. What do you make of this event? You would see the rising of the sun in completely different ways, depending on whether you believe the earth is at the centre of the universe or not.

Relativists use this example to show that even simple ideas like the rising of the sun have within them preconceived notions, often culturally based, that mean one man's rising sun is another man's turning earth. The way human beings perceive things is a product of culture.

4. Relativism argues that **truth lies in the ideas of the masses**. The American philosopher Pojman puts it this way:

   Truth is with the crowd and error with the individual. (Louis P. Pojman, Ethics: Discovering Right and Wrong, *Wadsworth Cengage Learning, 2009)*

   This comment describes only one type of relativism. It may appear as both a strength and a weakness. Pojman implies that the views of the crowd are good since the selfishness of the individual is weakened by the needs of the group. An example of this might be the traditions of football supporters who congregate on a match day. They are a tightly knit micro-society, bound by their common devotion to their club. Pojman suggests that the views of the crowd filter out the selfishness of the individual. Pojman's statement can, however, be seen in a negative way. Groups may not necessarily filter out personal prejudices. They might magnify them.

5. In the case of subjective relativism, the individual's character determines his or her moral framework. Hugh LaFollette, an American relativist philosopher, makes the point that most ethical theories ignore the **personality of the individual** who makes moral decisions. Subjective relativism puts personality to centre stage. Again, this may be both a strength and a weakness.

Weaknesses of relativism

The following criticisms of relativism can be made:

1. Relativism fails to appreciate that **certain moral values are universal**. This is a criticism made by the philosopher Stephen Law among others. There is a distinct problem when relativism is related to certain issues that some societies consider to be immoral but which other societies consider to be morally good. When the Spanish conquered Mexico in 1521 they found human sacrifice widely practised among the Aztecs. Furthermore human sacrifice and cannibalism were perceived as morally just. For the Spanish conquerors this was profoundly disturbing. Most cultural relativists have difficulty in condemning these Aztec practices, preferring to criticize the conquistadors for their imperialism. A few though, including Clyde Kluckhohn (1905–1960), argue that cultural relativism reveals the universal nature of moral law. He wrote:

Every culture has a concept of murder. (Clyde Kluckhohn, 1995, 'Ethical Relativity: Sic et Non', Journal of Philosophy 52:663–77 cited in Mark Timmons, Moral Theory: An Introduction, *Rowman & Littlefield, 2002)*

The heart of a sacrificial victim being offered to the Sun-god, in the form of an eagle. The picture is taken from an Aztec manual on how to perform human sacrifice. The conquistadors found the idea of human sacrifice morally repugnant.

Yet the Aztecs practised human sacrifice on a wide scale but did not regard this as murder, in exactly the same way that in China and in some states in America the death penalty is not seen as morally wrong.

To think about

Can there be any universal moral values in a multicultural, multi-ethnic and relativist society?

2. It argues that the job of ethics is **essentially descriptive**. The British philosopher Simon Blackburn attacks this view. Morality cannot and should not be essentially descriptive. He argues that if ethics just describes and analyses the customs of different societies it would not be possible to condemn corrupt, evil or foolish actions. There has to be a role in ethics for moral judgements. This would not be possible if the non-judgemental and culturally sensitive approach is followed.

3. It views culture as the sole influence on human life and therefore on morality. Moral problems are often complex. They are determined by a variety of issues. To see relativism as the single moral factor of any society is to ignore other problems. Relativists wish to create a society that is multicultural in nature. It is argued that relativists believe that a multicultural society will be tolerant and morally good, as people know more about each other's cultures. This has not been the case in human history, as there are more than just cultural problems that divide human beings from each other.

4. It creates a distinct problem over its opposition to cultural imperialism. What is the difference between **social reform** and moral imperialism? Cultural relativists reject any interference by one culture in the morality of another. What does this mean for social reform? Take the example of William Wilberforce and his campaign against the slave trade. Would the social reformer be seen as intolerant rather than being a courageous innovator? Moral progress becomes ethical interference by one society on the values of another. This prevents human progress and therefore a society's culture becomes rigidly fixed in the past.

Deontological and teleological ethical approaches

Imagine it is a Saturday evening and your parents want you to go with them to your uncle's fiftieth birthday party. You don't really want to go. Your mates are going to a friend's house. You are faced with a dilemma. What should you do? You decide to go to your uncle's party. You know it will not be that exciting; family parties never are. Yet you must go! Why? The answer is that you go out of a sense of duty, duty towards your parents and towards your uncle. You do not want to let them down. This approach to ethical decision-making is called deontological, from the Greek word *deon* meaning 'duty'. Deontological ethical theories maintain that moral decisions are made out of a sense of duty.

Suppose, however, you were faced with the same dilemma but this time you knew that your uncle always threw good parties and that you would have a great time. The choice now is between which party is likely to give you the most pleasure. Utilitarianism is one example of a teleological or consequentialist form of morality. The consequences of an action determine whether it is the right thing to do, whether it maximizes pleasure or not. Therefore you decide to go to your uncle's party because your attendance there will please your extended family and their friends while not going to your friend's house will only bring sadness to a few.

Deontological ethics is duty-based while a teleological ethical theory looks solely at the consequences of an action – the end result or *telos*. Details of the strengths and weaknesses of a deontological ethical theory are given in Chapter 3 Kantian ethics. The strengths and weaknesses of a teleological approach to ethics are examined in Chapter 4 Utilitarianism.

Key terms

deontology – a moral system based on duty. What is moral is what you have a duty to do.

teleology – designed for or directed towards a final end.

Key point

Deontological ethics is duty-based, while a teleological approach is based on the end result of a moral decision.

Objectivism and subjectivism

Consider again the questions that ethics tries to address. Among them is 'how is it possible to know what is good or what is right?' There are two ways of looking at these questions. Some writers argue that moral truths are simply social conventions or the particular attitudes of an individual or group of individuals at a certain time. These are known as subjectivists, since moral norms are based on personal opinions. The other group argues that moral concepts have an objective meaning independent of human attitudes. Therefore, for example, justice is not a matter of personal opinion or even the collective views of a group of people. This view is known as objectivism.

> ## Key point
>
> An objectivist argues there are universal moral truths. They are true today; they may not be true in years ahead. A subjectivist claims that moral truths exist but that they are statements of personal or social beliefs. They are not objective.

The approach of the moral objectivist lays down certain universal and therefore absolute values. Modern moral objectivists do not argue that these are fixed eternally but rather they are certain until they are held to be false. Accordingly, to compare a moral law with the law of gravity, scientists might discover for whatever reason gravity does not exist. Nothing may be eternally fixed. Human beings cannot know.

The nineteenth and twentieth centuries witnessed a long debate between those who believed that ethical truth was found in the self, in the subjective 'I' (in 'me'), and those who argued that it could only be discovered in the 'other', in objectivity. The approach of the moral objectivist lays down certain universal and therefore absolute values.

Moral subjectivism makes the claim that moral statements refer not to objective qualities or values but solely to human attitudes. They are true because human beings think they are. The human mind therefore constructs morality. Subjectivism is also known as **cognitivism**. Subjectivism can either be individual or interpersonal. Therefore relativism may be seen as subjectivist since it is determined by either individual or collective views.

One advantage of subjectivism is that it sees morality in terms of the individual's value system. This seems to fit in with a person's experiences. You compare the values of other people and other societies on the basis of your own moral position. It is argued that human beings do not naturally view other people's morals by a series of objective criteria. What is more you regard your particular moral assumptions as true, if only to you.

Practice exam questions

(a) Explain moral relativism.

The (a) question tests your knowledge of a subject. The starting point for this essay could be the assertion that moral relativists reject the idea that there are any universal moral norms. They argue that there is no such thing as a moral absolute; a moral norm that is applicable universally in time and space. You might then wish to go on to describe the **two basic types of moral relativism**. The first of these is **cultural relativism**. You could outline broadly the four distinct theories – **diversity thesis, dependency thesis, conventionalism and the pyramid theory**. Each one of these can be tackled in a couple of sentences. The second type of moral relativism is **subjective relativism**, based on the individual rather than on cultural developments. You could use the ideas of Richard Rorty to illustrate this.

(b) 'Relativist theories offer no convincing reason for people to be moral.' Discuss.

The (b) question tests your evaluative skills. You could start with the idea that relativist theories reject the idea of universal moral values. If moral values differ from society to society this might make them feel arbitrary and therefore support the statement that relativism does not offer a convincing reason for people to be moral. Relativist theories are essentially descriptive. A cultural relativist position makes it difficult to criticize practices that, you might argue, all societies ought to find morally wrong. In subjective relativism, morality becomes a question of personal choice. To counter the statement you could argue that relativist theories promote peace and understanding in a multicultural and multi-ethnic world. This may seem like a basic convincing reason for being moral.

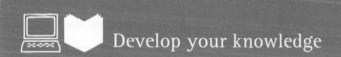 Develop your knowledge

There are numerous good introductions to ethics. Among these are:

Ethics: An Essay on the Understanding of Evil by Alain Badiou (Verso Books, 2002)
Ethics: Discovering Right and Wrong by Louis P. Pojman (Wadsworth Publishing Co., 1998)
A Companion to Ethics by Peter Singer (ed.) (Blackwell, 1993)
Ethical Theory by Mel Thompson (Hodder & Stoughton, 2005)
The Puzzle of Ethics by Peter Vardy and Paul Grosch (Fount, 1999)

Introduction

There is no such thing as a single Natural Law theory. There are a variety of theories of Natural Law that have developed since the time of the ancient Greeks. At the core of Natural Law is the belief that God has (or the gods have) ordered the universe in a certain way. It works in what appears to be an orderly and purposeful fashion and, it is argued, this structure and order is not accidental. It is deliberate and this has important implications for the human race. Human beings have a duty to conform to the Natural Law which God has made. Therefore, to keep to the Natural Law is morally good. To go against that law is morally bad.

Natural Law is principally a religious ethical system but it is not completely so. It is possible to be an atheist and still believe in Natural Law. Hugo Grotius (1583–1645), the Dutch Protestant philosopher, argued that even rational atheists were able to accept Natural Law. He wrote:

And what we have said [about Natural Law] would still have great weight, even if we were to grant, what we cannot grant without wickedness, that there is no God. (Hugo Grotius and William Whewell, Grotius on the Rights of War and Peace: An Abridged Translation, *John W. Parker, 1853)*

Therefore it is possible for atheists to accept Natural Law if they remove God from the equation and insert nature instead.

To think about

Do you think there is natural order in the universe? Where do you see evidence of order in the world around you?

There are problems with the Natural Law theory; two of these problems need to be considered from the outset and they divide Natural Law philosophers. The first major problem is what does the word 'natural' refer to when it is used in the term Natural

Law? Here there is a division of opinion. Some writers argue that 'natural' refers to human nature while the majority of Natural Law theorists argue that it refers to the whole universe.

There is a further division among Natural Law philosophers. The term Natural Law is both descriptive and prescriptive. Some scholars maintain that these two elements of Natural Law should be separated. They argue that Natural Law is the best explanation of the way in which the universe works, but that human beings are under no obligation to follow completely the route laid by Natural Law.

Aquinas

St Thomas Aquinas (1224/25–1274) was a prolific writer. Among his greatest achievements was the development of the Natural Law theory.

Before Aquinas the theology and philosophy of the medieval Church was often confused and contradictory. Aquinas attempted to give Catholicism a logical order and structure that it previously lacked. His philosophy is based on two fundamental authorities, the Bible and the writings of Aristotle. Earlier writers, such as Anicius Manlius Severinus Boethius (470/75–524), had relied heavily on the ideas of Plato. This led to the physical world being regarded as a shadow; as in the analogy of the cave, it was of no lasting value. For these writers, existence was just a step on the way to heaven.

Aquinas saw things differently; he looked to Aristotle for his inspiration. According to Aquinas, the natural world does matter. As Colin Morris puts it:

Thanks to the union of Aristotle and Christianity in the works of Aquinas, it was henceforth possible to look at man either *as a natural being* or *as a being designed for fellowship with God, whereas before the former could not be conceived separately from the latter. (Colin Morris,* The Discovery of the Individual 1050–1200, *Medieval Academy of America, 2004)*

The idea of Natural Law was central to the changes made to Western thought by Aquinas. His development of Aristotle's teleology gave the universe a natural order and structure. Human beings were placed firmly within this order. God was shown to be the creator of a logical and beautifully-crafted scheme of things. Natural Law was God's order set within the parameters of the universe.

Key terms

descriptive – describing how things are.

prescriptive – instructing how to act.

teleology – designed for or directed towards a final end.

Key term

Torah – the Torah contains the first five books of the Old Testament, the so-called books of Moses. The books are Genesis, Exodus, Leviticus, Numbers and Deuteronomy. These books have within them the Mosaic Law, which is central to Jewish ethical tradition.

Key point

There is no single Natural Law theory, yet all theories of Natural Law are based on the idea that nature has an inbuilt teleology.

The influence of the Bible on Aquinas

A lot is made of Aristotle's influence on Aquinas. However, it must not be forgotten that Aquinas developed Aristotle's theory only because it was consistent with the Bible. Biblical support for Natural Law relies on the writings of St Paul (4BCE–CE62/64). His letter to the Romans is generally regarded as his most important work. The letter concentrates on the nature of God's law, and how human beings are to be saved from sin. In Romans 2 Paul explains why both Jews and Gentiles are under this law. His argument is straightforward. First, he argues that Jews are under the laws of the Torah, the first five books of the Old Testament. The Torah includes the Ten Commandments (Exodus 20 and Deuteronomy 6). Among these commandments are:

You shall not murder.
You shall not commit adultery.
You shall not steal. (Exodus 20:13–15)

Jewish people follow such laws because God gave them to Moses on Mount Sinai. They are part of God's law. Yet Paul continues his argument by referring to non-Jews. Gentiles do not kill or steal yet they do not know the Ten Commandments. They are ignorant of the Torah, yet they keep the commands. How can this be? Paul argues that God has given humanity two laws – the Law of Moses (the Torah) for Jews and the Law of Nature for Gentiles. In Romans 2 Paul writes:

When Gentiles, who do not possess the law, do instinctively what the law requires, these, though not having the law, are a law to themselves. They show that what the law requires is written on their hearts, to which their own conscience also bears witness; and their conflicting thoughts will accuse or perhaps excuse them on the day when, according to my gospel, God, through Jesus Christ, will judge the secret thoughts of all. (Romans 2:14–16)

God's law being written into nature is a by-product of Creation. Paul finds it impossible to separate morality from the material creation of the universe.

God, who is omnibenevolent and all-loving, created a perfect world to mirror his love and goodness. Moral laws are therefore inbuilt into Creation. The world may have fallen because of original sin, but the divine law is still found imperfectly rooted in the matter of Creation.

To think about

'The law only condemns a person. It can't reform the individual.' Is this also true of Natural Law?

Aristotle's idea of function, purpose and end

The Bible taught Aquinas that God had created the universe with order and purpose. Having discovered this through Scripture, Aquinas developed these ideas. His explanation of how Natural Law works is taken from Aristotle.

Aristotle argued that the universe contains both rational forms and material substance. The two are joined together; you cannot separate forms from substance. In his *On Physics* and *On Metaphysics* Aristotle sets out these ideas on the nature of animate (living) things. He argues that all things have (a) material substance and (b) a reason for their nature.

In exactly the same way human beings possess a body and a soul. The soul is the rational form behind both human beings in general and behind the particular individual. The soul or form comes first and is unchanging because it is conceptual. The body, which is always changing, develops to accommodate the form.

This idea is equally true of parts of the body as it is of the human being as a whole. Each organ has a material substance and a rational form; a body and a soul. Aristotle explains this by reference to the eye. How did the eye develop? Aristotle asserts that the idea of sight must come before the existence of the eye. He cites the story of a partially sighted man. The man is walking along and sees on the ground a ball of jelly. He says to himself that this looks like his other eye. He picks it up and inserts it into the empty socket of his other eye. But it is just a lump of jelly and he sees nothing through it. The lump of jelly may look the same as an eye but it does not possess the rational idea of sight. It is simply jelly.

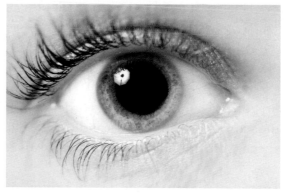

In Aristotle, for the eye to function it requires the material substance of the eyeball and the rational form of sight.

The example of the eye reveals Aristotle's view that everything in nature has a function, purpose and end. Elsewhere he gives the example of a house to develop his argument. A house also has a function, purpose and end, but as it is manufactured, human beings determine these.

Key term

eudaimonia – Greek for happiness, flourishing or a state of contentment.

Teleological chart: Aristotle

Function	Purpose	*Telos* (end)	Final end
Sight	To see	Eye that sees	Eudaimonia (happiness/contentment)
Protection	To protect from the weather	House that protects	Eudaimonia (happiness/contentment)

In both cases, eye and house, eudaimonia is the final end. Eudaimonia is the final end of all things; it can be defined as **happiness**. It is best understood as the contentment which comes when a thing achieves its purpose.

Since every animate object is designed to achieve eudaimonia, it follows that if everything worked efficiently and effectively this would lead to a harmonious relationship between everything. Take your body as an example. If one organ does not function properly it has a knock-on effect on other organs of the body. Aristotle argued that everything in nature has a harmonious relationship with everything else. This is like the keys on a piano; they exist separately but their end is achieved when they work harmoniously with each other. A happy person is someone whose organs function properly and in harmony with each other. A happy society is one where all individuals and groups work for their own good in relation to everyone else.

This harmoniousness is Aristotle's inbuilt law. The process consists of:

1. There is a reason for everything.
2. These reasons are contained within the rational forms.
3. The reasons do not exist physically but conceptually.
4. Material things are then mixed with the rational forms.
5. The material substance and the rational form exist in tandem.
6. Material substance and rational form are of equal worth.
7. They exist to complement each other.
8. They have different functions.
9. Human beings have body (**soma**) and soul (**psyche**).
10. Other things have **material substance** and **rational form**.

Aristotle's Natural Law brings order out of the state of flux. It points to a link between the natural order of things and morality. It is teleological since everything moves in a specific direction to an end, which leads to happiness.

Aristotle hints that there is an unmoved mover at work in the universe. Christian writers saw in Aristotle's philosophy support for the biblical notion of a God who brings order out of chaos. God's hand is at work, creating a structure for existence based on the function, purpose and end of all things. Aquinas adopted and developed Aristotle's understanding of Natural Law.

Extension note

The X factor: order out of chaos

Early medieval society was often in conflict. Marriage, family life and property rights were not yet fixed and therefore disputes between illegitimate siblings were common. Bloodshed and family feuds were normal. During this time the Church, with its legal system, was the only source of stability. The Natural Law theory spearheaded the Church's moves to regulate society and to make Christian Europe peaceful yet secure.

The role of Jesus as the foundation stone of Christian society was crucial. This was often expressed symbolically. The first letter of Christ in Greek is *chi*, which appears as X in the Greek alphabet. From the eighth century the letter X became symbolic of Christ and of the benefits the Church believed God brought in Christ. These benefits all contain the letter X. In Latin they are LEX – LUX – PAX – REX (law – light – peace – king).

God's law brought, as Alfred the Great among others put it, the king's law of justice and peace. An X was placed on the obverse side of coins to show that the Anglo-Saxon kings were ordained to follow God's law. Before the Battle of Hastings, King Harold had coins minted with the X of Christ and pax (peace) stamped on them.

Aquinas' ideas of purpose and perfection

1. The perfection of Creation

Aquinas, using Aristotle's philosophy and the Bible, transformed attitudes to Natural Law. His starting point is the nature of God as Creator. Two points should be noted. First, God is changeless and, thereby, rationally consistent. He cannot change his mind or do something that contradicts his eternal nature. Secondly, God is good and therefore it follows that Creation must be good since God cannot create anything that runs contrary to the divine nature.

Thomas Aquinas (1224/25–1274), known as Doctor Angelicus (Angelic Doctor). Aquinas merged the philosophy of Aristotle with the doctrines of the Christian Church to create a systematic form of Christianity.

Aquinas asserts that:
1. Nothing with God is accidental or by chance.
2. God made Creation.
3. Creation therefore was not caused by chance.

4. Creation happened for a reason.
5. The Bible states (in Genesis) that Creation is good.
6. Thus Creation exists to reveal God's goodness.
7. What is true of the whole of Creation is equally true for what exists within Creation.
8. Everything has a reason for being.
9. Everything is created to reveal God's goodness.
10. Natural Law regulates everything.
11. Therefore Natural Law exists to reveal something of God's nature.

The material universe, therefore, points to the omnibenevolent and all-loving divine nature from which it emerges. Reflecting Aristotle, Aquinas believed that the universe and every part of it have a natural teleology. This teleology of all things conforms to God's eternal law. Natural Law is the method by which human beings share in God's eternal law.

2. The primary and secondary precepts

Aquinas developed Aristotle's teleology. He agreed with Aristotle that eudaimonia is the natural end of man and of all Creation. He gave this a moral connection, believing that human happiness can only be achieved by pursuing certain goods.

Key point

Aristotle and Aquinas saw the natural end of man and Creation as eudaimonia. However they differ in what they mean by this. Aristotle viewed eudaimonia as the contentment attained when something achieves its purpose. Aquinas saw it as achieving heaven and thereby being in union with God.

Christians are called to be perfect just as their God is perfect. Christians therefore have to live in accordance with the Natural Law. As Aquinas put it:

Good is to be done and pursued, and evil is to be avoided. (Thomas Aquinas, Summa Theologica, *Hayes Barton Press, 1947)*

Following this law will make people happy and content, because they will be close to God their creator. This eternal relationship with God is, in Aquinas, the *telos* of all human life. In the *Summa Theologica*, Aquinas sets out the **fundamental goods** to which all human beings, being made in God's image, are inclined. They are:

- the preservation of life
- human procreation (reproduction)

- the advancement of knowledge and learning
- living in a peaceful and harmonious community
- the worship of God.

To achieve heaven it is necessary for each person to live a life in harmony with these goods. It is part of human nature to wish to preserve life, to have children, to gain knowledge and to live in harmony and peace with other people. These are known as the primary precepts.

Key term

primary precepts – general rules inbuilt into human beings as a consequence of being made by God.

Extension note

Cardinal virtues and capital vices

The word cardinal is derived from the Latin *cardo* meaning 'hinge'. Aquinas asks us to imagine a box with four hinges. The box is moral goodness, which the Natural Law contains. The four hinges are the four cardinal virtues of justice, prudence (showing care and thought for the future), temperance (moderation or restraint) and fortitude (courage in pain or adversity). Yet Aquinas' virtues are not as simple as that. Aquinas divides each of the virtues into different parts. Imagine these as screws, which ensure that the virtue is held fast to Natural Law. There are eight screws in the hinge of prudence. They are – caution, circumspection (being wary and unwilling to take risks), foresight, ingenuity (being clever and inventive), memory, passivity, reason and understanding. Aquinas argues that it is not possible for a person to be prudent without any of these. Aquinas divides the other three virtues in a similar way. Consequently, being virtuous is a very hard path to follow.

Later medieval writers added the further three virtues of faith, hope and love (charity) in order to parallel the capital vices. These virtues are taken from Paul's first letter to the Corinthians, while the original virtues appear in the works of Plato. The seven virtues and seven vices first appear together in Dante's (1265–1321) *Divine Comedy*, which was written shortly after Aquinas' death. The vices are anger, avarice (greed for wealth), envy, gluttony (greed), lust, pride and sloth (laziness).

The **cardinal virtues** relate to all five of the primary precepts. Aquinas contrasts these with the seven **capital vices** which act to undermine the primary precepts.

The primary precepts are descriptive. Aristotle believed human reason or wisdom should be used to move from what *is* to what *ought to be*. Aquinas' theory suggests that human beings have an obligation to:

1. create general laws that reflect these moral goods and virtues
2. abide by these laws.

It is the job of the secondary precepts to set out the way in which the primary precepts can be implemented. This requires reason and argument.

Key term

secondary precepts – any rule that is rationally deduced from one of the primary precepts. Thus suicide is morally wrong because human beings have a natural inclination to preserve life.

Key point

Primary precepts describe the general rules that human beings are inclined to follow; secondary precepts are the practical application of these in specific areas.

Aristotle did not intend his teleological framework for nature to set down strict moral laws. It was a framework; descriptive not prescriptive. In the same way, Aquinas does not say how the primary precepts should be enforced in every situation. In Part III of the *Summa Theologica* Aquinas uses a method of argument and counter-argument to develop his moral philosophy. He shows, in this section, how difficult it is to put the primary precepts into practice. Below are a few examples of the way in which a description of human life can become a moral prescription.

Primary precept	Possible secondary precept
Life is about gaining knowledge, wisdom and understanding.	Refusing education to girls is morally wrong. Education should be free to all.
Life is about being co-creators with God, being procreators.	Masturbation is morally wrong. IVF should be permitted.
Life should be preserved and human dignity sustained.	Suicide is morally wrong. Transplant surgery should be permitted.

3. Reason discovers God's law

You may have noticed how, in Aquinas, the primary precepts are descriptive and the secondary precepts demand a response; they are prescriptive. Aquinas needed to explain how it is possible to move from a description of what Natural Law is to a prescription of how human beings should behave in life. Following Aristotle and the biblical view that human beings are created in the image of God, Aquinas believed that human beings are rational creatures. They have inbuilt into them an ability to work out rationally how life is to be lived morally. Human beings can understand the principle of function, purpose and end.

Rational debate, as Aquinas presented in his *Summa Theologica*, will lead human beings to understand how Natural Law works. It will also lead them to see beyond the laws of nature to God's eternal law. Yet, human beings can never fully grasp this eternal law.

Aquinas believed that four laws exist; the Natural Law is just one of these. The laws are:
• **Eternal law** – God's wisdom, unknown to human beings.
• **Divine law** – God's law as revealed through the Scriptures.

- **Natural Law** – God's law as revealed through nature and interpreted by reason.
- **Human law** – laws made by societies for the good of people.

Such laws must be examined rationally with care. This is not simple, yet Aquinas believed that it is possible to understand those that conform to God's eternal law and those that do not. Aristotle again plays an important role in his interpretation. Aquinas makes the function, purpose and end of Aristotle's teleology more complex. The complexity is seen in the chart below.

Key term

reason – the ability to analyse an argument, to criticize it and to calculate logically its strengths and weaknesses.

Teleological chart: Aquinas

Term	Material cause	Efficient cause	Formal cause	Final cause	End A leading to End B	End B
Meaning	Object – What changes?	Method – What event causes change?	Function – What process is involved in the change?	Purpose – For what purpose does change take place?	End – What is the result?	Final end – What is the common aim?
Example 1	Student/ Teacher	Tutorial	Education	Knowledge	Examination success, but to what purpose?	True happiness which lies in oneness with God
Example 2	Man/ Woman	Intercourse	Relationship	Procreation	Baby, but to what purpose?	True happiness which lies in oneness with God

The chart shows Aquinas' understanding of natural teleology. It begins with the **material cause**. This is simply the physical form or process that undergoes change. If we are making a cup of tea, the material cause is the various material objects that go into creating a good cup of tea – milk, sugar, tea, water, electricity and a kettle.

The **efficient cause** is the method by which change occurs. It is called efficient because Creation is a product of the nature of God. God is efficient. Simply put, things change by means of a process that is the simplest possible method to achieve it. The cup of tea again illustrates this. The efficient cause is the method by which the tea is made. To make your cup of tea you need to be efficient. You need to put the right amount of water in the kettle, make sure that the water boils, add a tea bag. Efficiency is required or you will not produce the best cup of tea.

The **formal cause** is the underlying process involved in the change. As far as the cup of tea is concerned, this involves the way in which water boils and the effect that water has on the tea bag.

The **final cause** is the purpose of the cup of tea. It has been made to quench thirst and thereby to give pleasure.

When the cup of tea has been drunk it has fulfilled its **end**. Its *telos* (end) has been to give pleasure to the person drinking the cup of tea. Eudaimonia is an Aristotelian idea. Aquinas wants to go further. The ultimate pleasure as Aquinas sees it and the one for which human beings were designed is union with God as Creator. Thus end B is that ultimate inter-relationship with God in heaven.

4. Moral perfection and heaven

One thing should be noted from the teleological chart for Aquinas. Aquinas' world was centred on the idea of salvation and the reward of heaven in a way that modern Western society is not. The *telos* of a thing must, therefore, be related to the final end of humanity which is eudaimonia; for Aquinas true happiness is achieving heaven. Here Aquinas parts company with Aristotle. For Aquinas the true *telos* of human beings is not, as Aristotle suggested, realizing their potential or blueprint in this world. For Aquinas heaven is the destiny for all human beings' souls.

Aquinas did not believe that eventually all will be saved. He believed that God grants the gift of eternal life to those who love God and therefore follow God's Natural Law. Hell waits for those who do not live by the precepts of God's Natural Law.

Even before the rise of Protestantism there were writers who attacked Aquinas' view that obedience to law is rewarded by eternal life. In the fourteenth century the English philosopher, William of Ockham (1285–1347/49) attacked Aquinas' teaching. He argued that faith matters more than human reason. He also argued that if a person obeys God's law then God must reward him with eternal life. This means that human beings control God. For example, if you live a good life and you give to charity, you expect heaven at the end of it. It would be a strange God who sent Adolf Hitler to heaven and Mother Teresa to hell, yet God cannot be controlled by humans.

To think about

'If I live a good life I *deserve* a heavenly reward.' Discuss the implications of this statement.

Martin Luther (1483–1546) and John Calvin (1509–1564), the fathers of the reformation, developed this and other criticisms of Aquinas' Natural Law theory.

Key point

Aristotle and Aquinas agree that happiness is the final end of humanity. Aristotle's happiness is concerned with fulfilment in this life, whereas Aquinas is concerned with fulfilment in the next life, in heaven.

5. Discovering what is immoral

Using Aquinas' teleology, it is now possible for moral wrong to be calculated rationally. Moral wrong includes anything that causes the end to be different from the formal cause (see table on page 35). This can be clearly seen in Aquinas' **Just War theory**, which we look at in more detail in Chapter 9 War and peace. There is no point fighting a war, however well meant and just it may be, if the end result leads to the destruction of the country that you are fighting to protect. In such a case, the final cause for fighting the war is protection of the country. If the end is its destruction, then going to war would be an immoral act.

The example of the Just War theory raises another aspect of Aquinas' Natural Law theory. **Circumstances** may lead you to do something that may appear morally wrong at first sight. Lying is one such example. Aquinas believed that lying is contrary to Natural Law because it undermines life within a peaceful community. Yet there may be situations in which not telling the truth would be necessary if your function, purpose and end are to be met. Imagine, for example, you are a doctor in a society that sentences medics to death (as in Cambodia under the Khmer Rouge government). Do you lie when you are asked whether you are a doctor? You do not tell the truth. This is not because you want to lie; but you lie (a) to preserve your life, so that (b) you can fulfil your function in life which is to cure the sick. As a result, Aquinas allowed for some bad actions to be moral.

There are some actions that will always be wrong because they do not conform to the moral nature of humanity as being made in the image of God.

Aquinas and Natural Law: a summary

In summary, Aquinas' Natural Law theory is:

1. God is a good and all-loving Creator. He created the universe for a reason.
2. The Creation reflects the Creator through God's eternal law which governs it.
3. God orders the universe through law, of which there are four types – eternal, divine, natural and human.

4. Human beings share in God's eternal law through obedience to the Natural Law.
5. Natural Law is both descriptive and prescriptive.
6. Natural Law is teleological.
7. The end of human life is happiness, which means being a moral being in harmony with God.
8. To follow Natural Law means obedience to certain moral goods, which are: preservation of life, procreation, social life and harmony, pursuit of knowledge and worship of God.
9. These goods are not made by people but come from God.
10. These moral goods are known as the primary precepts.
11. Actions are moral if they conform to the primary precepts within a teleological framework.
12. Some actions, because they are contrary to the moral goods, will always be morally wrong even if for the greater good.
13. Some actions, because the function or purpose of the act conflicts with the moral end, are morally wrong. They may be justified as for the greater good if circumstances necessitate.
14. Human laws must reflect either directly or indirectly on Natural Law.
15. Some human laws may conflict with Natural Law. A Christian is not obliged in conscience to obey such laws.

Extension note

The law of double effect

Aquinas' Natural Law theory is an **absolutist** theory since it lays down what should or should not be done. Some actions will always be morally wrong since they conflict with the natural end of human life, which is to be with God. Thus rejection of God (blasphemy) is always wrong. However, some actions are less certain. For example, a patient suffering from terminal cancer lies dying in a hospice. The dying person cannot speak and is lying in a comatose state. Suddenly the foot of the patient twitches. The nurse realizes that the patient is suffering pain. A doctor is called and morphine is administered to the patient who is already near death. The morphine hastens death and a few minutes later the patient dies. In this situation the morphine kills the person but it was administered with the intention of relieving suffering. The twitching foot was an indication of pain. This is an example of the **law of double effect**. You do something with a good intention but it has another consequence. It is the **intention** that determines the morality of the action. If the morphine was administered with the intention of killing the patient, as it was in the majority of deaths caused by serial killer Harold Shipman, it would be murder and therefore always morally wrong. The problem is how do you judge intention?

To think about

What is Natural Law? Is it possible to accept the Natural Law theory without believing in God?

Later developments of Natural Law theory

An important criticism of Natural Law is to be found in the views of the early Protestant Reformers, such as Luther. Early Protestants rejected Aquinas' Natural Law theory because it was based on, in their opinion, three false assertions.

1. First, Aquinas based Natural Law on God's Creation. Most Protestants rejected the idea that the laws of nature reveal God's law. The Fall of Adam and Eve in the Garden of Eden created a clear break between God and the natural world. Creation, Luther argued, is fallen and corrupt. How can a corrupt world reveal God?

2. Their second objection is to the importance Aquinas gives to human reason. The early Protestants condemned the Catholic Church for the stress it placed on human reason. Reason, like the world itself, was depraved, fallen and sinful.

3. Third, Protestants criticized the importance Natural Law gives to doing good. Can a corrupt person do good works and enter heaven? No, Luther argued, the corrupt individual can only do corrupt works. Luther believed that doing good and obeying the Natural Law cannot save you; only the grace of God can bring salvation.

However, some Protestants developed Natural Law theory. They did not do so on the basis of the Catholic teaching of Natural Law, but turned instead to the ideas of the ancient **Stoics**. This group of ancient Greek philosophers saw life as a struggle in which human beings must rise above the tragedy and trauma of life. They can only do this by living a virtuous life, an upright existence. The Protestant Natural Law theorists took on these ideas, while rejecting the teleological framework of Aristotle and Aquinas. They believed God had set the universe in a perfect order and Christians were called to follow this Natural Law. The moral virtues were vitally important otherwise human beings would descend to the state of barbaric animals. This was not, despite the Fall, what was natural to human beings.

One of the most important Protestant Natural Law thinkers was Hugo Grotius. He developed Aquinas' Just War theory in his work *The Rights of War and Peace*, which remains one of the most important pieces of writing on the morality of warfare (see Chapter 9 War and peace).

Key terms

the Fall – the story in Genesis 3 of Adam and Eve's fall from grace. Christian writers, from Paul onwards, saw the events of the Fall as the defining moment when human beings set themselves apart from God.

grace – a gift or favour of God.

Extension Note

New Natural Law theory

Since the 1960s a New Natural Law theory has emerged. The New Natural Law theory is very different to the approach of both Aristotle and Aquinas. John Finnis and Germain Grisez developed this New Natural Law theory in America and Canada. They argue that both the ancient philosopher and the medieval theologian spent far too much time and effort constructing a big picture of the way in which the universe works towards a natural *telos*. Both failed, in doing so, to look at the way in which the individual's moral route through life should be governed. They also argue that, by focusing on the big picture (metaphysics), earlier Natural Law scholars had ignored very basic practical things that will aid the individual's journey through life.

The year 2009 marked the fiftieth anniversary of the M1. Imagine that this motorway is your life and that each junction is a moral issue en route. Finnis and Grisez argue that both Aristotle and Aquinas are concerned about your journey. They are interested in where the M1 starts and ends, the design of the bridges and the way that the road surface has been made. They are not interested in how you actually get from London to Leeds. The New Natural Law approach, they believe, is concerned with your car and the way you drive it to the destination. Grisez argues that in order to reach your destination (heaven) you need certain goods, or qualities, to assist your journey. Aquinas had listed these as the virtues. Grisez goes further. He argues that goods come in two forms: practical goods (practical qualities that will help or impede your ability to be virtuous, for example wealth or talent), which affect moral goods (virtuous qualities, for example prudence or justice). Therefore, for example, there is not much point in being generous to your neighbour, if you have no money!

Another New Natural Law philosopher, Joseph Boyle, argues that human reason should be directed towards actions that contribute towards 'communal well-being and flourishing'. Boyle lists the moral goods required for the journey. They are the traditional virtues, such as justice, love and mercy. He also lists those practical goods that human beings require. These are, what he calls, self-evident basic goods. They include life, health, knowledge, aesthetics, work and play, friendship and marriage. They also include harmony with God, choices and the ability to choose in life, feelings and behaviour. It follows that no one has the right to remove these goods from anyone else. No one, he goes on to argue, has the right to take the life of another as the gift of life is a basic good. This means that, for Boyle, abortion and euthanasia are immoral acts. Warfare and capital punishment are also regarded as immoral acts. How would Boyle's views work in practice? Take, for example, a prisoner. Boyle argues than no one has the right to remove goods from another. Therefore, prisoners have the right, not to liberty, but to work, play, health and knowledge whilst in jail.

Unlike Aquinas, New Natural Law philosophers do not rate moral goods higher than practical goods nor do they rank moral goods in a certain order. All are individual parts of the car that will take you through your life. All are necessary. As a result New Natural Law philosophers refuse to set one good against another. They also argue that, unlike traditional Natural Law theories, their system is agent-centred. Aquinas looked at the road; they look at the car and the driver.

Natural Law: strengths

There are a number of strengths to the Natural Law theory. The most important of these are:

- Its **universal application**. This is important in a multi-ethnic and multicultural world. The application of the Natural Law theory unites major groupings within the world's monotheistic religions. Consequently, there is a common approach to issues, such as abortion and euthanasia, between Roman Catholic, Muslim and Orthodox Jewish scholars. Aristotle's understanding of Natural Law was vitally important to both Aquinas and to Muslim medieval writers; this link creates a point of dialogue between Christians and Muslims.
- Values such as the **preservation of life, procreation, social life and harmony and pursuit of knowledge are considered ethically good by most societies in the world**. These norms create the basis for dialogue between religious and non-religious that, it is argued, prevents the fragmentation of society along ethical lines.
- The importance it places on the **ultimate goal of human life**; a *telos* that is not hedonistic in character. Some Natural Law philosophers, including Pope Benedict XVI, argue that the Natural Law theory gives a counterbalance to modern materialistic and hedonistic trends in society.
- The stress it puts on the value and worth of life in general and of human life in particular. The **sanctity of human life** is central to its teleology.
- The link between the body and the soul emphasizes the **importance of the physical body in morality**. This in turn leads to bodily issues, such as the status of the foetus and the plight of the elderly, being taken seriously.
- The stress it places on **rightness of character**, through pursuit of the cardinal virtues.

Key term

hedonism – the pursuit of pleasure.

Natural Law places emphasis on harmony in the natural world; an example is the reciprocal relationship between the bee and the flower.

- The emphasis it places on **social harmony** in pursuit of the ultimate good. Continental political philosophers, unlike those in the Anglo-Saxon world, often assert that Aquinas was the father of democracy. By this they mean that at the heart of the Natural Law theory is the idea of the **common good**, that all individuals and groups in society work in harmony with each other.
- The emphasis it places on **natural harmony**. The harmonious nature of the natural world is an important feature of environmental ethics today.

Natural Law: weaknesses

Despite its strengths various criticisms have been made of the Natural Law theory. The first three criticisms are fundamental. They are:

- **Is it possible to judge what is natural?** For example, a person is being kept alive by artificial means. The individual has been in a coma for many years and there is little evidence of brain activity. What is to be done? Is it right for the preservation of life to be the number-one priority? Would that person already be dead if nature had taken its course? Modern medicine has blurred the distinction between what is natural and what is not.

- **Are ethical decisions reached rationally?** It has been argued that human beings do not think through moral actions. They do not review the Natural Law in making a decision. Instead they act spontaneously or out of a sense of duty. If you love someone you will do things that put your own self-preservation at risk.
- There is often **conflict between different parts of the Natural Law**. This is not just in the case of the law of double effect. In other situations one virtue may have to be bypassed in order for another cardinal virtue to be kept. For example, can you always be both just and prudent? Sometimes, people can put their own lives in danger when fighting for justice.

Other criticisms that can be made include:

- Some Christian writers, most notably the Swiss theologian Karl Barth (1886–1968), argue that **Natural Law not only limits human beings but it also restricts what God can do**. Following the ideas of St Augustine (354–430) and Martin Luther, Barth argues that Christianity is first and foremost a religion of revelation. Human reason can only be used to understand God's revelation. In his *Church Dogmatics* he goes further. Barth argues that human nature is corrupted by original sin and, therefore, it is impossible for human beings to behave morally without God's grace. The prominence of reason in Aquinas' Natural Law theory is rejected.
- The contemporary American philosopher Kai Nielsen puts forward the idea that the **Natural Law theory assumes that all human beings are similar**. This assumption runs contrary to modern studies of human behaviour. Present day research suggests that human beings may have different *hard-wiring*, due to genetic and other considerations. Most, for example, are naturally heterosexual but some are born to be homosexual. Natural Law philosophers cannot accept this without destroying the whole basis of the theory.
- Peter Vardy, the English ethicist, argues that while the parameters of the Natural Law theory may be correct, it is impossible to apply the broad picture to specific and complex cases. **Individual moral problems do not easily fit into the Natural Law framework**.
- The Natural Law theory **limits human freedom**. Critics of Natural Law theory assert that conformity to Natural Law prevents human beings from taking into account exceptions. For example, Natural Law forbids abortion; it does not take into account circumstances such as pregnancy as a result of rape or underage sex. Total obedience to Natural Law makes human beings robotic.
- All Natural Law theories can be criticized on the basis of the naturalistic fallacy. This is the idea that just because nature is a certain way it does not follow that this is how things ought to be; the idea that you cannot derive an *ought* from an *is*. It does not follow that human beings ought to follow a particular course of action just because nature has a certain order and structure.

Key term

naturalistic fallacy – the idea that just because nature acts in a certain way it does not follow that this is how things ought to be.

Practice exam questions

(a) Explain Natural Law theory.

You could begin answering this question by looking at Aristotle's Natural Law theory. You could look at Aristotle's theories on the nature of animate beings, of function, purpose and end, and eudaimonia. You could then look at how Aquinas developed this theory from a Christian point of view and made it more complex. You might want to consider Aquinas' four causes, the cardinal virtues and the primary and secondary precepts.

(b) 'Natural Law is not the best approach to morality.' Discuss.

In support of this statement you could argue that nature does not have within it an ethical teleology. Modern scientific views dispute the idea that function and purpose to an end exist within nature. You may want to mention the **naturalistic fallacy** which concludes that just because nature works in a particular way does not mean that this is how things ought to be. You might wish to include a practical illustration, but keep this brief. For example, Natural Law theory runs contrary to contraception. Yet it might be argued that AIDS has spread more rapidly in societies that limit the use of the condom. AIDS kills and therefore it shows a lack of empathy to ban the condom. You could also make a case for Natural Law as a good approach to morality, for example by stating that it shows respect for all human beings and for Creation. You could argue that Natural Law theory avoids subjective interpretations and that this protects the vulnerable, for example in the case of the Natural Law approach to euthanasia (see Chapter 7 Euthanasia).

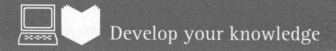 Develop your knowledge

There are numerous good publications on Natural Law. Among these are:

The Encyclopedia of Ethics by Lawrence C. Becker and Charlotte B. Becker (Routledge, 2001)
Natural Law and Natural Rights by John Finnis (Clarendon Press, 1990)
'Natural Law' by K. Haakonssen in *Three Rival Versions of Moral Enquiry* by Alasdair MacIntyre (Duckworth, 1990)
Ethics: Discovering Right and Wrong by Louis P. Pojman (Wadsworth Publishing Co., 1999)
A Companion to Ethics by Peter Singer (ed.) (Blackwell, 1993)
The Puzzle of Ethics by Peter Vardy and Paul Grosch (Fount, 1999)

3

Kantian ethics

Introduction

The seventeenth century was a period of intense warfare throughout Europe. The religious divide between Catholic and Protestant states made conflict inevitable. As a result of this conflict, certain ideas began to develop which were to free ethics from the domination of religion. These ideas include the importance of:

- human reason in determining moral truths
- individual freedom and autonomy
- a sense of duty or obligation to act morally.

These three ideas come to the fore in the writings of Immanuel Kant.

Kant is generally regarded as the outstanding philosopher of the eighteenth century. Kant developed a philosophical theory known as transcendental idealism. A fundamental aspect of transcendental idealism is the view that concepts or ideals, such as beauty and justice, do exist and that they have a universal meaning. Transcendental idealism is therefore opposed to relativism, where the meaning of concepts depends on the attitudes of a particular culture, society or individual.

> ## Key point
>
> Kant's morality is based on a firm belief that morality exists universally; it is independent of human experience.

Kant was not a relativist. He argued that it is incoherent to believe that justice can mean one thing in a specific country or time period and something different in another society or era. Kant believed the meaning of such concepts is a priori, independent of and prior to human knowledge, and that they transcend human experience. These concepts and the laws that govern them are not discovered by observation of nature or by an understanding of human psychology. It is human reason alone that gives

Key terms

transcendental idealism – Kant's theory that humans construct knowledge by imposing universal concepts onto sensory experiences.

relativism – the theory that there are no universal truths; truth is relative to the subject and can vary from person to person and society to society.

a priori – can be known without human experience.

Immanuel Kant (1724–1804) was the eighteenth century's greatest philosopher.

Key terms

empiricism – the idea that knowledge can only be gained by analysing sensory experiences of the material world.

moral law – in Kantian ethics a rule for how you should act, based on a maxim.

autonomous individual – a person who is free to choose.

humanity knowledge of moral truth. Therefore Kant rejected empiricism, the idea that morality can be discovered through the observation of human nature or through the way the natural order works.

Kant rejected the idea of happiness or contentment as the basis of morality. He believed that human beings cannot fulfil their lives by concentrating on happiness; morality is more important than the selfish desire for personal happiness. For Kant, such desires are morally dangerous and lead the human race down a false path. Kant regarded those philosophers that try to turn happiness into a higher value as no better than those who view morality as 'eat, drink and be merry, for tomorrow we die'. The problem with happiness as the basis for morality is that it is based on feelings and desires and that it is subjective; what makes one person happy might make another person unhappy. Kant was determined to discover the essence of moral truth, which he believed was objective in nature and based on reason, not feelings.

Moral knowledge comes through the power of human reason and rational debate. All human beings have the ability to argue rationally; some use this ability and others do not. Kant believed that human beings are not by nature moral creatures. They have the capacity to be moral and they discover this through reason. Kant believed that he had discovered the method by which rational human beings could discover the moral laws. His system creates a method. Once learnt and implemented, Kant believed, these rules would set humanity free to be autonomous individuals.

Key point

Whether you are a king or a commoner you are under the same moral law. All human beings are morally equal and each person must determine rationally his or her moral framework.

Extension note

Kant, walks and Königsberg (Kaliningrad)

Kant was born near Königsberg (now renamed Kaliningrad) in East Prussia. He spent most of his life living in the city and its suburbs. He is buried in its cathedral. Kant loved the city and seldom left it. Each day, in the suburbs to its south, he went for a very long walk. Year after year, day after day, he walked the same route. He met the same people en route but he never spoke to anyone. He covered his mouth with a scarf that protected him from what he believed were the germs of those he passed. Kant's walks kept him fit and he lived to the advanced age of 80.

Kant's walks symbolize the rigour and exact nature of his philosophy. He hated lack of precision. Everything had to be logically structured and coherent. His walks followed a similar plan. They were well organized, starting and ending at the same time each afternoon, summer and winter. His intellectual rigour was replicated in the discipline of his exercise.

Kant saw himself as the Socrates of the modern age. Like Plato's Socrates he believed that truth was revealed only by the careful dissection of arguments. Rational argument alone would reveal error. Kant created a system of thought that he believed, if used, would cut through subjective uncritical judgements and the errors of empiricism and romanticism. He viewed British Utilitarianism with derision and romanticism with contempt. The dryness and strict logic of his method was, like his walks, untarnished by contact with human beings. Subjective feelings have no rational moral basis; when love enters the room, morality exits.

From maxims to moral laws

Kant believed that there are universal moral laws, which are created by God. Yet Kant rejected the Divine Command theory as a basis for knowing these laws. God's universal moral laws, he asserted, cannot be known through direct revelation. Instead, Kant believed that human reason has the ability to uncover them.

This discovery starts with a series of maxims. These are subjective moral principles that, Kant believed, can be deduced by all rational human beings. Sit down, look at the moral life and imagine the sort of ethical principles that society needs. One of these might be the principle that lying is wrong. Kant then goes on to argue that through trust, which is the idea of good will towards others, these basic principles can be developed into moral laws to govern society. For example, laws such as libel or slander are developed from the maxim that lying is wrong. In order to develop these laws, there must be **good will** between human beings. Each rational human being must, in a moral society, live his or her life with a sense of trust and good will to others. Trust and good will are central to Kant's belief that human beings have the ability to turn subjectively-based ethical maxims into moral laws.

Key terms

maxim – a moral principle, subjective in origin, which demands practical application.

Extension note

Trust, the will and good will

Kant believed that human beings approach moral issues in two separate ways. They have natural instincts, which lead them into selfish acts. They also have rational minds, which make them realize that there are moral principles (maxims) that ought to control human behaviour. This division within human beings creates a problem. It leads to the struggling will, in which the human being is uncertain of what moral decision to make. Trust is crucial in resolving this ethical dilemma.

Trust is an important element in the applicability of the universal principle. The rational human being must trust his or her ethical decision-making. The individual must not allow his or her thoughts to be clouded by emotional impulses, even when these seem to be morally good. Therefore Kant rejects concepts such as sympathy or love as bases for ethical decision-making. The moral agent must rise above such emotions, however good they may appear.

What is it that drives human beings forward? Earlier writers, such as Dante, spoke of the human soul's journey towards God. Kant, though, is concerned with the human will. The precise meaning of the will in Kant is hard to define. This is because he tries to fuse the objective, rational nature of logical thought with the subjective qualities of a human being's drives. It is the human will that makes choices in life and drives humans forward, using practical reason.

This forward movement (teleology) relies on trust. Trust as defined by Kant is essentially the idea of good will. Kant's good will is independent of the object of the moral action. It makes decisions based on reason and logic. It does not need detailed knowledge since ignorance of the object of the moral decision brings with it clear thoughts rather than the emotional nature of sympathy, which can cloud judgement.

The Categorical Imperative

Key term

Categorical Imperative – something human beings are duty-bound to do, whatever the circumstances.

How are God's moral laws to be known? How can we know if a maxim, which is subjective in origin, is morally right? Kant's solution lies in the use of the Categorical Imperative.

The Categorical Imperative has three tests that show whether a moral maxim is to be accepted as a universal law. These tests are:

- the universal law principle
- the principle of humanity as an end not a means
- the principle of the universal kingdom of ends.

Key point

The Categorical Imperative lays down the moral maxims that should be followed in life.

The universal law principle

In his *Groundwork for the Metaphysics of Morals* Kant gives the formulae that control morality. The first is:

Act only on that maxim whereby which you can at the same time will that it become a universal law. (Immanuel Kant, Groundwork for the Metaphysics of Morals, *Broadview Press Ltd, 2005)*

The basis of this idea is that when making moral decisions no one should do anything that he or she would not accept as a universal law for everyone in every situation. Maxims can be tested by seeing if they can be applied regardless of the circumstances and individuals involved. Kant gave examples from life of maxims that should be seen as moral laws. The first of these is the issue of **suicide**. Kant argued that there is a universal law that suicide is always wrong. He argued this on the basis that if you, in a state of suffering and despair, were to sit down and think about the moral principles involved in taking your own life, you would decide that it was contrary to the universal principle. Why? You would have to reflect on whether, in all situations, you would wish people to take their own lives. For example, would it be a good idea for healthy people or individuals bullied into a state of despair to commit suicide? The answer would surely be no.

Telling lies is another example of Kant's universal principle in action. He argued that it is never morally acceptable to lie. However, you might decide that it is morally right to lie in a particular situation. Let's illustrate this. Imagine that you are walking down a street. A man passes you and turns left at the junction ahead. A minute later another man brandishing a gun also passes you. He stops and asks which way the first man went. What do you do? Do you lie, either by saying he turned right when the man actually turned left or by saying 'I don't know' when clearly you do? Kant said never lie. You must tell the truth. His argument is that if lying were turned into a universal law it would mean that it would be morally right to lie in any situation. Since human relationships are grounded in trust, it would be impossible for any trust between people to exist.

A further example Kant gave is the issue of **borrowing money**. Here again Kant concludes with the universal principle that all debts must be paid, however difficult that might be. Indeed, if you borrow money and then get into dire straits, you must still pay back what is owed. This is true even if such payment brings harm to your family. This is because if debts were not paid, normal business transactions would not be possible. The credit crunch that began in 2007 illustrates the problems that can occur when people cannot repay their debts. In some respects the element of trust is to be found in the lending of money, as with the telling of lies.

Key point

The universal law principle states: '*Act only on that maxim whereby which you can at the same time will that it become a universal law.*' (Immanuel Kant)

The principle of humanity as an end not a means

Kant, in the *Groundwork for the Metaphysics of Morals*, defines the next formula as:

So act as to treat humanity, whether in your own person or in that of any other, in every case at the same time as an end, never as a means only. (Immanuel Kant, Groundwork for the Metaphysics of Morals*)*

This Kantian principle argues that you must not use others in pursuit of an ethical end. As an example, imagine you propose a hydroelectric power scheme on the Turkish banks of the Tigris River. Lower down the river Turkish and Iraqi communities would suffer as a consequence of the reduction in the water supply. The benefits of the dam for some areas would be great, but by harming some people in order to achieve the general good you would be treating those people as a means not an end. Therefore such a dam would be morally wrong.

Kant noted the illogical nature of projects that use people in pursuit of the general good. It is self-contradictory for you to act in a way that devalues the worth of the human being, whilst seeking to do something for the good of humankind.

Kant's principle of humanity as an end has a further meaning. It refers not only to other people but also to the moral agent. Kant regarded self-worth as important; you cannot undervalue yourself when seeking a moral end. Thus it would be wrong for *x* to starve in order to give to *y*, since *x* is of equal value to *y*. It may be admirable to help others but not at the expense of self-destruction or self-harm. Shakespeare's *Timon of Athens* illustrates this. Timon's generosity to others in good times leads to him becoming destitute himself. His kindness results in his own destruction.

Key point

The principle of humanity as an end not a means states: '*So act as to treat humanity, whether in your own person or in that of any other, in every case at the same time as an end, never as a means only.*' (Immanuel Kant)

The principle of the universal kingdom of ends

The last of the three formulae that form the basis for the Categorical Imperative is the notion of the kingdom of ends. Kant wrote:

Act according to the maxims of a member of a merely possible kingdom of ends legislating in it universally. (Immanuel Kant, Groundwork for the Metaphysics of Morals*)*

The **kingdom of ends** appears under various guises in the *Groundwork for the Metaphysics of Morals*. Kant is describing a state of affairs in which all members of a society desire the same good; a society that the moral laws are designed to achieve. These goods are the common ends of humanity. Kant wants to achieve a state of affairs where conflict is removed and all human beings realize their common aims.

How is this achieved? Consider the following scenario. You meet a group of people from your area because things are chaotic in your town or village. You need to sit

Key term

Hypothetical Imperative – something human beings ought to do, to achieve a certain end.

down with them and draw up moral principles (maxims) that will establish a good, moral society. When you discuss your ideas with the other people in the room, you suddenly realize that they share your ideas. You meet them and, slowly but surely, you draw up laws for your society.

Kant believed that most human beings are rational people. They prefer the moral life to the immoral. Kant knew that it is not possible to realize this in life; but the process must be attempted. The universal kingdom of ends must be pursued.

Key point

The principle of the universal kingdom of ends states: '*Act according to the maxims of a member of a merely possible kingdom of ends legislating in it universally*.' (Immanuel Kant)

To think about

Can you put the universal law principle, the principle of humanity as an end not a means and the principle of the universal kingdom of ends in your own words, presenting them as three bullet points?

The Hypothetical Imperative

Kant asserted that not all moral issues are determined by the Categorical Imperative. Those that do not fall within the ethical tests of the Categorical Imperative are determined by the Hypothetical Imperative. The Categorical Imperative is a command that must be obeyed. The Hypothetical Imperative refers to commands that ought to be obeyed to achieve a certain aim.

The Hypothetical Imperative is concerned with moral ends. The moral agent examines how a moral end is to be achieved. Simply put: if I want x, then I ought to do y.

The Hypothetical Imperative is conditional on the practicality of the aim. If the agent does not want that aim, then it lapses. It may be that the moral agent decides that the moral aim is not feasible. In this case the moral action may not be implemented. If, though, the rational person concludes that it is possible then he or she ought to act.

For example, the moral aim might be the elimination of poverty in Africa. This might be achieved, or certainly helped, by cancelling the huge debts that some African countries owe. This action is not determined by the Categorical Imperative. If we were to apply the universal law principle we would see that abolishing debt is not universally moral. It would not be right to cancel all debts, in every situation. This action is covered by the Hypothetical Imperative. *If* we want to eliminate poverty *then* we ought to drop the debt owed by poor African countries.

Key term

deontology – a moral system based on duty. What is moral is what you have a duty to do.

To think about

Which kinds of action are bound by the Categorical Imperative and which by the Hypothetical Imperative?

Duty

Kant's moral philosophy is deontological. It is a system of morality based on duty. Kant was not the first philosopher to make moral obligations the centre of his ethical system but he is, perhaps, the most important.

A soldier who risks their life for their country does so because it is their duty.

In his *Groundwork for the Metaphysics of Morals*, Kant asserts that human beings give the most praise to those who perform an action simply because they are required to. They act from duty alone. For example, the carer who dedicates ten years of their life to care for a sick and paralysed parent or the soldier who risks their life for their country. Both act from a sense of duty. Kant argued that this sense of moral duty can be converted into a series of universal moral laws that all human beings ought to follow.

Key point

For Kant morality is based on duty, not on emotions or ties of love.

Kant's ethical position is duty based, deontological. This is not an ordinary sense of duty but something more extreme. It is, as Kant puts it, like the duty to preserve your life:

> *. . . a wretched man . . . longs for death and still preserves his life without loving it – not from inclination or fear but from duty. (Immanuel Kant,* The Moral Law: Groundwork of the Metaphysics of Morals, *Taylor & Francis, 2005)*

This is **extreme duty**. It is done at a cost to self. It rejects happiness as a basis for moral decision-making.

The strengths of Kant's deontological morality are that it takes account of the responsibility that we have to others and it recognizes the universality of morality. However, duties sometimes conflict.

Imagine you are a young man or woman with a partner and a young baby. One day you are walking along the street and you see someone being attacked. You recognize the attacker as a criminal who the police have warned the general public not to approach. What do you do? Do you confront the violent attacker? Or, do you stand aside and watch the attack whilst phoning for police assistance? It is praiseworthy to act. You have a duty to act, but you also have a duty to your family. You tackle the assailant but you are killed in the encounter. You have done your duty and the media praise you, but you have left behind a partner and baby.

Kant did not recognize this problem with the deontological approach. He argued that a conflict of duties is 'inconceivable', as duties are universal and do not discriminate. Imagine that you are in the midst of a bush fire. Forest areas are ablaze around you and you can see a row of houses in flames. From the attic of the nearest house you hear a person calling for help. You are duty-bound to respond but you know your mother is stuck in a burning house at the other end of the street. What do you do? Kant is firm. You must try to save the person in the nearest house. Your mother will have to wait. Why? Kant argued that the duty to save life is universal and therefore should not discriminate in favour of a loved one.

To think about

Can you see a conflict of duties in the above scenario? Should you have a greater sense of duty to your family than to your neighbour?

Taxonomy of duties

Kant had a low regard for the value of human nature. He viewed our natural inclinations as being contrary to reason. This low estimation of human nature means that the concept of duty is raised to a new height. Duty saves human beings from self-delusion. It is as if human beings perform duties despite themselves *not* because of themselves.

Kant regards duty as always being towards an object, whether this is another person or oneself. In his *Groundwork for the Metaphysics of Morals* he lays down:

1. the link between these duties and virtue
2. the nature of these duties.

Allen W. Wood, in *Kant's Ethical Thought* divides these duties into two categories: duties to oneself and duties to others. He lists the duties to oneself of rational people as:

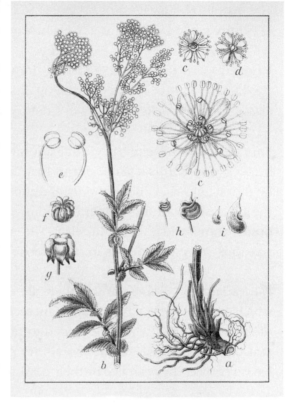

Taxonomy is the science of classification; it is usually used to classify plants and animals. Kant used this principle to draw up a list of duties that human beings have to perform in order to be moral agents.

- *as an animal being*
  - *against suicide*
  - *against lust*
  - *against drunkenness*
  - *against gluttony* (greed)
- *as a moral being*
  - *against avarice* (greed for wealth)
  - *against lying*
  - *against servility* (acting in a manner that undervalues yourself). *(Allen W. Wood,* Kant's Ethical Thought, *Cambridge University Press, 1999)*

According to Wood, the duties to others of rational people are:

- *to love by beneficence* (generosity/charity), *gratitude and sympathy*
- *to respect as individuals and equals. (Allen W. Wood,* Kant's Ethical Thought*)*

Extension note

Taxonomy

The Swedish botanist Carolus Linnaeus (1707–1778) published his work *The System of Nature* while Kant was at university. Kant read the work and drew on its ideas.

Linnaeus was the first scientist to draw up a taxonomy of plants, a system of classification into which everything fits. Taxonomy is the law or structure of classification; it is key to Darwin's theory of evolution.

Kant uses the principle of classification to draw up two taxonomies. The first can be seen above. It is a list of duties that human beings have to perform in order to be moral agents. This taxonomy of duties points human beings towards achieving the highest good. It is sometimes known as a transcendental taxonomy, as these duties transcend everything else. The second taxonomy is Kant's taxonomy of passions, a list that points in the opposite direction, towards insanity.

Patrick Frierson points out that there are empirical aspects in Kant's thought, one of which is his interest in psychology. Kant sees a stark distinction between the psychology of the moral agent who is dedicated to reason and achieving the highest good, and that of the irrational, whose morals are products of their passions. Human beings have a choice; they can live by their passions or they can live by reason.

In 1791 a rich Austrian woman wrote to Kant, stating that life was not worth living. She had kept a secret from her lover and on disclosing it had lost his affections. Maria von Herbert was a fervent follower of Kant and wrote to the great philosopher for advice. Kant replied that she should not brood over her loss: 'the value of life, insofar as it consists of the enjoyment we can get out of people, is generally overestimated, whereas life, insofar as it is cherished for the good that we can do, deserves the highest respect' (Immanuel Kant, *The Cambridge Edition of the Works of Kant: Correspondence*, Cambridge University Press, 1999). Two years later she wrote again. Her relationship troubles are resolved, but she can't shake off a feeling of intolerable emptiness. Her only desire is to 'shorten this so useless life of mine' (Immanuel Kant, *Correspondence*) Kant never wrote to her again. He bundled up her letters and sent them on to the daughter of a friend as a warning, as he saw it, against letting your fantasies run away with you. Maria von Herbert committed suicide in 1803.

To think about

Is it easier to let your passions rule you than to be led by reason alone? Why is this a problem for Kant's ethical theory?

The *summum bonum* in the moral community

Kant's moral system is designed to create a moral community in which all moral ends are reconciled. This will be a slow, perhaps ineffectual, process. It has a teleological and religious basis. Kant is clear that the implementation of the ethical principles in his moral system will lead to a unity of ends and the purposeful transformation of human society.

Conflicts are resolved as this unity is achieved. The analogy of a game of chess illustrates this. The world at present is like a game of chess being played between two grandmasters. Both have different goals and the game is about conflict. But suppose a time comes when these grandmasters look at a chess problem and join together to solve it. Conflict would be resolved and the kingdom of ends would be created. Kant, in his *Critique of Practical Reason*, called this state of affairs 'the highest good' or, in Latin, the *summum bonum*.

Kant believed that this *summum bonum* consists of the resolution of two different ends. He described these two ends as **good** and **well-being**. By the former Kant meant **moral goodness** or **righteousness**. The latter is meant to convey the idea of **contentment**. The individual is truly moral when he/she is both good and happy with that state of affairs. Kant does not mean that happiness is a basis for moral well-being. He means by this that human beings must do good and be happy that they live a life which is praiseworthy. A moral society is one in which rational beings are ethically upright and are content with this moral position. Since most human beings are incapable of resolving these ends in this life, Kant argued that *summum bonum* is not reached until after death. The nature of this afterlife, as with the nature of God, is not examined. It is impossible for any human being to define that which, until after death, cannot be known or understood. In the *Critique of Practical Reason* Kant adds the idea of the **consummation of moral good** to his idea of the *summum bonum*. This new phrase suggests that happiness and moral goodness will work in heaven in tandem, like parallel rails on a railway track.

Key terms

teleology – designed for or directed towards a final end.

summum bonum **–** the highest good, which is only achievable in the moral community.

Key term

autonomous individual – a person who is free to choose.

universalizability – the principle that moral values are universal and therefore universally applicable.

Teleology in Kantian ethics

Kant believed that the consequences of an action should not be the basis of a moral action. Yet, at the same time, Kant was clear that there is an inbuilt goal to which nature and history aspire – that is the kingdom of ends. Kant imagined that all rational creatures have within them a germ that predisposes them towards a moral end. This **predisposition to moral reasoning** is, as Kant put it, the 'ground for the determinate development' of humanity. Humankind progresses towards perfection and the kingdom of ends.

Kantian ethics: strengths and weaknesses

Kantian ethics has many strong points. They are:

1. Unlike other ethical theories it does not view all human action as being morally based. **Most actions do not require a moral litmus test**. This frees up the moral decision-making process to concentrate on what is important. It recognizes that many actions, however moral, should not be performed because they are not based on a universal moral law.
2. It emphasizes the worth of each human being as an autonomous individual, with the freedom to act morally.
3. Human equality and harmony are central features of Kantian ethics.
4. It puts **pressure on the individual** to act in a moral and logically coherent manner.
5. It emphasizes the **dignity and worth of all human life**. As a result activities such as pornography and slavery are seen as immoral in themselves.
6. The emphasis on **duty** appears to fit in with human experience.
7. Equal treatment of individuals **eradicates bias** towards family, friends or nation that sometimes influences decision-making.
8. The principle of universalizability emphasizes that moral actions cannot be just in one society and unjust in another.

Extension note

The problem of duty
The Nuremberg trials are renowned throughout the world. Less well-known are the war crimes trials that took place in Vienna, Austria, at the end of World War II.

The details of one trial held there reveals one problem with a moral system based on duty.

At the end of the war an atrocity occurred in a village high up in the Tyrolean Alps. The war was ending. To conceal the existence of Nazi death camps, soldiers were ordered to march those left alive inside the camps around the countryside. The soldiers were, by this stage of the war, old men and teenagers. The prisoners were ordered out of the camps and marched each day so that, through exhaustion and starvation, one by one they died. To the Allied troops they would look like refugees that didn't survive. The Nazi soldiers reached a village high up above the valley of the river Inn. The soldiers were fed up. They were far from home and they too had no food. They went to the mayor of the village and sought the advice of the town council. The solution was an atrocity. The prisoners were rounded up and put into a hay cart; the cart was then pushed over the side of the mountain down into the valley below. All those on board perished. The soldiers had done their duty. The mayor and the town council had likewise done their duty to the Nazi soldiers. Yet the plea of doing one's duty was not an excuse either in Vienna or Nuremberg.

Kant's deontological ethics is based on duty but it contains other elements that, in the example above, conflict with the plea of 'I was just doing my duty'. Kant's **taxonomy of duties** means that duty is not to be followed blindly, but there is a list of precise duties which are vital. As a result, an appeal to duty for duty's sake is invalid. The individual must act to respect others and to value their autonomy. Clearly, on the Austrian mountain slopes, they did not.

Modern criticisms of Kant include:

1. Does the teleological nature of Kantian thought undermine the whole basis of its ethical theory? This is the **problem of compatibilism**, which appears to be a contradiction in Kant's thought. Compatibilism is the idea that human beings are both free and at the same time bound by moral and physical laws. On the one hand Kant is in favour of human freedom and autonomy but, on the other hand, he implies that the moral agent must obey the principles given in the Categorical Imperative.
2. There is **no place for love and personal relationships**; it is too cold and logical.
3. **Consequences are ignored** but they matter in deciding the best (most moral) way to proceed.
4. **Do a priori moral laws actually exist?**

5. **Are moral laws essentially products of environment and culture**? Kant does not take into account, nor could he develop, modern ideas in sociology and psychology.

6. The issue of **moral luck**. Thomas Nagel and Bernard Williams (1929–2003) argue that Kant's moral philosophy is not fatally flawed because it does not take into account the consequences of a moral decision. Rather it is damaged because it ignores the circumstances of a moral action. This is known as moral luck. An individual may think that they are doing good by doing *x* but the circumstances of their actions may result in harm being done. Another person may do exactly the same action but the result is a moral good and not harm.

7. The **law of double effect** may not be so morally certain. For example, should a terminally ill patient be given painkilling drugs to ease their suffering if the administration of these drugs will cause them to die sooner? Or, should the harm in shortening life be the crucial factor and the patient allowed to continue to suffer in pain? Philippa Foot, among others, has made this criticism.

Practice exam questions

(a) Explain Kant's theory of duty.

Kant's ethical system is deontological, that is based on duty. Mention could be made of Kant's view that there are certain universal and absolute moral principles. These are grounded in the Categorical Imperative and human beings are obliged to conform to these moral principles. This leads on to Kant's view that (as a result of using the Categorical Imperative) there are certain basic duties that human beings have in life. You could examine Kant's understanding of duties to self and duties to others. You could also discuss the idea of extreme duty.

(b) 'Kant's ethical theory has no serious weaknesses.' Discuss.

You could start by considering criticisms of Kant's ethical theory. For example, Kant rejected happiness as a basis for ethical decision-making and argued that you should not favour loved ones in doing your duty. This leads to the criticism that his ethical theory is cold and impersonal. Kant's theory is non-consequentialist and does not take into account the results of an action. You could also mention the problem of compatibilism and the question of whether a priori moral laws actually exist. In a good answer you might discuss whether you consider any of the criticisms to be a serious weakness to the ethical theory. For example, a counter argument to the criticism that the theory is non-consequentialist could be that consequences are not predictable anyway. Therefore you might not consider this a serious weakness.

Develop your knowledge

There are a number of excellent books and relevant sections on Kant's moral philosophy. These include:

A Companion to Kant by Graham Bird (ed.) (Blackwell, 2006)
A Companion to Ethics by Peter Singer (ed.) (Blackwell, 1993)
The Puzzle of Ethics by Peter Vardy and Paul Grosch (Fount, 1999)
Kant's Ethical Thought by Allen W. Wood (Cambridge University Press, 1999)

4

Key terms

a priori – can be known without human experience.

a posteriori – known by logical deductions made from observation and experience of the material world.

empiricism – the idea that knowledge can only be gained through rational analysis of the observation of sensory experiences of the material world.

Introduction

Utilitarianism is the most important ethical theory to originate in Britain. While Kant developed his view that human beings were rational animals who can develop a moral society based on reason, far away in Edinburgh and London a completely different view of morality was created. Kant based his moral philosophy on what he regarded as a priori knowledge. In Britain, by contrast, a new moral philosophy was based on a posteriori knowledge; on the view that ideas are products of human experience. Utilitarianism was the most important ethical product of this empirical approach to knowledge.

Utilitarianism is the belief that the rightness of an action, rule or principle is to be judged by its presumed consequences. Utilitarians, in coming to a conclusion about the rightness of an action, rule or principle, are forced to answer two fundamental moral questions. These are **what is good?** and **what is right?**

The principle of Utility

Utilitarians base goodness and rightness on human experience. For them what is good is that which produces pleasure, happiness, contentment or welfare and what is right is that which maximizes one or more of these things. Utilitarians call the method for maximizing good the **principle of Utility** and they use the term optimific to describe the achievement of this maximization.

As John Broome puts it:

Utilitarianism contains a theory of good and a theory of right. It is characteristic of the utilitarian theory of right that rightness is derived from goodness. (John Broome, 'Can there be a preference-based utilitarianism?', Justice, Political Liberalism and Utilitarianism: Proceedings of the Caen Conference in Honour of John Harsanyi and John Rawls, *ed. Maurice Salles and John Weymark, Cambridge University Press, 1998)*

Extension note

The greatest good of the greatest number

Francis Hutcheson (1694–1746) was an Ulster Protestant who studied at the University of Glasgow. There he read the works of Bishop George Berkeley (1685–1753). Hutcheson noted that Berkeley, in one of his more obscure works, argues that human experiences give rise to either pain or pleasure. Berkeley gives the illustration of a man putting his hand in front of a fire. The fire, at a distance, produces the pleasure of warmth and light. However, what was pleasure becomes pain as the hand draws closer to the source of the heat. Hutcheson notes that particular sensory experiences therefore create what he calls **simple ideas of approbation or condemnation**. Things that create pleasure you approve of, whereas experiences that cause pain make you condemn them. Hutcheson goes on to argue that people prefer a happy and contented society to constant social change and financial turmoil. Hutcheson writes:

> *The highest moral approbation, is the calm, stable, universal good will to all. (Susan M Purviance, 'Hutcheson's aesthetic realism and moral qualities',* History of Intellectual Culture, 2006, Vol 6, No 1 *available from www.ucalgary. ca/hic/issues/vol6/2* [accessed 01/06/2010])

The maximization of happiness would lead to a calm and stable society. This Hutcheson called:

> *The greatest good of the greatest number. (Bernhard Fabian,* Collect Works of Francis Hutcheson, *G. Olms, 1971)*

Modern utilitarians often disagree over what is good and what is right. These differences of opinion have resulted in four different strands of Utilitarianism in contemporary society, three of which are examined in this chapter. They are:

1. **Act Utilitarianism** (also called **extreme Utilitarianism**)
2. **Rule Utilitarianism** (also known as **restrictive Utilitarianism**)
3. **Preference Utilitarianism**.

Utilitarianism, in whatever form, is a teleological ethical theory as each action or rule is judged on whether its end (*telos*) result maximizes good. It is also consequentialist since the consequences of an action or rule is the sole criterion to judge whether it is right or wrong.

Key terms

optimific – the maximization of pleasure, happiness, welfare or whatever concept(s) a particular utilitarian thinks is essential for human fulfilment and well-being.

teleology – designed for or directed towards a final end.

consequentialism – the consequences of an action solely determine whether it is the right thing to do.

Key point

The highest moral approbation is the calm, stable, universal goodwill to all ... the greatest good of the greatest number. (Francis Hutcheson)

Origins

The experience of the English Civil Wars (1642–1651) demonstrated, for many people who lived through it, that human beings were often violent and immoral animals. As Thomas Hobbes (1588–1679) wrote at the time:

The life of man [is] solitary, poore, nasty, brutish, and short. (Thomas Hobbes, Leviathan, *Penguin Classics, 1985)*

Hobbes' analysis of the human condition was bleak. Christians saw it as a threat to their understanding that man is made in the image of God. A growing number of non-believers saw it as an overly pessimistic view of human nature. In the century that followed the publication of Hobbes' *Leviathan* both Christians and non-believers tried to create a new moral system based not on the Bible, but on the laws of nature. Some of these were Christians who believed that the laws of nature were products of the divine hand at work in the universe. Among this group, known today as the **theological utilitarians**, was the writer John Gay (1685–1732) as well as William Paley (1743–1805), who developed the teleological argument for the existence of God. The others were a growing band of sceptical non-believers, known collectively as the **classical utilitarians**. Jeremy Bentham (1748–1832) and John Stuart Mill (1806–1873) are the most important of these. Both groups, through observation, agreed that:

• in nature things and actions either cause pleasure or pain
• pleasure is good and pain is bad
• the utility (meaning usefulness) of an action or thing is to be judged solely on the basis of whether it maximizes pleasure (happiness)
• an action or thing should either directly or indirectly lead to the pleasure or happiness of the maximal number of people in society
• all human beings prefer pleasure to pain and this preference is built into nature's laws.

Jeremy Bentham

Jeremy Bentham is regarded as the father of classical Utilitarianism. Bentham developed an ethical philosophy grounded in individualism. Each human being was free to create his or her own morality based not on God but on nature.

Bentham called himself a **non-theist**. He rejected the term atheist, as he thought it was impossible for any human being to know whether God exists or not. As a non-theist Bentham rejected morality based on divine authority. He believed that there is one single basis for ethics and that is nature. Nature replaces God as the sole higher authority to which human beings must turn in order to understand themselves, the world and moral life. Bentham, however, never attempted to explain what he meant by nature. He assumed that no explanation was required. Bentham developed from this view the idea that morality is the maximization of pleasure in society. He wrote:

Jeremy Bentham (1748–1832) ordered in his will that his mortal remains should be stuffed and kept within the precincts of University College London, where they can be seen today. The face is a replica. He is wearing his favourite hat and sitting on his writing chair.

> *Nature has placed mankind under the governance of two sovereign masters,* pain *and* pleasure. *(Jeremy Bentham,* An Introduction to the Principles of Morals and Legislation, *W. Pickering, 1823)*

Bentham believed that not only is humanity under these twin masters, but that every human should prefer pleasure to pain. Bentham gives no reason for this preference. He argues that it is *fundamental* and needs no evidence. However, he does explain that pleasure and pain are not just physical sensations; they are also the psychological state that comes from feeling pain or pleasure. It might be argued that some people prefer

Key terms

sentient – able to experience sense or feeling.

Hedonic Calculus – system of calculating whether an action will maximize pleasure and minimize pain.

pain, whether physical or psychological. The answer to this is that such people do not see pain as pain but rather as pleasure. For example, a hermit might suffer hardship by living in a cave all his life, but he regards suffering as a stepping-stone to the pleasure of a heavenly reward. For the hermit, the physical pain is psychological pleasure.

Key point

Nature has placed mankind under the governance of two sovereign masters, *pain* and *pleasure.* (Jeremy Bentham, *An Introduction to the Principles of Morals and Legislation*)

Bentham follows up his view that human beings are under the mastery of pain and pleasure by arguing that what is good for the individual is right for human society and for all sentient creatures, that is animals as well as humans.

Utilitarian theory was not enough for Bentham. He believed that theories are worthless unless they have practical application.

The Hedonic Calculus

Bentham's application of his moral theory led to the construction of a method. All actions are to be calculated in terms of the **maximization of happiness** and the **minimization of pain**. This method is known as the Hedonic Calculus or **felicific calculus**. Bentham states that there are seven basic tests for calculating whether an action will maximize pleasure and minimize pain. They are **PRICED F**:

1. **Purity** of the sensation, meaning that it is not followed by sensations of pain.
2. **Remoteness** or nearness of the sensation.
3. **Intensity** of the sensation.
4. **Certainty** of the sensation.
5. **Extent** of the sensation, meaning the number of people affected.
6. **Duration** of the sensation.
7. **Fecundity** of the sensation, meaning the chance it will produce other pleasurable experiences.

Bentham uses the word **sensation** instead of experience or action. By this he means that pain and pleasure are products of the senses: seeing, hearing, touching, tasting and smelling. It is for each person to sit down and calculate whether a particular action will maximize pleasure. The Hedonic Calculus is the test for all practical decisions.

To think about

What do we mean by 'happiness'? Can it be defined? How can you test happiness?

Criticisms of Bentham

Bentham's ideas are not without their problems:

1. He views **all pleasures as being of equal value**. It follows that the happiness of a person clubbing on a Thursday night is the same as that of a carer doing unpaid social work for the elderly. A Benthamite approach maintains that both get pleasure from what they do. They are either happy or they are not. Their activities either give pleasure or not. For him it is impossible to speak of higher or lower pleasures.

To think about

Are all pleasures of equal value?

2. Bentham rejects the idea of **human rights** or, as they were called at the time, **natural rights**. He describes human rights as 'nonsense upon stilts'. Rights lead to conflict and not harmony. It would be wrong to allow the rights of an individual or group to frustrate actions that might lead to the general happiness of society.

3. His theory has the **logical consequence of allowing what common sense might regard as evil as a good**, if the purpose of that action maximizes happiness. Bentham supported William Wilberforce and others in their opposition to slavery and the slave trade. Yet Bentham's view of the maximization of happiness would make voluntary slavery a moral good. This could even apply to involuntary slavery if the slaves were significantly in the minority. An unemployed person might become a slave as a means of survival. His action would benefit himself and, by increasing productivity, society. All would therefore be happy as a consequence of this slave economy.

4. Bentham's theory is based on **nature**. It is argued that this application of the **eighteenth-century concept of nature** to morality is outdated. Scientists today

Key term

naturalistic fallacy – the idea that just because nature acts in a certain way it does not follow that this is how things ought to be.

have a different understanding of the natural world, which is a product of Darwinian evolutionary theory and quantum mechanics.

The use of nature as the basis of morality is, as Mill states:

Irrational because all human action whatever, consists in altering, and . . . improving, the spontaneous course of nature. (John Stuart Mill, Nature; The Utility of Religion; and Theism, *Kessinger Publishing Co., 2004)*

Mill argues that what benefits human beings get from the natural world are a result of how we harness nature, and not from following nature's laws.

5. Utilitarianism commits the so-called naturalistic fallacy.

This suggests that just because nature has x it does not follow that a person ought to do x, whatever x is. In the case of Bentham x is the principle of Utility, of pain and pleasure. Therefore, just because in nature people prefer pleasure to pain it does not follow that people ought to do that which is preferred.

6. Bentham's theory requires a **great deal of knowledge** in order to make a moral decision. It is argued that, because Bentham is concerned with long-term happiness in society for the maximal number of people, such knowledge is impossible. Few, for example, foresaw the credit crunch of 2008 yet an understanding of the future of the global economy is a necessity in calculating what decision would lead to the maximization of pleasure in society. Is it possible for ordinary people to make judgements if so-called experts could not see the impending financial disaster three weeks before it happened?

7. Bentham's theory requires a **great deal of time**. Bentham was a gentleman, which in the nineteenth century meant someone rich enough not to have to work. It can be argued that only the rich have time to sit down and calculate the general good in every situation or for every decision. The Victorian factory worker, by comparison, was not in any position to look at every action in a utilitarian way, even if he or she had the freedom and education necessary so to do.

8. There is a **lack of humanity** in Bentham's Utilitarianism. Mill, following his mental breakdown at the age of 20, used this criticism. Mill suggested that Bentham was a cold person who only understood one half of human nature, the calculating side. Critics have pointed to Bentham's development of the model prison and the workhouse system as examples of Bentham's lack of humanity and compassion. Both were designed to bring order to the penal and welfare systems, based on the principle of Utility. Today both are seen as cruel and degrading institutions that caused suffering to minorities for the benefit of the majority.

9. The American philosopher Robert Nozick (1938–2002) criticized Bentham's **hedonism**. Do pleasurable experiences lead to human contentment? Nozick believes not and he gives an illustration to prove his point; those who know the film *The Matrix* will be familiar with this analogy. Nozick states 'suppose there were an experience machine that would give you any experience you desired' whilst you were 'floating in a tank, with electrodes attached to your brain' (Robert Nozick, *Anarchy, State and Utopia*, Blackwell, 1974). Nozick questions whether you would want to be plugged in to such a machine. He is convinced that most people would not want to be. This, for Nozick, raises the question of whether pleasure rules human nature. As in the film *The Matrix*, it may be that qualities such as self-worth, freedom, personal identity and integrity are more important to human beings.

Extension note

The panopticon

Bentham was a practical philosopher. The principle of Utility was not important unless it was put into practice. During the last two decades of his life he wrote a number of books on practical issues. These reveal his view that human beings have no natural rights and that the interests of the individual must be limited for the benefit of the general happiness of the majority. In the words of Gertrude Himmelfarb:

The greatest happiness of the greatest number might thus require the greatest misery of the few. (Gertrude Himmelfarb, Victorian Minds, Ivan R. Dee, Inc., 1995)

Bentham designed the **panopticon** (meaning 'all-seeing') prison with cells arranged around a central well with a control centre, from which prisoners could be observed at all times. No prisoner was ever out of sight of a prison officer and, through a system of hard labour, silence and harsh physical punishment, every inmate would be on their best behaviour. The lack of privacy was crucial. The old prisons allowed inmates to do what they liked as long as they were locked away from the general public. The new system of total control was designed to educate the prisoner, through fear, to behave for the good of the population at large. The prison control centre might be left unmanned and still the prisoner would behave, as they would not know if someone was watching them or not. Prisoners would learn to behave for fear of returning to prison again. Crime would thereby be reduced and the principle of Utility served.

General happiness was created at the expense of freedom.

To think about

Do you think prisons should be designed for the benefit of society or for the prisoner? How is this question related to Utilitarianism?

John Stuart Mill

John Stuart Mill (1806–1873) was a leading figure in Utilitarianism.

John Stuart Mill is probably the most important of the classical utilitarians. Influenced by Bentham and by his father, James Mill, he rejected the simplistic view of pleasure that the Benthamites put forward. His early affection for Bentham turned into contempt. He wrote that Bentham remained 'a child all his life' and that his views were both infantile and cold.

Mill did not reject everything that Bentham and his father, James Mill, taught. The young Mill wanted to improve Utilitarianism and not destroy it. Mill rejected the idea of the individual's application of the Hedonic Calculus. He put forward the idea that what each individual wants, in terms of happiness, is what all human beings truly desire for themselves and for others. This creates what Mill called the aggregate of individual happiness. Mill believed that this aggregate creates the possibility of a system that can maximize happiness in society. Bentham's simple rule of applying the Hedonic Calculus to each individual action is replaced by what Mill called the logic of practice. To explain this Mill compared the roles of a judge and a legislator.

A judge sticks rigidly to the law in coming to a moral decision. For example, a driver is involved in an accident on the motorway and kills a family of five in the collision. He is jailed for five years because this is the maximum sentence allowed for causing death by careless driving. This may not seem fair or just but it is the law. Mill sees Bentham's Hedonic Calculus in the same way. The rigid application of this calculus inevitably leads to the creation of the model prison and the workhouse; systems that Mill found degrading and immoral.

Mill, who was an MP for many years, compared the role of a judge with that of a legislator. An MP does not stick rigidly to the law. He or she bases decisions on the logical application of general principles that are grounded in experience. This is what Mill means by the logic of practice. A legislator might, for example, believe that CCTV cameras should be in every street so that crime would be dramatically reduced for the common good, but would it be right to do this? Would general principles of privacy and liberty be infringed by having a police camera outside every front door?

The different roles of the judge and the legislator illustrate for Mill the fundamental divide between his application of Utilitarianism and that of the Benthamites. Mill was a legislator and Bentham was a judge.

Here, four main points should be noted. They are:

1. Mill rejected **Bentham's simplistic view of the causes of human happiness**. Mill argued that actions themselves do not make people happy; it is necessary to have the right conditions as well. For example, you might be a wealthy family man or woman living in a prosperous suburb in an emerging economy but when you go out you are afraid of speaking your mind for fear of the national secret police. On the face of it you should be happy as you have a loving family, wealth and security, but you live under the cloud of a dictatorship. Happiness is therefore causally complex.

2. This led Mill to develop basic principles that must be upheld to ensure that the **conditions for happiness** are met. The most important of these principles is **liberty**. Freedom or liberty comprises three elements. They are: a limit to the power of society over the individual, freedom of thought and speech, and the right to be an individual. The individual should be free to do whatever they want providing they do not cause harm to another person. Mill notes that those who stood out from the general opinions of their contemporaries have often been proved correct, for example Galileo and Socrates. Progress would not have been made if their views had been totally suppressed.

3. Mill believed that forcing the minority to accept the decisions of the majority does not produce the greatest good for the greatest number. What is good for society is overall **individual happiness** not the suppression of minorities. Society should have the self-confidence to allow individuals to flourish. The result, when it does, is the combined total of individual happiness to create 'the greatest good of the greatest number'. This is known as the **principle of universalizability**; meaning

Key term

Golden Rule – the Golden Rule of Jesus is 'do to others as you would have them do to you' (Matthew 7:12). It can also be expressed as 'love your neighbour as yourself' (Mark 12:31).

what is good for one person is good for all people. This does not mean that what makes you happy should be the same as everyone else. It is rather that society is content when all are happy in their different ways. Mill illustrates this theory by the so-called Golden Rule of Jesus: 'In everything do to others as you would have them do to you' (Matthew 7:12).

4. Individual happiness goes hand in hand with human equality. Mill was a leading campaigner for women's rights and for **universal suffrage** (the idea of one person, one vote). Mill's belief in individual happiness led him to reject Bentham's denial of natural rights. Bentham considered human rights to be 'simple nonsense... nonsense upon stilts' (Jeremy Bentham, *Rights, Representation and Reform: Nonsense on Stilts and Other Writings on the French Revolution*, Ed. Philip Schofield, Catherine Pease-Watkin and Cyprian Blamires, Oxford University Press, 2002); whereas for Mill, **human rights** create the conditions in which happiness can be maximized.

Key point

The principle of universalizability is expressed in the Golden Rule: 'In everything do to others as you would have them do to you' (Matthew 7:12).

Mill's Utilitarianism is very different from that of Bentham. He regards happiness as a state of mind resulting from the application of a series of basic principles in society. Denial of these basic principles, such as liberty, will result in the absence of what Mill calls the **aggregate of individual happiness**. Human progress is guaranteed when these basic principles are applied.

Utilitarianism is **teleological**. The idea of human progress is central to the application of the principle of Utility. Mill was a Victorian; he lived in a fast-changing world of human progress in industry, technology and in democratic government. He was convinced that human nature is not static but progressive. Human beings are not satisfied with remaining still but constantly desire a better tomorrow in order to be truly happy.

Key point

The promotion of happiness is the ultimate principle of Teleology. (John Stuart Mill, *A System of Logic, Ratiocinative and Inductive, Being a Connected View of the Principles of Evidence, and the Methods of Scientific Investigation,* Parker, Son & Bourn, 1862)

Higher and lower pleasures

This idea of human progress affects Mill's attitude to Bentham's Utilitarianism. Mill rejects the idea that all pleasures are the same. Human progress is the key. Some pleasures are satisfying but do they improve the person? A person who goes to the pub on a Saturday night may be enjoying themselves but is he or she improving his or her Quality of Life? Is progress being made?

Mill argues that some pleasures make people happy because they are progressive. These are the **higher pleasures**. Mill does not list what he considers to be higher and lower pleasures but he makes it clear that philosophers understand both types of pleasure. Higher pleasures therefore include such things as philosophical insight, educational development, self-improvement, empathy towards others, listening to music, generosity and even reading this book!

Lower pleasures include eating a meal, drinking, sexual intercourse and so on. They make the individual happy but the pleasure gained does nothing for the person's progressive nature. They are fleeting: here today and gone tomorrow. They are, as Mill puts it, '**worthy only of swine**' (John Stuart Mill, *Utilitarianism*, Longmans, Green, Reader and Dyer, 1867). Continuing his swine analogy, Mill wrote:

Is it better to be a happy pig or an unhappy philosopher?

*It is **better to be a human being dissatisfied than a pig satisfied**; better to be Socrates dissatisfied than a fool satisfied. And if the fool, or the pig, is of a different opinion, it is because they only know their own side of the question. The other party to the comparison knows both sides. (John Stuart Mill,* Utilitarianism)

This famous quote is an attack on Bentham's simple hedonism but it is also an assault on all those who look to lower pleasures as their source of happiness. These fools, as Mill sees it, are in all sectors of society, from the wealthy banker interested only in making money to the impoverished poor, who spend life creating ever-larger families. All are fools because they live in a world in which there is 'the absence of high feelings. . . the absence of interest' (John Stuart Mill, *Autobiography*, Elibron Classics, 2005). These though are the minority of the human race.

Mill differed from Bentham who believed that all pleasures are of equal value. Bentham, for example, regarded reading poetry and playing music as less important than playing the child's game of push-pin. Why? A child's game can be played by anyone. Poetry and music are understood by a few. The utilitarian principle of 'the greatest good of the greatest number' means that a child's game is much more useful (utilitarian) than the arts of poetry or music. Mill, on the other hand, regarded reading poetry as one of the higher pleasures. Push-pin was a trivial game that was a lower pleasure.

Criticisms of Mill

Mill's Utilitarianism has been criticized on a number of levels. The main criticisms are:

1. Mill's psychological approach is a product of nineteenth-century attitudes about human nature, which are discredited today. Mill has a very optimistic view of human nature and believes in individual autonomy. These views are in marked contrast to the ideas of contemporary scientist Richard Dawkins, who asserts that human behaviour is heavily determined by our genes.

2. Mill's higher and lower pleasures are meaningless terms. People either get pleasure from something or they do not.

3. Mill's notion of the teleology of happiness, which suggests that higher pleasures lead to human progress, is weak. Progress can be made equally by lower pleasures as by higher pleasures.

4. There is an arrogance in Mill's ideas of higher and lower pleasures. His comment that lower pleasures are 'worthy only of swine' suggests intellectual arrogance.

5. Mill rejected the simplicity of Bentham's ethical theory, but produced a view of Utilitarianism that is too complex. Many consider that Mill is a Rule utilitarian but this is only partially true. There are always exceptions to any rule. Mill cites the Golden Rule of Christian thought ('In everything do to others as you would have them do to you' (Matthew 7:12)) as a rule but there are exceptions. For example, Mill rejects the right of a person to self-harm or to harm another consenting adult and asserts that a human being cannot become a slave to another person even if they wish to do so. As a result, liberty is a right but only up to a point; there are always exceptions.

6. The complexity of Mill's Utilitarianism means that the morality or otherwise of various issues cannot be easily or quickly resolved. Mill regards this as releasing human beings from the simplicity of the Hedonic Calculus. Critics of Mill argue that it prevents people from judging the merits of particular projects or situations which demand rapid solutions. The simplicity of Bentham's calculus is replaced by, what Mill calls, the **plurality of causes** and the **intermingling of effects**. The original purpose of Utilitarianism, which was to answer questions about what is good and right in a particular situation, is no longer possible.

Similarities and differences between Bentham and Mill

The tables below outline the most important similarities and differences between the views of Bentham and Mill.

1. Similarities

	Similarity between Bentham's Utilitarianism and Mill's Utilitarianism
1	Belief in the pain/pleasure calculus as inbuilt in human nature.
2	Belief that happiness is the highest goal of human beings.
3	Belief that human society exists to create happiness.
4	Belief in human progress.
5	Rejection of religion and the Divine Command theory.
6	Rejection of concept of a priori moral truths.

2. Differences

	Bentham's view	Mill's view
1	It is the **quantity** of happiness that is important.	It is the **quality** of happiness that matters.
2	All pleasures are of same value.	There are higher and lower pleasures.
3	Focused on the individual.	Emphasis on the aggregate of individual happiness.

(*continued*)

	Bentham's view	Mill's view
4	System of Hedonic Calculus based on experience.	System based on the application of logic to practical situations.
5	Considers human rights to be nonsense.	Believes that without individual liberty society's happiness is not possible.

Key term

Act Utilitarianism – theory that individual actions must be determined by the amount they increase general utility or happiness, based on the principle of 'the greatest good of the greatest number'.

Act Utilitarianism

Act Utilitarianism is also known as **extreme Utilitarianism**, as the value of an act is the amount it increases general utility or happiness. Rules and moral maxims are only to be kept if, in all probability, obedience to the law will lead to a net gain of utility. Human beings ought, in most situations, to obey moral rules as they are designed to maximize **expected utility**. In cases where there are no rules or the existing laws seem to be contradictory, rules can be set aside. In such cases, Act utilitarians approach what to do in different ways. The most important are:

- An action is right if, and only if, it promotes happiness.
- An action is right if, and only if, it causes pleasure and the absence of pain.
- An action is right if its utility is greater than nought.
- An action is right if, when compared to available alternatives, it maximizes utility.

Act utilitarians no longer view happiness or pleasure as the basis of their approach. They have a broader view of utility based on a variety of attributes for what makes people content.

The originator of modern **Act Utilitarianism** was the philosopher Henry Sidgwick (1838–1900). His work, *The Methods of Ethics*, is the final utilitarian work to be based on the idea that morality is the greatest happiness for the greatest number. Sidgwick addresses the same questions (**what is good?** and **what is right?**) as the earlier utilitarians. He argues that hedonism, the pursuit of pleasure, is the best of a series of alternative theories about **what is good?**

This conclusion is reached empirically by examining how human beings reach decisions about their lives. How do you imagine your life to be in 20 years' time? Surely you imagine your life being happy and successful with your dreams fulfilled. Sidgwick imagines that this dream of a better tomorrow is part of human nature. Human beings want a pleasurable existence, where the individual's psychological state of well-being is realized. Sidgwick adds that this state cannot be created by accident. It involves willpower and the ability to act on what you believe. You cannot be happy if you do not control your destiny.

To think about

Do you agree that dreaming of a better tomorrow is part of human nature?

The second question (**what is right?**) divides utilitarians today. Sidgwick's answer is complex and very different from previous utilitarians. He argues in favour of a sort of common-sense intuition, which forms the basis of his Act Utilitarianism. Rules are framed by a common-sense understanding of what is right or wrong, for example, the maxims 'never lie' or 'never steal'. Sidgwick maintains that if you look carefully at these rules/maxims they are really utilitarian values, as they have a basis in hedonism. Therefore, 'never lie' would be seen as 'If I lie no one would trust me and I would not be able to trust anyone else. This would be painful to me'. Again, 'never steal' would be seen by the reflective person as 'If I steal I would leave myself open to either theft or imprisonment, both of which would be painful'.

However, Sidgwick does point out that, after reflection, an individual might decide that it is best to lie or to steal. She or he will have calculated that the net effect of lying or stealing is more pleasurable. Moral rules are rules of thumb, useful indicators that in certain circumstances can be set aside.

This view of morality creates a problem. Imagine that you are walking along a canal towpath. You see a young person struggling in the water in danger of drowning. Common-sense intuition tells you to save the young person. Utilitarian reflection assures you that a rescue will produce more pleasure than pain. You dive into the cold water and save the young person; he and his family are grateful and you feel happy that you have done a good deed. As a result, pleasure is maximized. However, several years later, you discover that the person you saved became a serial killer. He is now serving a life sentence for scores of brutal murders. What was a good act, as it maximized happiness at the time, becomes an action that brought more pain than pleasure.

The logic of Sidgwick's ethics is that the same act can be seen as both moral and immoral. How is it possible to know in advance whether an action will have a net benefit or deficit? Sidgwick's solution to this problem is that an act may be both moral and immoral at different times. When making a moral decision, you must respond to the immediate consequences of your actions. It is not possible to be certain about the long-term effects of what you decide.

This is one of the strengths of modern Act Utilitarianism. It allows exceptions to a particular rule or law if the exception appears to maximize human welfare. It also takes into account the lack of knowledge that may exist when coming to a moral decision. In these types of circumstances Act utilitarians distinguish between **objectively right**

Key terms

principle of justice – Sidgwick's idea that justice is as important as happiness in determining the utility of an action or moral rule.

Rule Utilitarianism – theory that life is too short to judge every action on the basis of 'the greatest good of the greatest number'. Instead rules exist, which are based on the maximization of happiness principle, that make it easier to act.

and **subjectively right acts**. An objectively right act is one that turns out to be the right decision on the basis of net benefit. A subjectively right act is what you decide to do, on the basis of the information you have at the time.

It is also possible for an Act utilitarian to decide to do one thing in a particular situation and the exact opposite a few hours later. This has led to a charge of moral inconsistency. Sidgwick sought to counteract this criticism by adding one further element to the theory. This is the principle of justice. Sidgwick followed the ideas of Mill by citing the Christian Golden Rule: 'In everything do to others as you would have them do to you' (Matthew 7:12). Sidgwick's theory develops this further by making justice a central plank of Utilitarianism. Justice is about equality of action. In considering any action the individual has to take account of not only whether the deed has a net benefit (more pleasure than pain) but also whether what will be done is just to all the parties concerned. This saves Sidgwick from the earlier criticisms but it creates a new one: what is special about justice? Later Act utilitarians add further virtues to solve this problem, but in doing so, it is argued that they have stopped judging each action separately. They have created moral norms to judge acts. Rule utilitarians develop this further.

Rule Utilitarianism

Rule Utilitarianism is in marked contrast to Act Utilitarianism. While Act utilitarians regard laws and maxims as rules of thumb that can be disregarded in some circumstances, Rule utilitarians argue that moral laws must be obeyed. These rules are selected on the basis of whether they will maximize general good or welfare in society. J.O. Urmson and Richard B. Brandt in America and John Austin (1790–1859) and Stephen Edelston Toulmin (1922–2009) in the UK developed Rule Utilitarianism. They did so in response to the criticism that Utilitarianism was too complex to be useful in making moral decisions. Rule utilitarians are agreed that there is a process by which acts can be judged as immoral. They argue that this method sets the conditions by which moral decisions ought to be made and that will, they believe, lead to the condemnation of some actions and the praising of others.

The basic assumptions of Rule Utilitarianism are:

1. General moral rules exist in order to achieve benefit for the majority of people in society.
2. Rules prevent
– the selfish use of utilitarian principles
– a subjective notion of what constitutes happiness or pleasure.

3. Rules have consequences on actions and Rule utilitarians believe that actions must always be guided by the general rules that create the maximization of pleasure or happiness.
4. Rules ensure that the motive of an action is not guided by self-interest or delusion.
5. Modern Rule Utilitarianism is largely influenced by the notion of the maximization of social benefit or welfare.
6. Rules do not always need to be acted upon. A country has, for example, the right to self-defence. It will only need to keep this rule if it is under attack. Since it is a powerful country it is never attacked. Thus the rule exists but is never needed.
7. Rule utilitarians take into account the consequences of actions and not only the good likely to be produced by a single moral decision.

Several criticisms have been made of Rule Utilitarianism. These fall into four distinct areas. They are:

• How it is possible to **universalize the concept of general benefit** or happiness? This is important since the rules within Rule Utilitarianism are universally applicable. In some societies an action might be morally beneficial to that country's system whereas in another society it would be morally harmful.

• How is it possible to create particular moral rules that maximize happiness or **social benefit throughout the world**? Can, for example, the right to personal property always be justified in a world of starving millions?

• Do not **moral laws often conflict**? The right to be free from hunger and want seems logical yet, it might be argued, destroying the rainforests to provide food for the world's population goes against other utilitarian rules about protecting the earth's resources.

• How can the benefit for the maximal number of people be deduced from following a rule if the consequences of actions are not known? **Future benefits of any action are unpredictable**.

Some scholars argue that Bentham was the forerunner of Act Utilitarianism and Mill of Rule Utilitarianism.

Preference Utilitarianism

Preference Utilitarianism is based on a belief that what is morally right is *not* actions that maximize human welfare, nor is it obedience to certain moral rules that have the same effect. Preference utilitarians, such as Peter Singer (1946–), believe that a right action is one that maximizes the preferences that individual human beings make in life.

Key point

In deciding what is good and what is bad for an individual, the ultimate criterion can only be his own wants and his own preferences. (John C. Harsanyi, 'Morality and the theory of rational behaviour', *Utilitarianism and beyond*, Ed. Amartya Sen and Bernard Williams, Cambridge University Press, 1982)

Preference utilitarians argue that every human being wants a good life. In this Singer is regarded as a modern follower of Bentham. Singer goes so far as to argue that this desire is inbuilt into the evolutionary process and transcends societies. Preference utilitarians go on to argue that individual preferences relate to the need for a good life. John C. Harsanyi (1920–2000) argued that there is a distinction between manifest and true preferences. A manifest preference is what you prefer, which is based on immediate desires and needs. A true preference is based on reflecting on all the information known and on the likely consequences. True preferences, states Singer,

Preference Utilitarianism encourages you to consider overall happiness or overall suffering of all sentient creatures. Can we balance the suffering of battery farmed animals against the loss in earnings of the farmer and the price the customer will have to pay for their eggs?

are those that a person would accept if 'they were fully informed, reflective, and vividly aware of the consequences of satisfying their preferences' (Peter Singer, 2002, 'A Response to Martha Nussbaum' available from www.utilitarian.net/singer/by/20021113.htm [accessed 01/06/2010]).

Singer believes that all ethical decisions are based on 'trade-offs dependent on empirical calculations' (Singer, 'A Response to Martha Nussbaum'). The word trade-off is important. He argues that one of the great strengths of Utilitarianism is that it does not give a clear-cut answer of what is right or wrong but provides a means of approaching ethical issues. Singer believes that society is made up of a collection of individuals, each with their own preferences. Trade-offs have to be made for the general welfare. Some preferences have to be rejected or deferred so that the general good is maintained.

Key term

paternalism – the idea that a person or group in authority is qualified to make decisions in the best interests of another person or group.

Extension note

Preference Utilitarianism, chickens and trade-offs

It is important to note here that Singer includes all sentient creatures and not just human beings in his ideas. Singer gives the following example of a trade-off. Battery farming brings a lot of suffering to hens. In return the intensive production of battery farming brings benefits to the profits of the farmer and to the consumer who buys cheap eggs. A trade-off would occur if battery farming were abolished. The consumer would suffer from higher prices for eggs while the farmer's profits would diminish.

Singer argues that Preference Utilitarianism is the best method of approaching this issue. Singer states that 'we can minimize overall suffering by calculating whether, for instance, banning battery cages for laying hens would, in the long run, save more suffering in hens than it causes in factory farm owners, and people who have to pay a little more for their eggs' (Singer, 'A Response to Martha Nussbaum'). He campaigns against battery farming, arguing that when society understands the cruelty involved, it will think that the higher cost of eggs is a price worth paying. It will have accepted the trade-off.

Preference utilitarians maximize good through the maximization of individual preferences but this raises important issues, which have led to the criticism of Preference Utilitarianism.

These issues include:

1. At what stage do you judge people's preferences? Harsanyi addresses this by arguing that there is a difference between **manifest preferences** and **true preferences**. Manifest preferences are based on what you happen to prefer due to immediate needs. True preferences are those you would have if you had all the facts and evidence to make a calculated decision on what you prefer.

2. Harsanyi's distinction between two sorts of preference raises the issue of who decides whether a preference is manifest or true. Critics have called this a **paternalistic** feature of Preference Utilitarianism; it assumes that the preferences

Key term

principle of equal consideration of interests – idea in the work of Singer that individuals' preferences must be rooted in the notion that what I prefer must consider other people's interests and that what other people prefer must have regard to my interests. This is applicable to all sentient beings.

of policy makers and so-called experts are true while those of non-experts like you and I are just manifest, because the experts know more.

3. Preferences are not static things. People change and therefore so do their preferences. When there were only fish and chip shops in the UK, people preferred fish and chips. Now there are Indian restaurants and takeaways some people prefer chicken tikka masala. Preference is therefore a consequence of what is available rather than what people really prefer or want.

4. The concepts of **love and relationships are absent** from Preference utility. Preference Utilitarianism is based on the maximization of preferences, on universalizability, the idea that the individual will prefer something because it is good not just for that individual but also for all individuals. Singer, in his *Practical Ethics*, calls this the principle of equal consideration of interests.

5. Universalizability of preferences and the principle of equal consideration of interests raise a further issue. Welfare is a central feature of Preference Utilitarianism. Preferences are formed on the basis that what you prefer will benefit everyone. Therefore, it is argued, an individual's preference for inexpensive jeans will be beneficial to those who produce the jeans in the developing economies. In the same way a personal preference for eco-friendly commodities will benefit all – it is 'the greatest good of the greatest number'. Yet critics argue that in a world of limited resources, it is not possible to accept a link between a person's preferences and the general welfare. For instance, a person may prefer expensive meals every day, which benefits those who produce them; but would that preference disadvantage those living in poverty?

6. Human beings do not live a life of preferences. Preference utilitarians believe that sentient beings are constantly making decisions. This may not be the case. Anne Maclean, in her book *The Elimination of Morality*, criticized the Preference utilitarians including Singer over this. She argues that, while some moral judgements can be made rationally, it is wrong to argue that all ethical decisions should be based on philosophical enquiry. Keith Crome puts it more clearly by arguing that there is 'a limit to the role of rationality' (Keith Crome, 'Is Peter Singer's utilitarian argument about abortion tenable?', *Richmond Journal of Philosophy* 17, Spring 2008). Perhaps life is making the best of a bad situation rather than working out preferences? Perhaps life is about going with the flow?

Singer justifies his Preference Utilitarianism by arguing that when informed preferences are fulfilled human beings enjoy a good life. This is what he desires for himself and therefore, he argues, this must be logically true for all human beings, other things being equal.

To think about

'In the end, Utilitarianism is simply a moral justification for individual or group selfishness.' Discuss.

Utilitarianism: strengths and weaknesses

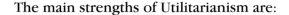

The main strengths of Utilitarianism are:

* It tries to relate human psychology and experiences to a method of discovering what is the right thing to do.
* It is in essence a simple idea, which is easily understood and therefore possible for everyone to use.
* It answers the question of why human beings should be morally good by stating that it is in the individual's self-interest to be so.
* It implies that what is in my self-interest is to everyone's advantage, so that calculating personal advantage can only be done if the wider community is considered.
* It is progressive and argues that, if implemented, the world would be a better place.
* It supports the idea of human welfare and can be used in a variety of areas of life, from personal morality to world economics.
* It takes into account the consequences of any action or moral principle. These are the determining factor. End results matter. This is a common-sense view.
* It does not rely on what many see as out-of-date religious bases for morality.
* It is morality for a democratic age, based on 'the greatest good of the greatest number'.
* It takes into account other sentient beings besides humans including animals and their pleasure.

The main weaknesses are:

* It is based on an outdated concept of nature. It can also be criticized for committing the naturalistic fallacy.

- It is concerned with the greatest number and therefore ignores the plight of minority groups.
- It does not take into account the intentions of people but rather focuses on the action or principle.
- It ignores the notion of doing something out of a sense of duty.
- It ignores the importance of love and human or animal relationships in morality.
- It ignores the idea of self-sacrifice as a moral virtue yet, at the same time, it tolerates the sacrifice of individuals for the common good.
- It focuses on supposed consequences that are hard to predict because of the limitations of human knowledge.

Practice exam questions

(a) Explain the main differences between Act and Rule Utilitarianism.

The starting point of your answer could be a clear definition of Act Utilitarianism. In Act Utilitarianism it is actions that maximize human welfare – moral laws should only be used as a rule of thumb. In Act Utilitarianism the Hedonic Calculus, not obedience to law is crucial. You may want to illustrate this by using the ideas of Bentham or Sidgwick. You might then mention that many utilitarians argue that it is not possible for any human being to look at every issue on a case by case basis. These scholars developed Rule Utilitarianism. You could examine the Rule utilitarian belief that there are certain laws that must be obeyed as they ensure the maximization of human happiness. You could mention Mill's use of the Golden Rule of Jesus and thinkers such as J. O. Urmson.

(b) 'Utilitarianism has no serious weaknesses.' Discuss.

You could start by looking at supposed weaknesses of Utilitarianism. These might include that it is consequentialist in nature, and that consequences can be difficult to predict. You could also look at Kantian criticisms that while happiness and welfare are important for human beings this is not and ought not to be the basis of morality. You could mention that Utilitarianism ignores the ethical state of the moral agent for the idea of the greater good, and that working for the greater good may involve the suffering of the minority. The best answers might give counter-arguments to these criticisms and consider how serious they are as weaknesses.

Develop your knowledge

There are a number of books that consider Utilitarianism, including:

Ethics: Inventing Right and Wrong by J.L. Mackie (Penguin Books, 1990)
Ethics: Discovering Right and Wrong by Louis P. Pojman (Wadsworth Publishing Co., 1999)
A Companion to Ethics by Peter Singer (ed.) (Blackwell, 1993)
John Stuart Mill by John Skorupski (Routledge, 1991)
Utilitarianism: For & Against by J.J.C. Smart and Bernard Williams (Cambridge University Press, 1973)

5

Key terms

denomination – refers to the different branches of the Christian Church.

liberal Christians – Christians that believe in the centrality of the individual conscience in moral matters and in social justice.

Introduction

There is no such thing as a single Christian approach to ethics. Christians have, since the creation of the Church, disagreed over ethical issues. These disagreements occur for a variety of reasons. The first divisions are those that have occurred within the Church over the centuries. Today there are many denominations each with differing views of Christianity. These differences may not be great but they do have an effect on the way in which ethical values and moral issues are perceived.

There are also divisions that do not relate to which denomination a person belongs to. There are divisions within the Churches, caused largely by differing interpretations of the Bible and tradition, between what are known as traditionalist and liberal Christians. However, there are, despite these divisions, a kernel of beliefs that unite all Christians and also represent the basis for dialogue between Christians and with non-believers.

Christianity: Sources of authority

The Bible

The Qur'an states that Christians are 'People of the Book' (5:19) (*The Koran*, Penguin Books, 2000). The **Bible** is the book being referred to. It is true that all Christians regard the Bible as the Word of God, but what is meant by that expression has been a matter of controversy from the beginning of the Christian Church. The Bible can be understood as containing hidden moral or spiritual meanings beyond the literal meaning of the text. Each passage is therefore open to many complex interpretations.

Fundamentalist Christians hold that the Bible is literally the Word of God. They assert that God's message was directly conveyed to the Bible's various writers. They believe that all that is necessary for salvation can be found within the Scriptures. The various writers whose work is to be found within the Bible were inspired to write what they wrote. The expression salvation history, first put forward by the German biblical scholars Julius Wellhausen (1844–1918) and Karl Graf (1815–1869), conveys the idea that there is a common theme that runs throughout the books of the Bible. God reveals himself by a series of **covenants** (agreements between God and human beings). The first are to be found in the book of Genesis and the last in the Incarnation of Jesus. From this point, with the establishment of the Christian Church, further covenants become unnecessary. The biblical covenants demonstrate God's love for his world and his people. The Bible is therefore seen as the document that will point human beings towards a right relationship with God.

However, it can be argued that even fundamentalists do not follow all the teachings of the Bible which were written for historical times. For example, few Christians today conform to the laws of Moses, despite the fact that Jesus told his disciples to follow them. For instance, Christians do not observe Jewish dietary laws nor do they have their male children circumcised.

Extension note

The Bible belongs to everyone? A woman in court

In 1559 a woman was arrested for not attending church. She was brought before her local church court. This was the end of the first year of the reign of the Protestant queen, Elizabeth I. It was clear from her words to the court that the arrested woman was guilty. She was not an educated woman but her words to the court suggest that she was intelligent. She told the court that in all things religious the world had seen great changes. Today, she said, every man had become their own god, reading the Bible and interpreting it in their own way.

The point is not whether she was a Catholic, attached to the religion of Elizabeth's half-sister Mary Tudor, or not. We will never know. What her words demonstrate is that she had identified a changing attitude to the Bible. The Bible was now widely available in English. The Church, whose clergy had set up the first printing presses, had lost control of its sacred text. Now ordinary people were able to read and evaluate it.

Key terms

fundamentalism – the belief in the strict literal interpretation of Scripture and sacred texts. In Christianity this is the belief in the literal interpretation of the Bible.

salvation history – the idea that the Bible documents God revealing himself in history as Saviour.

Key term

synod – an assembly of the clergy and sometimes the laity in a particular Church.

To think about

'The Bible is too important a document to allow the person in the street to interpret it.' Discuss.

For Protestants the Bible is the focal point of authority. Consequently, for Protestant Christians any belief or doctrine must be supported by evidence from Scripture. Shortly after Luther began the Protestant Reformation in 1517, he identified two Latin phrases that everyone could understand. They are:

- *per sola fide* (**by faith alone**) – concerns salvation, as it is by faith alone that a person is saved.
- *per sola scriptura* (**by the Bible alone**) – concerns the authority of the Bible.

Put the two phrases together and it is clear what all the fuss was about. No longer would the Church be the vehicle of salvation. Each human being would find his or her own faith through the Bible and be saved by it.

Some Protestants believe that the interpretation of Scripture and the accompanying authority lies in individual church groups. These are small congregations that discuss the Bible and create, within their small community, a consensus view about Christian doctrine.

Other Protestants take a different route. They hold to the idea that the Bible is the sole body of authority but that it must be interpreted wisely. By this they mean that there must be guidance on what Scripture means and that an educated clergy and, more recently, laity can best provide this. Such churches have a central structure, with an assembly of elected members at its core. This assembly, sometimes known as a synod, discusses matters of faith and morals as well as practical issues of governance. Such structures are not without their critics. Is it possible for an assembly to discover the mind of God or the faith of the Church?

Tradition and reason

The Church of England is an amalgam of various traditions; it incorporates both the traditions of medieval Roman Catholicism and the fundamentals of Reformation Protestantism. Due to this mix of traditions, Anglicans are divided over where authority lies. Some Anglican Christians believe that the Bible is the sole source of authority. These are known as Evangelicals or, more traditionally, the Low Church. Morally these

Anglicans are often, though not universally, opposed to gay rights and to women priests and bishops. Their reading of the Bible is the basis of their objection to these things.

The Church of England includes two other groups. They are (a) Anglo-Catholics or, more traditionally, the High Church and (b) liberal Anglicans. These Anglicans do not have a single source of authority for making moral decisions. They use three agreed sources of authority. They are:

- the **Bible**
- the **traditions of the ancient Church**, as laid down in the writings of the Fathers and the First Universal Councils of the Church
- **reason**.

The first source of authority is self-explanatory. The other two require analysis. From the first century CE to the fifth century CE Christian leaders (the Church Fathers) met regularly to discuss matters of beliefs and morals. They wrote down what they agreed. Sometimes they put their ideas down in statements of belief, called **creeds**.

> ## Extension note
>
> ### The age of the Fathers
> The polytheistic religion of ancient Rome did not die; it had to be killed. It was the so-called Church Fathers that through their writings and the example of their lives buried the ancient religion of the Romans. If you have already completed the Philosophy section of this course you will know something of the life of two of them – St Irenaeus (130–200) and St Augustine of Hippo. There were tens of thousands of such people. Some lived simple lives in caves throughout the Mediterranean world. There were, before the rise of Islam, hundreds of thousands of monks living in the caves of Syria alone.
>
> Some lived in communities in the major cities of the Roman Empire. Their moral teaching is useful in understanding how Christian ideas developed; for example, ideas about sex and marriage and how virginity became valued in a way that is not found in Jewish tradition.

The last source of authority is **reason**. The ancient Greek writers, such as Plato and Aristotle, believed that truth could be revealed through argument and structured debate. The free male Athenians spent vast amounts of time discussing issues. Reason is the skill of using the mind to analyse information, find what is relevant and what is

Key term

Church Fathers – any of the great bishops, early philosophers and theologians and other eminent Christian teachers of the early centuries. They are divided into the Latin Fathers, such as St Augustine of Hippo (354–430), and the Greek Fathers, for example St Basil the Great (330–379).

Key term

magisterium – the teaching authority of the Roman Catholic Church.

not, and then to deduce from this truths. These truths are the best possible fit. They may not be eternally true but they attempt to solve the problem in the immediate.

Christians believe that God created reason. This faculty is linked with the image of God to be found in every human being. Reason is a central feature of Aquinas' thought, which is the basis of modern Catholicism.

Reason is regarded as important by most Anglicans, because it helps with Christian responses to moral issues that did not exist in the Bible, or with re-evaluating old problems. Christian social reformers used reason to attack the slave trade, even though there are a number of biblical passages that recommend slavery.

The magisterium of the Church

The Roman Catholic Church is by far the largest of all the Christian denominations. Its sources of authority known as the magisterium are similar to those of the Church of England, although the difference lies in the position of the pope. The pope is considered the successor of St Peter and holds a huge amount of power to decide the beliefs of Roman Catholic Christians worldwide. He does this in three distinct ways. The first is through **sermons** and **pastoral letters** to the faithful in Rome, to which all Roman Catholics should listen. The next method is through **encyclicals**. These carry the weight of the authority of the Church. They are papal letters addressed to all the bishops of the Roman Catholic Church and the faithful everywhere in the world. Some direct the faithful to consider while others expect obedience. The latter group are known as statements *ex cathedra*. These are very rare and cannot be questioned by members of the Church. There have only been four since 1854.

To think about

'Morality is a private matter. No one should tell me how to live my life.' Discuss.

The inner self

Christians of all denominations find help in making moral decisions through two things that are essentially individualistic in nature. These are **private prayer** and the

conscience. The first disciples were taught to pray by Jesus. He taught them what today is called the **Lord's Prayer** (or *pater noster* meaning 'Our Father'). The prayer includes one moral statement about forgiveness. Private prayer among Christians helps them to contemplate where they have gone wrong and what they must do to live a loving and caring life, in service to others. These are central themes of the Gospel. Christians also believe that they gain insight into morality through the human conscience. This, for many Christians, is the voice of God within. The idea of the human conscience is examined in the A2 part of this book.

A further source of authority for most Christians is the sacraments and other services of the Church. The services, especially the **Eucharist** (Holy Communion and the Mass), are designed to enhance the loving and caring aspect of the Christian community. Sacraments have a moral as well as spiritual agenda. The words of the services are often used by Christians to express what they regard as moral truths. For example, the words in the marriage service:

Those whom God has joined together let no one put asunder.

Key point

The main sources of authority for Christian ethics include the Bible, Church tradition, reason and the inner-self.

Christianity: Main ethical principles

At the heart of the Christian religion are a number of shared beliefs. These are to be found in the creeds of the Christian Church. One of these is the **Apostles' Creed,** which is accepted by all Christian denominations, irrespective of their other differences. The creed is a summation of the main principles of Christianity. It is possible to use this creed to construct not only the main beliefs of the Christian faith but also the main ethical principles of Christianity.

The Apostles' Creed is a statement of Christian beliefs.

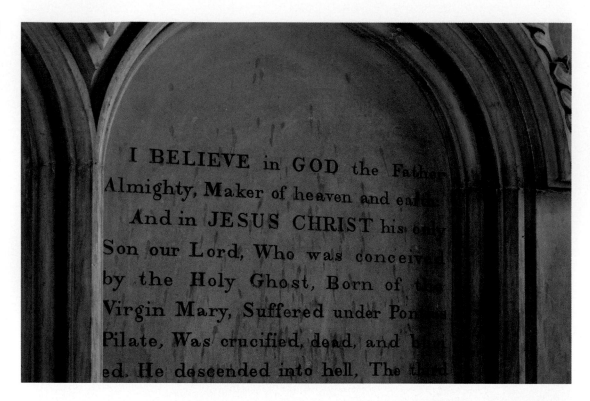

God as father and the Divine Command theory

Ethical principles in Christianity have developed from the Christian understanding of God. Christians believe that God is Father, Son and Holy Spirit. This belief in the Holy Trinity has moral implications. The Apostles' Creed opens with the words:

I believe in God the Father almighty, creator of heaven and earth. ('Apostles' Creed', Encyclopædia Britannica. Encyclopædia Britannica Online. Encyclopædia Britannica, 2010. Web. 3 Mar. 2010, http://search.eb.com/eb/article-9008045)

Two fundamental beliefs stand out. They are that God in Christianity is an omnipotent deity and that, as father, he is the creator of all things. This brief summary of faith should be linked with the opening chapters of Genesis. God made the universe through his Word and, since he is perfect, his Creation was without fault. The moral perspective to this is that Christians are bound to respect God's Creation, like tenants respecting the property of their landlord. Christians are called upon to go further. They must understand that everything they have in the end belongs to God. They must therefore live their lives in conformity to the will of God or, more accurately, to the nature of God as revealed through the Bible and the teachings of the Church.

An acceptance of God's omnipotence has moral implications. Christians recognize that they are, in the end, powerless. This sense of helplessness led to the development of an ethical theory, **theological voluntarism**. The word voluntarism comes from the Latin word for 'will'. Human beings ought to do what God wills. The theory falls into four parts. They are:

- God is all-powerful and therefore has total freedom to do whatever he wishes.
- God chooses not to act arbitrarily, which would be inconsistent with his nature.
- Therefore, God orders the universe by his Divine Law.
- Human beings, being powerless, have an obligation to obey God's law.

The theory can be understood by a simple illustration. Imagine that God is a general in the army and that Christians are his soldiers. The soldiers wait on the battlefield of life. They know that the general has the strategic plan that will enable them to be victorious. What should they do? Should they follow the orders, however strange the commands might seem at the time? The clear answer is that they should for their own good if nothing else. They know that, by doing so, victory will be achieved.

Key point

According to the Divine Command theory humans should live their lives in conformity to the will of God as revealed in the Bible and the teaching of the Church.

Strengths of the Divine Command theory

Theological voluntarism or the **Divine Command theory**, as it is sometimes called, has certain strengths. They are that:

1. It conforms to the Christian understanding that God is omnipotent. This is the idea of **divine sovereignty**.

2. It conforms to the Christian idea that **God is Creator** of the universe and, in consequence of that creativity, expects human beings to live in a particular way. This means that Christians have a duty of care to the environment.

3. It is an **objective moral system**, not based on human preferences or outcomes. This, it is argued, gives it that **universalizability** and **impartiality** which other ethical theories often lack.

4. It emphasizes the **virtue of obedience**, **obligation**, in Christian thought. The American scholar Robert Adams has developed this idea in his study of the Divine Command theory. It is also consistent with the concept of Christians being called to be, in the words of Paul, 'slaves of Christ' (Ephesians 6:6).

Criticisms of the Divine Command theory

Theological voluntarism is not without its critics. The most important criticisms are:

1. The Euthyphro dilemma. This is an important criticism of the Divine Command theory. In *Euthyphro*, one of Plato's first and smaller works, Plato tackles the issue of religious piety. In the work, Socrates asks Euthyphro a question:

   Is the pious loved by the gods because it is pious, or is it pious because it is loved? (Plato and Aristophanes, Four texts on Socrates: Plato's Euthyphro, Apology, and Crito, and Aristophanes' Clouds, *Cornell University Press, 1998)*

   Plato persuades Euthyphro to argue that piety is that which is loved by the gods. He has fallen into a trap. Imagine Euthrypro going to the temple to offer a sacrifice; he performs a pious act. The gods see the sacrifice being performed and are pleased. Why are they pleased? Are they pleased because they love piety because it is pious? Or are they pleased because he has performed an act that the gods love which means it is pious?

   This is the dilemma. Do moral values (piety) come from an independent moral code other than the gods? Or, do the choices of the gods dictate what is good (pious)? If morality comes from an independent source beyond the will of the gods, then gods are not all-powerful, they too can be judged on moral grounds, and morality is independent of religion. If the gods dictate what is morally good then it follows that gods can command an act that would, by human standards, be viewed as immoral and it becomes a moral act because the gods have willed it. This view raises the question of whether gods are inherently good and moral.

   Plato's dilemma was not a major problem for the ancient Greeks. The gods of ancient Athens were not all-powerful nor were they all-good. It does, however, present a problem for monotheistic religions in which God is omnipotent, omnibenevolent and the source of moral law.

Extension note

The Euthyphro dilemma

William of Ockham, the English medieval philosopher, tried to solve the problem posed by the Euthyphro dilemma by asserting that what God wills is morally right. As a result God has total power to make what common sense regards as evil morally good. This would allow crusaders to kill people because they are doing God's will. Ockham saw the problem and created a way out. This is the idea of *de potentia ordinata* (God's ordained power). God has total power (*de potentia absoluta*) but he limits himself. He agrees to abide by his own moral framework and voluntarily limits his power to act. God has power, Ockham argues, to make good evil and vice versa but he chooses not to exercise this power.

Ockham's solution was rejected by the Protestant reformers of the sixteenth century because, they argued, it placed a limit on God's freedom, in practice if not in theory. As a consequence, they claimed, God was no longer omnipotent.

The American theologian, Robert Adams, a contemporary supporter of theological voluntarism, argues that obedience to God depends on there being a consistency between God's nature, as expressed in Scripture, tradition and in the life of Jesus, and what God wills. Simply put: if God says do *x* and it does not appear to relate to God's nature then God cannot be telling you to do it. Jesus commands that Christians love their enemies. Would he then order you to kill them all?

It might be argued though that Adam's theory does not get to the heart of the Euthyphro dilemma. Peter Geach, for example, argues that the Divine Command theory is unnecessary. If what God commands is not right then the fact that God commands it is no reason for obedience to the order. Conversely, if it is right it is morally good not because God commands it but because it is right in and of itself. Since God will always command what is morally good, the role of God in moral decision-making is an unnecessary distraction.

2. To what extent is the Christian religion about obedience to laws? It is argued that the God of Christianity is fundamentally a loving God. Therefore the early Christians rejected the legalism of the Torah. They had, it is argued, a more open response to moral issues. Liberal Protestant scholars, such as Ernst Troeltsch (1865–1923), emphasize the non-legalistic nature of Christianity.

3. Some writers disagree with the idea that obedience is a virtue. They ask whether God wants human beings to live by the principle of obligation. They see something perverse in the idea that God has set human beings free from sin in order to enter into slavery, as slaves of Christ.

4. The question of human free will is another problem. God gave human beings free will. Some people argue that to expect obedience runs contrary to God's intention for humanity at Creation.

5. The problem of knowing God's will. It is argued that it is not possible for human beings to know what God desires.

Key term

supervenience – the idea that the rights and wrongs of a practical moral issue are consequent on a concept or religious belief.

6. The problem of **supervenience**. This problem relates to the difficulty of logically moving from a non-ethical belief to an ethical statement. For example, 'God made human beings in his own image, therefore abortion is wrong'.

7. The German philosopher Gottfried Leibniz (1646–1716) raised the problem of the value of goodness in and of itself. His argument centres on two things:

   - The first of these is the devaluation of acts of goodness. If goodness is solely that which God commands then it follows there is no intrinsic value to a good action, in and of itself. A person does something good because God commands it and not because that action is something morally right.
   - Leibniz raises another problem. If God wills a person to do the opposite of what God has already willed then both acts, despite being contrary, would be morally good. It is argued that this is rationally absurd.

8. The problem of God's freedom. So far objections to theological voluntarism have centred on the human situation. Critics of the theory argue that it also limits God. The God of Christian belief is omnipotent but he is also unchanging. Therefore God must act consistently; his laws must be consistent with his nature. This creates a problem, for instance:

   - God wills x to do y and promises x that z will happen if he does y.
   - x does y.
   - God therefore has to give the result z to x or God would not be consistent.

It is argued that God is no longer all-powerful, since he is forced to give z to x. If he denied z to x then he would be an arbitrary power and therefore would not be the God of Christian belief. William of Ockham tried to solve this problem by arguing that God has both **absolute power** (*de potentia absoluta*) and **ordained power** (*de potentia ordinata*) (see Extension note, pages 94–95).

Jesus

The Apostles' Creed continues with these words:

I believe in Jesus Christ, his only Son, our Lord. ('Apostles' Creed', Encyclopædia Britannica)

The central ethical principles of Christianity can be found in the life and teaching of Jesus. Christians believe that Jesus is the incarnate Word of God, which means that he is God in human form. This belief is unique to Christianity. Certain moral consequences follow. It also means that the words of Jesus, as recorded in the Gospels, are uniquely special to Christians.

There are many passages of moral guidance in the Gospels. Jesus was a Jewish teacher, a rabbi, and therefore an interpreter of the Torah. He was not a moral philosopher. His message, as recorded in the Gospels, is therefore quite different to later writers of ethics. Its central theme is love of God and love of others.

Jesus lived at a time in which the Jewish people were under Roman rule. The Jews were under no illusion about the power and authority of Rome. They hoped to restore their freedom under God but they knew that this would be a hard task. Some imagined that the Romans could be defeated and, a few decades after Jesus was crucified, these Jews rose in revolt against Rome (CE69). They were crushed. Others looked to a different sort of kingdom, in which God would rule men's hearts and minds. This was a spiritual kingdom. Whether this kingdom would have led, in the mind of Jesus and his followers, to the Day of Judgement is a matter of opinion. What is true is that many of the early Christians thought that God's kingdom was coming soon and in their lifetime. The teaching of Jesus is therefore designed to prepare people for the **kingdom of God**.

The different Gospel writers accentuate certain themes in the teaching but all place morality within the context of the coming kingdom of God and the need for believers to be prepared. This gives the teaching a certain eschatological context, which often means that what Jesus says is hard to put into practice. Set, however, within the context of the imminent arrival of God's kingdom the words make sense. Why, for example, hoard wealth and make money if God's kingdom is about to happen?

Amos Wilder (1895–1993), in *Eschatology and Ethics in the Teaching of Jesus*, argues that Jesus' moral teaching is designed to do three things.

1. To instil in the listener a sense of guilt and the need for urgent repentance.
2. To promote the idea that the kingdom of God has been or will soon be realized.
3. To teach the attributes that a true disciple needs in the kingdom.

The Sermon on the Mount (Matthew 5–7) addresses the central moral questions of what is meant by the term 'good' and what the moral agent ought to do.

Jesus tells his followers to suffer with dignity the insults and lies of their persecutors (Matthew 5:11). They are told to:

Love your enemies and pray for those who persecute you. (Matthew 5:44)

Key term

eschatology – study of ideas about the end of life/time and the Day of Judgement and resurrection.

The stoical qualities of patience, prudence and perseverance are praised. Later Christian writers, such as St Augustine of Hippo, will point to these qualities as those that a true disciple should have. The self-effacing martyr became, during the period of persecution, an illustration of what discipleship means.

The Golden Rule

Love provides the key to these stoical attributes. The Gospel writers are keen to show that the life of Christ is the story of the outpouring of God's love for humanity. The teaching of Jesus demonstrates this. The writer of Mark's Gospel states that Jesus was asked by a scribe which is the greatest of God's laws.

> *Jesus answered, 'The first is, "Hear , O Israel: the Lord our God, the Lord is one; you shall love the Lord your God with all your heart, and with all your soul, and with all your mind, and with all your strength."' (Mark 12:30)*

He adds to this:

> *The second is this, "You shall love your neighbour as yourself." (Mark 12:31)*

The concept of love of neighbour became the basis of what today is known as the Golden Rule of Christianity:

> *In everything do to others as you would have them do to you. (Matthew 7:12)*

The teaching of Jesus is one aspect of the Golden Rule. More important than this teaching is the way in which his message was put into practice. Christians see in Jesus an example of love in action. Each of the Gospel writers portrays Jesus' love in action in a particular way.

An interesting example is Luke's Gospel. Luke's writings on the ethical teaching of Jesus are concerned with those in poverty. From the outset of Luke's Gospel, some scholars believe, there is the idea that Jesus is a revolutionary figure who has come into the world to transform society. Leon Trotsky (1879–1940), one of the leaders of the Russian Revolution in 1917, argued that the words of the pregnant Mary at the beginning of Luke's Gospel (Luke 1: 47–55) make it one of the most revolutionary documents in human history. Mary's words to her cousin Elizabeth are startling. Speaking about God she states:

> *He has brought down the powerful from their thrones,*
> *and lifted up the lowly;*
> *he has filled the hungry with good things,*
> *and sent the rich away empty. (Luke 1:52–53)*

Key term

Golden Rule – the Golden Rule of Jesus is 'do to others as you would have them do to you' (Matthew 7:12). It can also be expressed as 'love your neighbour as yourself' (Mark 12:31).

Christians see Jesus as love in action.

This understanding of the life and teaching of Jesus is in marked contrast to traditional views. The ethical teaching of Jesus is not seen as concerned with personal salvation or discipleship but rather with the plight of the poor.

To think about

Offer explanations for the Bible quote: 'It is easier for a camel to go through the eye of a needle than for someone who is rich to enter the kingdom of God.' (Matthew 19:24)

The role of the Holy Spirit

The last section of the Apostles' Creed begins with the simple statement:

I believe in the Holy Spirit. (*'Apostles' Creed'*, Encyclopædia Britannica)

In many respects the Holy Spirit is that part of God that is hardest to describe or contemplate. Christian writers speak of the Holy Spirit as being the creative power of God present today in the world. According to Genesis 1 the Spirit of God hovered over the earth when it 'was a formless void and darkness covered the face of the deep' (Genesis 1:2), before the land separated from the waters. The Spirit breathed into the nostrils of Adam to give him life. Christian attitudes to God the Holy Spirit therefore are concerned with creativity. Paul writes: 'the fruit of the Spirit is love, joy, peace, patience, kindness, generosity, faithfulness, gentleness and self-control' (Galatians 5:22).

Christians believe that the creative nature of the Spirit inspires and encourages them to act for the good of others and for the planet, for example in work for those in poverty, the oppressed, in ecology and in their personal lives. Those Christians opposed to the exploitation of the planet use the creative nature of the Holy Spirit as an exemplar of how people should look after the planet. The Holy Spirit is seen as both the creative and sustaining nature of God at work in the world. This ecology movement has been called the **New Creation** movement, to illustrate the link between spiritual renewal and the revival of the planet.

Paul's moral teaching

The Apostles' Creed, after referring to the Holy Spirit, ends with a few short phrases. One of these is:

I believe in . . . the communion of saints. ('Apostles' Creed', Encyclopædia Britannica)

St Paul was one of the most important early followers of Jesus. In early life he was a Jewish rabbi who persecuted the first Christians. Later, after his conversion on the road to Damascus, he became a Christian missionary. He was, according to tradition, executed in Rome during the executions of Christians ordered by the emperor Nero following the great fire in the city in CE64.

Paul's ethical teaching is a mix of various philosophical and religious traditions of his time. Paul was an expert in the Torah. His writings also reveal the influence of Greek philosophy and Roman law. There is one overarching influence that runs throughout his moral statements; this is the personality and role of Jesus. Paul, unlike the other Apostles, did not know Jesus. He was in all probability a young student, in what today is modern Turkey, when Jesus was crucified. Yet, despite this, the life and work of Jesus dominate Paul's message.

Paul sees Jesus as the Messiah, the Saviour sent by God to bring humanity salvation. Christians are required not only to follow the teachings of their Lord but also to learn by his example. This is a theological necessity that has moral ramifications. As Paul said:

Let the same mind be in you that was in Christ Jesus. (Philippians 2:5)

And later Christians are told:

. . . work out your own salvation with fear and trembling. (Philippians 2:12)

An important feature of Paul's message is that Christian morality should imitate the lifestyle of Jesus. Love, kindness and generosity are central practical themes transposed from the teaching of Jesus into Paul's writings. They are not new ideas. What is new is the way in which Paul links fundamental theological concepts to his moral teaching. It is as if Paul is beginning to construct a moral system from his ideas about Jesus.

Many Christians use Paul's teaching about living in the imitation of Christ as a guide for making moral decisions. Some consider 'What would Jesus do?' if he were in their position.

Another theological concept that becomes a moral duty is Paul's use of the term the **body of Christ**. At first glance this term is quite straightforward. Paul uses it frequently, especially when dealing with the church at Corinth. This community was, by Paul's own comments, divided into warring factions. It was also not very moral. Paul wrote to the Christians at Corinth on numerous occasions. He appealed to them to be united in their faith in Jesus as the Christ. Unity is at the heart of the expression 'the body of Christ' (1 Corinthians 12:27). Paul, in his first letter to the Corinthians, develops the idea in different ways. They are that:

• Christians are part of a body, whose head is Jesus (see 1 Corinthians 11:2–4).
• The Eucharistic meal, the Holy Communion, is about community and not about division (see 1 Corinthians 11:17–34).

Key term

agape – one of the four words in Greek for love. Agape refers to communal love, which does not demand anything in return.

- The gifts of the Spirit are like organs in the body; Christians have different gifts, different tasks, and none is superior or less than any other (see 1 Corinthians 12). There is a symbiosis between the organs of the body in the same way that there should be a symbiotic relationship between all Christians, whatever their skills might be.
- There are three gifts to which all Christians should aim. These are faith, hope and love. The greatest of these is love (see 1 Corinthians 13:1–13).
- The division of the body, the church, is best repaired and unity restored by love, the chief gift of God's Spirit (see 1 Corinthians 14:1).

Paul's idea of 'the body of Christ' (1 Corinthians 12:27) has moral implications for Christians. They are to work together bonded by communal love, agape. What is more Paul implies that a Christian, as part of the Church, is a part of Christ. The Church is Christ in the world. This has ethical implications, in terms of behaviour, as Paul points out in the rest of the letter.

Love, for Paul, is the primary gift of the Spirit. This is a particular type of love. It is agape, which primarily means communal love, which is freely given and asks for no reward. Paul wrote:

Love is patient; love is kind; love is not envious or boastful or arrogant or rude. It does not insist on its own way; it is not irritable or resentful; it does not rejoice in wrongdoing, but rejoices in the truth. (1 Corinthians 14:4–6)

Situation ethics

Paul's understanding of the centrality of agape led in 1966 to the publication of *Situation Ethics* by Joseph Fletcher (1905–1991), a work on ethics that takes love (agape) as the test of all moral actions. It has its origins in the radical movements of the late 1950s and 1960s. During the 1960s, America was involved in a long and in the end futile war against communism in Vietnam. This war led to riots at various university campuses, as students protested against the war and the conscription of young men into the armed services.

Fletcher was an academic theologian who worked at several American universities before teaching at the Union Theological Seminary, where he trained future priests and ministers. He was a liberal, opposed to the war in Vietnam and an exponent of social reform. In divided America, Fletcher wanted to re-establish what he considered the most important feature of Christian morality – the law of love. Later, he was to reject Christianity, believing that the Christian Church was the wrong vehicle for conveying the message of communal love.

At the heart of Jesus' teaching was reconciliation, of God and man and between men. Such forgiveness and reconciliation has its foundation in what Fletcher called agape. This Greek word defines a particular type of love – communal love based on mutual acceptance. Such mutual acceptance destroys the social alienation that, so he believed, modern society creates. Although agape is not central in the Gospel tradition it does appear in Paul's First Letter to the Corinthians. In this letter Paul writes to a divided Christian community and appeals to them to unite their church in brotherly affection centred on Jesus.

Key point

Situation ethics takes agape (communal love which asks for nothing in return) as the test for all moral decisions.

Fletcher's application of agape to the modern world has its problems. He uses the term agapeism when explaining how it is to be used as a moral test in all ethical situations. Yet what does agapeism mean when applied to ordinary things and common situations? How can it be applied? Fletcher realized the difficulties in applying agape in life. He accepted that it is not easy to apply. Fletcher's solution is a compromise. He argues that Christians should search for a middle way between legalism and antinomianism, between those who adhere strictly to a moral system not based on consequences (for example, the Divine Command theory) and those who reject all systems and thereby are equally anti-consequentialist. He sets out, therefore, to create a limited consequentialism. There are four working principles to his agapeistic consequentialism. They are:

1. Pragmatism: to be right the moral decision must involve an outcome, which will work. What this means is that every action should be judged on the basis of agape and every result also on this criterion. Consider the following scenario. There is a severe food shortage in the Horn of Africa and people are starving. A worldwide appeal raises a large amount of money in order to feed the people of this region. The money is used to import wheat from countries in the European Union and America. Aid arrives and the wheat is distributed in the markets. People who were starving are now fed. An agapeistic act has been performed. Yet the delivery of aid has some hidden consequences that transform society. The wheat distributed as aid is free. The wheat produced by the local farmers is not. The farmers cannot sell their flour in the market place, as the inhabitants prefer free flour. The farmers cannot therefore buy seed for the next harvest and so nothing is grown. A culture of aid dependency is thereby created. What, at first, was an agapeistic act results in long-term economic and social problems.

2. Relativism: the circumstances of a situation always throw up exceptions. Fletcher understands that the concept of agape cannot be a strict test of what to do. It is rather a guide, a rule of thumb. This can be illustrated in the following example. An

Key terms

agapeism/ agapeistic – the use of agape as the test for making moral decisions.

antinomianism – the idea that chosen Christians are freed, by God's grace or predestination, from the obligation to observe moral laws.

consequentialism – the consequences of an action solely determine whether it is the right thing to do.

elderly person lies bedridden at home. Her son, the carer, notices that the woman is unable to drink. She is dehydrating and this causes her a great deal of suffering. He phones the consultant at the hospital to seek advice. It is not the first time that he has done this. The consultant says that he will admit the elderly woman back into hospital but that she will be back time and time again. The carer realizes that the consultant thinks enough is enough. He knows as well that this will mean the old lady will die. What should he do? As a situation ethicist he decided to apply the rule of agape and leaves the elderly person where she is. She dies in a few days. Her suffering ends. His decision haunts him. In another situation he might have decided otherwise. The one thing he knows is that using agape as a guideline is not easy. A relativist use of an absolute principle, the law of love, is hard to determine.

3. Positivism: Fletcher dismissed such ideas as Natural Law or Virtue Ethics because they are dependent on reason to discover the best way to act. Situation ethics is about making rational decisions based on agape. This rests on freely accepting to believe in agape, which is a matter of faith and not reason.

4. Personalism: the God of the liberal tradition is a personal deity. He is not a distant ruler or judge. Fletcher's God has a relationship with humanity. This understanding of God is applicable to human relationships. Agape is about a communal love in which there is no place for judgements or for legalism. Agape is relationship-centred. Fletcher uses Paul's ideas in 1 Corinthians 13 to draw out the idea that Christians should not sit in judgement on other people. He goes further. Paul, after discussing agape, lays down rules for the church at Corinth. Fletcher cannot. It is for each individual Christian to decide for him or herself how to approach moral issues.

The use of agape by Fletcher presumes certain fundamental principles, which are held by faith. Six basic premises exist within the above four principles.

1. Agape is the only good in and of itself. All other virtues are dependent on it.
2. All decisions should be made on the basis of agape.
3. Agape and justice are the same. As Fletcher puts it, 'justice is love distributed, nothing else' (Joseph Fletcher, *Situation Ethics: The New Morality*, Westminster John Knox Press, 1966)
4. Agape has no preferences for one person over or against another.
5. Agapeistic ends justify the means.
6. Agapeistic decisions are variable, as situations alter.

Strengths and weaknesses of situation ethics

There are a number of advantages to this form of liberal Christian ethics. Among these are that:

1. It is an attempt to develop the individual basis to morality, which has often been neglected in religious ethics. The divine will has often been interpreted as a command ethic that suppresses the individual to the teaching of the Church or to the teaching of the Bible.
2. It restores love to the centre of any moral decision-making process.
3. It values the exception and rejects the idea that every situation can be judged on the same moral bases.

However, the situation ethics theory also has its critics. Scholars have pointed out that:

1. It is difficult to give a particular action as morally right in a particular situation. There is a tendency towards vagueness.
2. The method inherent in situation ethics lacks objectivity and therefore it is possible for situation ethicists to use agape for self-advantage.
3. It does not distinguish between what is morally good and what is morally right.
4. It does not justify its own moral values. These values are asserted as a matter of faith.

To think about

'Love and do what you will' (St Augustine of Hippo, *Sermon on 1 John 4*). How could this quote be applied to situation ethics?

Fletcher's *Situation Ethics* is hard to place within the various ethical systems. Is it a normative ethical theory? Is it relativist? Is it an ethical theory based on the Divine Command? Is it consequentialist or deontological? Perhaps it would be best to see it as a compromise ethical system. On the one hand it is consequentialist in that the outcome of every situation is vitally important in deciding what to do. Yet the law of agape, which determines how to act in a given situation, prevents it from being entirely consequentialist. Many scholars argue that this tension between a law-based ethic and one based on consequentialism is its fundamental flaw.

Law and sin

The Apostles' Creed finally ends with these words:

I believe in . . .
the forgiveness of sins,
the resurrection of the body,
and the life everlasting. Amen. ('Apostles' Creed', Encyclopædia Britannica)

The idea of sin is central to Christian morality.

Most Christians believe in **original sin**. What this means has been defined in various, often conflicting, ways. The concept of original sin is an important aspect of the Christian moral framework. Traditionally original sin is a result of the Fall of Adam and Eve in the Garden of Eden. They ate the forbidden fruit from the tree of knowledge and, as recorded in Genesis 3, were sent from the Garden of Eden to live in the real world. Today most Christians take this story as a metaphor for the fact that human beings have an inclination to do bad things. Paul, in his letter to the Romans, states:

> *For I do not do the good I want, but the evil I do not want is what I do. (Romans 7:19)*

Both Augustine and Luther were to repeat these words as part of their own experience of life.

The problem of original sin plays an important part in Christian discussion of free will and determinism, which is examined at A2.

Are religion and ethics linked?

The chapter so far has set out both the bases for Christian ethical decision-making and also several ethical theories. One of those (the Divine Command theory) is objective, while situation ethics is generally perceived as a relativist approach to Christian ethics. It is necessary here to examine the relationship between religion and ethics. Some reference has already been made to the difficulty in connecting the two. This problem is not limited to Christian ethics.

Christian ethics makes certain moral assumptions about the nature of goodness, based on the principle that God is love. Christians are commanded to love one another yet there is a problem between the commands to love and how this is put into practice. There is no clear route. It is as if you have an idea of where you need to get to but in your car you have a satnav, a map and a set of directions all with very different routes heading in different directions. This is the problem with Christianity. The simple message has no single route and no distinct destination. Throughout the history of Christianity those who believe have differed on the route to be taken and, at times, on the destination. Some have emphasized the loving nature of God while others have stressed the vision of God as the judge of the universe. These differences create wide variations of attitude when it comes to practical moral issues, from homosexuality to war and peace.

There is also a further problem. This is how much attention does a Christian pay to secular ethics and to philosophical theories and how much to the revealed word of God in Scripture and/or the traditions of the Church. Christian ethical theory has never been simply a matter of God's revelation. It has involved the interpretation of faith using philosophical and ethical theories. This occurred in the New Testament. Paul's writings are influenced by both Platonic and Stoic ideas.

In the second century Quintus Septimus Florens Tertullian (*c.*160–*c.*240) argued for a complete separation between religion and philosophy; between revelation and human wisdom. His mantra,

> *What has Athens to do with Jerusalem? (Eric Osborn,* Tertullian: First Theologian of the West, *Cambridge University Press, 1997)*

meant what has philosophy to do with faith? Yet Tertullian did not keep to this and used Greek philosophical ideas to express his views. At the Reformation the reformers attacked the use of Aristotle to create the Natural Law theory of Aquinas. However, both Luther and Calvin used Platonic ideas to express some of their views.

Some Christians do try to maintain the separation. Fundamentalists argue in favour of a literal interpretation of Scripture yet, as has been pointed out, they do not maintain biblical laws on slavery. They maintain that their attitudes to slavery are based on certain biblical texts and have nothing to do with modern liberal attitudes.

Christianity has been affected by the moral secular values of contemporary society. Yet, at the same time, Christianity has shaped those values. In Chapter 2 Natural Law we looked at how Natural Law was central to the development of both later Utilitarianism and also natural rights, the predecessor of modern human rights legislation. Modern Virtue Ethics has also developed out of Aquinas' Natural Law theory. It can also be argued that Kant's deontological system would not hold together without a need for a God. The moral argument for the existence of God, you may remember, is the only one that Kant would accept.

Despite these links there are a number of contemporary secular ethicists who argue that religion and ethics do not mix. The Preference utilitarian, Peter Singer, in *Unsanctifying Human Life*, argues that Christianity's ideas on the nature of human life has been detrimental to a moral understanding of nature and has also been contrary to animal rights. Richard Dawkins, from a neo-Darwinist position, has argued in favour of determinism in morality that runs counter to the idea of free will in Christian thought. Other scholars have looked simply at the practice of Christianity and Church pronouncements on such matters as homosexuality, abortion and contraception, and have argued that Christian teaching is inappropriate to the modern world. Fletcher, the creator of situation ethics, later became an atheist because he viewed Christianity as detrimental to moral advances. In the nineteenth century various writers developed their ethics as an attempt to free morality from the straitjacket of religion. The Benthamite utilitarians were dedicated to a morality without God.

Some modern ethical writers have realized that this relationship is worth preserving. Richard Hare (1919–2002), the father of prescriptivism, towards the end of his life began again to look at the faith he rejected in his youth. His experiences of being a Japanese prisoner of war taught him that there are universal moral truths. These, he came to believe, were offered in the teaching of Jesus. J.S. Mill, though an atheist, also thought that the Golden Rule of Jesus was the kernel of morality.

Practice exam questions

(a) Explain a religious approach to ethics from one religion you have studied.

We look at several different Christian ethical positions in this book – Biblical and Church teachings, Divine Command theory, situation ethics and Aquinas' Natural Law. When answering this question you only need to examine one of these theories. Situation ethics might be a good theory to develop, as it is less broad-ranging than some of the others. You could explain the basic ideas behind the theory, as developed by Fletcher. You could look at the use of agape as the test for making moral decisions, and also the principles of pragmatism, relativism, positivism and personalism.

(b) To what extent is it useful to base morality on one religion you have studied?

Firstly you could briefly state the religious approach you will be analysing. If you want to argue that it is not useful, then you could look at the basic criticisms that have been made of Christian ethics. This could include criticisms based on philosophical issues, such as Plato's Euthyphro dilemma or Dawkins' neo-Darwinism. You could also consider the more practical issues of hypocrisy and inbuilt contradictions within religious ethical standards. You might want to set out the strengths of a religious approach, include issues relating to moral certainty and the practical question of where moral authority lies when there is no God. You might wish to point out that alternative sources of authority (such as nature) are not without difficulties. How you finally sum up might depend on whether or not you feel the weaknesses outweigh the strengths.

Develop your knowledge

There are a number of books on religious ethics. Here are a few:

The Moral Maze: A Way of Exploring Christian Ethics by David Cook (SPCK Publishing, 1983)

The Foundations of Christian Ethics by Michael Keeling (T&T Clark, 1994)

A New Dictionary of Christian Ethics by John Macquarrie and James Childress (SCM Press, 1990)

6

Key terms

embryo – unborn human, especially in the first eight weeks from conception, after implantation and before all organs are developed.

foetus – unborn human more than eight weeks after conception.

Abortion

Introduction

An abortion is the expulsion or removal of an embryo or foetus from the womb before it is able to survive independently. Sometimes this occurs naturally and this is known as a miscarriage. Induced abortions, where the foetus is removed deliberately by unnatural means, were illegal in England, Scotland and Wales until a 1967 Act of Parliament. The act stated that, with the consent of two doctors, an abortion could be performed up to and including the twenty-eighth week of pregnancy. In 1991 an amendment to that act reduced the time limit to 24 weeks. Abortions may be authorized after 24 weeks if:

1. there is grave risk to the life of the woman or risk of grave physical or mental injury to her by the completion of the pregnancy
2. there is evidence of severe foetal abnormality at birth.

Attempts have been made in recent years to (a) make the wording of these exceptions more precise in law and (b) lower the time limit in which most abortions are allowed to 22 weeks. All attempts to alter the law further have failed in the House of Commons. Those in favour of further changes have argued that medical advances in Britain and America mean that it is possible for a foetus to be delivered at 23 weeks and survive. Reformers also argue that what is meant by 'severe abnormality' is poorly defined.

The law on abortion was changed in 1967 for a number of reasons. The 1960s saw huge changes in social legislation in Great Britain. The Abortion Act was part of a progressive social agenda pursued by the Labour Government that included the abolition of capital punishment, easing of regulations on divorce and the legalization of homosexuality.

The reform of abortion laws was an important concern for the women's movement of the 1960s. The women's movement was a political movement that campaigned for women's rights. Feminists, such as Germaine Greer, argued that women had the right to control their own body. For some, the foetus was seen as being part of the female body in a similar manner to an organ. Feminists also made three other claims:

- First, they argued that making abortion legal would cut the number of deaths from so-called backstreet abortions.
- Next, they argued that unwanted babies often live an intolerable life of poverty and social deprivation and that the mothers who looked after such children were often abused and disadvantaged.
- Last, they saw the ban on abortion as part of the male domination of the legal profession and, more broadly, the control of women by men.

The present Abortion Act prohibits what is called abortion on demand. It lays down particular grounds on which two doctors can agree to the termination of a pregnancy. These grounds are:

1. that the pregnancy is no more than 24 weeks and that the pregnancy involves a risk of injury to the physical or mental health of the woman or any existing children in her family
2. to prevent grave permanent injury to the physical or mental health of the woman
3. the pregnancy involves risk to the life of the woman
4. there is a substantial risk that the child would suffer from such severe physical or mental abnormalities as to be seriously handicapped.

The basis of the law is to protect the mother from suffering the consequences of an unwanted pregnancy. The law in Britain is fundamentally different to that of the majority of countries in the European Union. In most countries abortion is permitted, often on demand, up to 12 weeks into a pregnancy. In Britain there are about 200,000 abortions each year. Abortion is still illegal in Northern Ireland. Each year about 1500 women come to Britain for an abortion from the province.

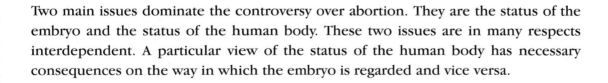

The status of the embryo

Two main issues dominate the controversy over abortion. They are the status of the embryo and the status of the human body. These two issues are in many respects interdependent. A particular view of the status of the human body has necessary consequences on the way in which the embryo is regarded and vice versa.

Key terms

personhood –
the attributes
that make a
human being
an individual.
This is partly
the character of
the individual
and in part it is
those things that
give the human
being freedom
from others, for
example, the
right to make
decisions.

sentient –
able to
experience sense
or feeling.

There is general agreement that from conception the foetal material is a member of the species *Homo sapiens*, since genetically the embryo is biologically human. The argument centres on whether this embryo is a human being in miniature. Many philosophers, including Michael Tooley and Peter Singer, argue that the embryo is not a human being but it has the potential for becoming a human being. This notion of **human potentiality** is important. Potentiality recognizes that the embryo is on the road to being a human being without the expectation that it will achieve that destination. Therefore it is allowable to abort an embryo. Some scholars point out that the body naturally rejects some embryos and as a result there should not be a link drawn between potential and its realization. This is just how life is. Many people have the potential to be Olympic athletes but few achieve it.

Some thinkers counter this argument by stating that it is wrong to make a comparison between failure to realize potential and the prevention of potentiality. If a person chooses not to realize his or her potential this is a matter of personal judgement. Being prevented from realizing potentiality is, for the embryo, not a matter of personal choice.

Various scholars, as well as the Supreme Court in America, have considered the potentiality criterion as the best option in judging whether abortion is moral and ought to be allowed in law.

Personhood

The issue of potentiality raises the issue of what is a 'person'. This is the question of **personhood**. Scholars who argue in favour of abortion point to the status of the embryo, and later the foetus, as a non-person.

Personhood, it is argued, implies an ability to make decisions and to be in some way both independent and also a social being. This twofold argument follows the views of John Locke (1632–1704), the British empiricist. Locke claimed that human beings are **sentient**. For Locke, sentience includes the capacity of choice (free will) and also individuality and a social nature. Sentience also includes the **principle of reciprocity**. To be a person you must be able to give and take from a relationship. It is claimed that a foetus does not have these qualities. It is therefore not a person in the usual definition of the term. It is assumed that the **foetus is not a rational being** capable of choice. There is also the presumption that the foetus is in some way on the road to personhood but is not yet a person. It lacks consciousness and those other qualities that are required for personhood.

Key point

Locke and other liberal writers argue that the foetus is not a human being as it lacks sentience: it is not able to choose, lacks individuality and is not a social being.

There are weaknesses in this argument. The most significant of these is the status of people affected by severe disability. Take, for example, a young man who is unable to move voluntarily. He is blind, deaf and unable to speak or communicate and has been bedridden from birth. How would this young man be classified? Is he a person in the same way in which an able-bodied young man is?

Those in favour of abortion, however, point out that even people with severe disabilities have an awareness of their situation. They have **sentience**. However, this is much harder to justify in the case of people in a coma, as the Virtue Ethicist Rosalind Hursthouse has pointed out. Such people are generally unaware of their situation and they are dependent on medical assistance. The sentience criterion has a further problem. Jeremy Bentham held that animals are sentient beings and this view is widely accepted today. Yet sentient animals are killed for food. It might therefore be considered illogical to state that a foetus can be killed because it is not a sentient being, if you consider it acceptable to slaughter animals which are sentient beings for food.

Singer and Tooley develop an alternative criterion that distinguishes the foetus from a human being. They argue that human beings have **self-consciousness** while a foetus only possesses consciousness. Consider the issue of **pain and pleasure**, so central to early utilitarian philosophers. Singer argues that a foetus may experience pain but does not understand it. The foetus cannot rationalize it. Human beings can understand their environment and make logical deductions from their experiences in a way that foetuses cannot. A scan might show a foetus in apparent pain. This only proves that the foetus has consciousness. It does not show that the foetus understands what pain is, what causes the pain and what can be done to relieve it. It might, though, be argued that the same is also true of those in a coma or of newborn babies. They experience pain but are, in all probability, incapable of rationalizing their experiences.

Tooley, in *Abortion and Infanticide*, adds another justification for abortion, based on his belief that the foetus is not a person. He calls this the **principle of moral equivalence**. Take a foetus and examine its physical attributes at the term an abortion is due to be performed. Compare its physical state with another creature, for example, a cat or dog. If human beings find it morally justifiable to experiment or kill another sentient being possessing similar characteristics to the foetus, then there is no moral reason not to abort. The reverse is also true.

Tooley's ideas have been criticized on two levels. The first is the difficulty of knowing the equivalence of different creatures. Second, even if this were possible, human beings, it is argued, are different from all other creatures.

To think about

List the things that make us a person. Does someone in a coma have all these qualities? Does this mean someone in a coma is not a person?

The status of the human body

Does a woman have the right to use her body as she chooses?

Abortion raises another important question; this is the status of the human body. Simply put: to whom does your body belong? This may seem a strange question. It is assumed by most people that they own their body. The importance of this question lies in the right of a woman to decide about what happens to her body, whether she wants an abortion or not.

It may appear at first sight that an individual owns his or her own body. The answer is not so straightforward. The teaching of Christianity and the earlier Platonist tradition, which stand behind many of the legal principles in this area, imagines that the material body is on loan to the individual. It is a gift of God:

Naked I came from my mother's womb, and naked shall I return there; the LORD gave, and the LORD has taken away; blessed be the name of the LORD. (Job 1:21)

This text was familiar to Locke. He developed what today is the basic liberal concept of body ownership. Locke's idea of personhood has already been discussed. His concept of body ownership stems from this idea of personhood. The individual is a rational being. Nature, which God made, has bequeathed to humanity certain rights. One of these is the right to own your body. Locke believes that without this right many of the features of personhood would not occur. The use of reason would not be possible if another controlled the individual's body. Additionally, human beings have a natural inclination to develop and improve their situation in life. This would also not be possible if someone else owned the body. Individuals should be free to work and enjoy the benefits of their labour.

Locke asserts that human beings possess things for a reason and that is to improve their lives. As a result property exists to be used for self-improvement. This is Locke's principle of **ownership-as-use**. Simply put, a thing belongs to an individual because that person uses it. If you do not use it, you lose it! Locke applies this idea of ownership-as-use to the body, implying that the body is property, like owning a car or a television. The body is there to be used for self-improvement and, by implication, to improve the lot of others.

Locke's ideas can be applied to abortion. His ideas, firstly, suggest that a woman considering an abortion has an absolute right to decide what happens to her body. Next they imply that the woman must also consider whether an abortion will improve her situation in life and that of her family.

Key term

property rights – idea that you have certain rights. One of these is that what you own is yours to use as you wish. This includes your body.

To think about

'I own my body. I can do whatever I want with it.' Do you agree with this statement?

There is a further reason why Locke's principles can be used in support of abortion. This is his understanding of the embryo/foetus. The foetus is no different to any other part of the woman's body. Locke believes that we have property rights over the body from birth to death. The individual does not lose any rights when anatomical changes occur. To use an analogy, you do not lose property rights to a car if you modify it or crash it. But should a woman's body be compared to a car?

Some scholars argue against the comparison of a thing and the human body. They reject the principle that the human body is ownership-as-use. Take the case of an individual in a coma. That individual cannot do anything and certainly not anything useful for his or her self-development. Does that individual cease being a person and therefore lose property rights over his or her body? Some argue that this is the case. Life-support machines can be turned off and intravenous drips removed without the

Key term

Quality of Life – idea that for life to be considered worthwhile a human being has to possess certain attributes, for example sentience, ability to communicate, to reason, to work and enjoy leisure, etc.

permission of the individual. Some scholars though are uncomfortable with such measures.

Abortion and rights

Human rights are an important reason for the legalization of abortion in many parts of the world. It is argued, on the basis of the woman's right to control her body, that the woman has a right to terminate a pregnancy.

Judith Jarvis Thomson, an American feminist philosopher, wrote, in *A Defense of Abortion*, that women should not be forced or obliged to give up the right to control their own bodies without consent. She illustrates this with the story of a woman who is kidnapped and who wakes up to find she is lying next to a famous violinist. The violinist has a fatal kidney ailment. His circulatory system has been plugged into that of the woman's. Allowing the violinist to stay plugged to the woman for nine months will cure the ailment. Unplugging the violinist will kill him. Thompson uses this rather outrageous story to question whether we are morally obliged to allow our bodies to be used however necessary to give another person the right to life.

Two other issues dominate the discussion of rights in relation to abortion. They are:

1. A right may not always be a moral good. It might be argued that the destruction of life is morally bad. It may be a right but it may also be bad. Therefore, it is argued, abortion should take place sparingly. Those who argue along these lines argue that society, by allowing something that is morally bad to occur frequently, damages its own moral foundations. As a result law has no connection with morality.

2. Does the foetus also have the right to life? This question reverts back to how the foetus is perceived. Is it a person or not? It would severely damage an argument in favour of the woman's right to an abortion were the rights of a foetus to be accepted.

Quality of Life theory

One of the most widely used expressions in medical ethics today is that of the Quality of Life. It is often used with regard to care for the terminally ill and in discussions regarding the elderly and disabled. Helga Kuhse argues that it is relevant to the issue of abortion. Following the idea of personhood, she maintains that there are certain qualities that human beings must have in order to live meaningful lives. The most important of these are sentience and self-awareness. This also includes the ability to act rationally, to communicate with others and to act morally. It can therefore be argued that, in certain situations, an abortion is a moral necessity if the foetus does not have the potential for this Quality of Life. Some babies are born with severe abnormalities that prevent them developing those qualities that she and, for example, Mary Anne Warren give for what constitutes a meaningful life. There are several objections, however, to this criterion. They are that:

1. There is no clear definition of what the term 'Quality of Life' means. Consider the following scenario. A severely disabled young person is taken to a swimming pool. The young person cannot swim, move their limbs, speak, hear or see and yet when that person enters the water a smile comes to their face. Does that person have a Quality of Life? It is argued that the term has no reference point. Who represents the base point for Quality of Life? Is it an able-bodied, active, healthy 20-year-old student? Is it a child?

2. Quality of Life is assessed not by the moral agent but by professionals. Should it be left to medical specialists to decide what a decent Quality of Life is? Some might argue that this is paternalistic. It is dependent on the views and judgements of medical professionals who may not deal with people with disabilities on a day-to-day basis.

3. There is no definition of whose Quality of Life is being examined in the case of abortion. Is it that of the foetus? Is it that of the pregnant woman or her family? Is it that of the doctors and nurses who perform abortions or who care for the severely disabled? Or is it that of the wider population whose taxes pay for abortions or for the medical care of those with severe disabilities? There would be huge divergences if all these groups were analysed in terms of the widely-accepted understanding of the Quality of Life.

4. The law places emphasis on the Quality of Life of the woman before that of any other group. Again, this is difficult to define. It is argued that what we consider decent Quality of Life varies from society to society and from person to person.

Key term

paternalism – the idea that a person or group in authority is qualified to make decisions in the best interests of another person or group.

Key point

Central to the arguments of pro-abortionists is the Quality of Life of the woman.

Sanctity of Life theory

The Christian religion emphasizes (a) the importance of life and (b) the Sanctity of Life. Genesis 1 states:

> *So God created humankind in his image, in the image of God he created them; male and female he created them. (Genesis 1:27)*

Later, 'God saw everything that he had made, and indeed, it was very good' (Genesis 1:31). The idea that human beings are made in the image of God is used to express the fact that human beings are different from other creatures; they are special. This concept can be also seen in the other story of Creation in Genesis 2, which states:

> *Then the LORD God formed man from the dust of the ground, and breathed into his nostrils the breath of life. (Genesis 2:7)*

Again this story shows that human beings are to be seen as unique among all the creatures of the earth. It is through **ruach**, which can mean the breath of life or the spirit of God, that humans are endowed with divine qualities. Human life is sacred and consequently for most Christians it is wrong to take life without just cause. There are some Christians who believe that taking any human life is wrong for whatever reason.

The problem is whether a foetus is a person or not. The answer to this question divides Christians. Some Christians argue that it is only when a foetus is physically independent of its mother that personhood begins. These Christians regard abortion as, in certain situations, the best of a number of imperfect moral alternatives.

Anti-abortion Christians, who argue against abortion, do so from the standpoint of the Sanctity of Life. They claim authority for their views on the basis of passages in the Bible which point to the foetus being a living human being at or shortly after conception. One key passage occurs at the beginning of the book of Jeremiah. Here the prophet is recollecting his call to the prophetic life when he was a young boy. He recounts how God spoke to him as a youth and said:

Before I formed you in the womb I knew you,
and before you were born I consecrated you. (Jeremiah 1:5)

Another passage where a foetus is referred to is in Luke's Gospel. Here Mary, the mother of Jesus, visits her cousin Elizabeth. Both women are pregnant. When the two women greet, Elizabeth's unborn baby (John the Baptist) moves in her womb: 'When Elizabeth heard Mary's greeting, the child leapt in her womb' (Luke 1:41). The text suggests that, as early Christians believed, John the Baptist understood the importance of Jesus as the Saviour before either was born. None of these biblical passages are about abortion; on the contrary, they point to an understanding that the foetus is a living human being.

Key point

Central to the arguments of anti-abortionists is the issue of the Sanctity of Life.

Various criticisms can be made of the use of the Sanctity of Life theory in relation to abortion. They are:

1. All life is special and human life is no different from that of other creatures. In *Unsanctifying Human Life* Singer argues that the sanctity given to human life has distorted morality. People find it easier to accept the use of healthy animals in experiments for cosmetics than the termination of an abnormal foetus.

2. While the life of a foetus is sacred, so also is that of the mother. The difference between these two sacred lives is that the foetus has potentiality while the mother has actuality. When there is a choice between preserving the Quality of Life of the mother, or saving the foetus, some would argue that although both are sacred, the mother's needs take priority.

3. A neo-Darwinian approach asserts that concepts such as sacredness are meaningless. Human beings are intelligent animals at the summit of the food chain. Survival of the human species is inbuilt into the evolutionary process. Abortion has to be allowed, as one method of controlling population in an overcrowded planet with limited resources.

Key terms

ensoulment – when the soul enters the foetus and it becomes a human being.

soul – the spiritual, non-physical part of a human being or animal regarded as immortal.

Ensoulment

The issue of when human life begins is for many Christians bound up with the question of **ensoulment**. The foetus, it is argued, does not become a person at conception but at ensoulment. This occurs when, following Aristotle's view of the **soul** as the blueprint for the material body, the foetus starts to show physical signs that its body and its soul are joined. Simply put: ensoulment occurs when the foetus takes on human characteristics, when it looks like a baby in miniature. It is at this point the soul and the body become one. Today it might be argued that this occurs when the foetus' nervous system has formed.

The precise time of ensoulment has been disputed. Some ancient and medieval writers, such as Aquinas, argued that it takes place at forty days. Forty is not a random number; it has biblical significance as it echoes the length of time Jesus was in the wilderness and the Israelites were in the desert after the Exodus. However, it has no biological significance. Other writers place ensoulment at eighty days. This seems to have been the position of Augustine, although he is not precise in his writings. In the early thirteenth century, Pope Innocent III (1160–1216) put ensoulment at the start of the thirteenth week of pregnancy (116 days). This late date can be explained by reference to the passage in Luke's Gospel when Elizabeth's baby leaps in her womb. This is known as the quickening, the first time the mother feels the foetus move in her womb. This is the moment that Innocent III thought that the foetus becomes a human being. Therefore abortions were permissible up to that time but not after.

Today the Roman Catholic Church does not believe that ensoulment occurs at this stage of pregnancy. Roman Catholicism teaches that it is at conception that ensoulment occurs. The Catholic Church at one point returned to Aquinas' forty-day rule, but reinstated the idea of ensoulment at conception in the *Constitution of the Holy See* in 1869. Since then Roman Catholic views on abortion have been firmly fixed. They were restated in 1968 by Pope Paul VI (1897–1978) in his encyclical *Humanae Vitae*. Abortion is against the teachings of the Roman Catholic Church because it teaches that ensoulment occurs at conception.

A number of criticisms can be made of the concept of ensoulment. They are:

1. That it is dependent on either an Aristotelian or dualist view that there is a body and a soul. Many scholars do not therefore accept the principle on which the concept of ensoulment is based.

2. Many fertilized eggs are conceived but are later naturally aborted by the body. What does this say about the nature of God as omnibenevolent if each one is already ensouled?

3. Even if the concept were valid, how can we know the precise moment when the soul becomes integrated into the body? Is it after forty days or eighty or when? Is it different for males and for females, as some medieval commentators believed?

4. Ensoulment does not have any biological or psychological basis. Would not the creation of the nervous system be a better and more obvious division? It might be argued that the best time to consider the foetus as a person is when its nervous system is developed enough for it to feel pleasure and pain.

Abortion in liberal Christian thought

The liberal Christian view on abortion developed in the early years of the twentieth century. By 1900 the movement to free women and to give them rights was well underway. At that stage women had few rights. In the 1920s liberal Christians began campaigning for female equality with men. In the 1960s this turned to issues such as divorce and abortion. Liberal Christians joined with radical secular groups to campaign for social reform.

In America the circulation of German Protestant theology led to situation ethics. In *Situation Ethics* Fletcher regards abortion as sometimes a necessary evil. He asserts:

- Abortion is not necessarily bad.
- It depends on the situation and it depends on the application of the law of love.
- An abortion is morally right or wrong depending on the amount of agape, unconditional communal love, which results from it and motivates it.
- An abortion might be morally right if the pregnant woman is very young, if the foetus is severely deformed, or if the pregnancy is the result of a rape.
- Equally an abortion might be morally wrong if it was performed because a woman was solely concerned about her career prospects.

The law of agape is the ultimate guide. However, it is argued that the theory is not without its problems. They are:

1. How is the quantity and quality of agape to be measured? It is argued that it will ultimately depend on the subjective opinion of either the mother or the practitioner.

2. Who should be included when calculating the quantity and quality of agape? Should we also consider the agape of the father, the foetus and the wider community?
3. The idea that love is the only criterion for abortion seems too simplistic.
4. It measures love in the immediate. Aborting or keeping the foetus may be the most loving thing to do at the time but what about the situation 20 years on?

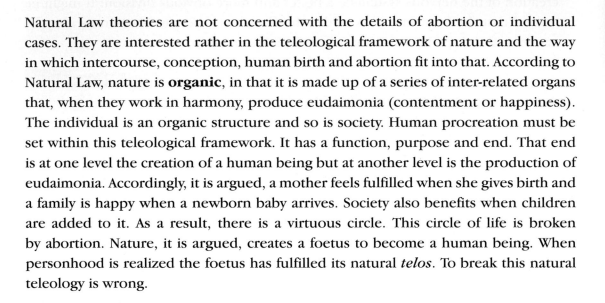

Abortion and Natural Law

Natural Law theories are not concerned with the details of abortion or individual cases. They are interested rather in the teleological framework of nature and the way in which intercourse, conception, human birth and abortion fit into that. According to Natural Law, nature is **organic**, in that it is made up of a series of inter-related organs that, when they work in harmony, produce eudaimonia (contentment or happiness). The individual is an organic structure and so is society. Human procreation must be set within this teleological framework. It has a function, purpose and end. That end is at one level the creation of a human being but at another level is the production of eudaimonia. Accordingly, it is argued, a mother feels fulfilled when she gives birth and a family is happy when a newborn baby arrives. Society also benefits when children are added to it. As a result, there is a virtuous circle. This circle of life is broken by abortion. Nature, it is argued, creates a foetus to become a human being. When personhood is realized the foetus has fulfilled its natural *telos*. To break this natural teleology is wrong.

Abortion is not a virtuous act because it breaks two of the primary precepts on which Natural Law is based: the principle of **reproduction** and that of **preservation of life**.

What is more, for sexual intercourse to be virtuous it has to conform to Natural Law. Sex is about reproduction and the virtue that comes from family life and from the very act of procreation. An abortion distorts this *telos*. The purpose of sexual intercourse has been destroyed.

Criticism of the theory revolves around:

1. Whether there is a teleological framework to life. Moral decisions ought to be made on the basis of the here and now and not concerned with some distant or illusory goal.
2. Whether being virtuous merely amounts to following laws found in nature. If, for example, Darwin's theory of evolution replaced the term Natural Law, would there be any virtue in a human being conforming to the law of natural selection?

3. Whether a woman's right to make decisions about her own body and future outweighs a foetus' right to life.

To think about

'Abortion is always wrong but it sometimes can be justified as the best solution.' Offer arguments in support of and against this statement.

Abortion and Kantian ethics

Kant's moral philosophy was not designed to tell the individual what to do. It is rather a theory that, when used, will help the free, rational, virtuous man or woman decide the best way to proceed.

An understanding of a Kantian view of abortion must take account of the three tests of the Categorical Imperative:

- Never treat someone as a means to an end but only as an end in themselves.
- Act only in accordance with that maxim by which you can at the same time will that it become a universal law.
- Act in accordance with the maxims of a universally legislative member of a merely possible kingdom of ends.

It must also consider:

1. the principle of duty
2. the rejection of happiness as a basis for moral decision-making
3. the rejection of love as a basis for moral decision-making
4. the importance of the individual and the immortality of his or her soul.

The following issues should be taken into account for a Kantian approach to the moral problem of abortion:

1. **The preservation of life** – The individual has a moral duty to preserve life. A comparison can be made between abortion and two ethical issues that Kant wrote about. He was critical of suicide, because human beings have a duty to preserve life. To take one's own life was therefore wrong. He was also critical of warfare and argued that rational human beings should work towards what he called 'perpetual

peace'. The preservation of life is again central to his understanding of war and peace. There is one reason for abortion that might be allowed. This is when the life of the mother is threatened by the continuance of the pregnancy. The preservation of her life is imperative.

2. **The principle of extreme duty** – Kant argues that some duties are so insignificant that they have no moral benefit. For example, you wear your own clothes to college or school and you give a pound or two to charity for the privilege. Has it greatly affected you? Will you lose sleep over giving away a couple of quid? It is doubtful. You have performed your duty at little cost. Kant says this is not what he means by duty. He is referring to things that are difficult or are performed against your natural instincts. It might be argued that bringing up a child in difficult circumstances would be an example of this extreme duty. An abortion might appear to be the easier option. Critics of this position argue that life is not an endurance test. Therefore, it is best for foetuses with severe abnormalities to be aborted rather than for the parents to live the often-difficult life of carers. Having an abortion might also be considered an example of extreme duty if it is deemed advisable by medical specialists, but goes against the natural instincts of the woman.

Key point

Kant's ethics is deontological. What you have a duty to do must come at a cost. If doing your duty costs nothing, then it is not a duty at all.

3. **Happiness has no part to play in any ethical decision-making.** A deontological approach to abortion is not interested in the happiness of the woman. Rather it asks her to consider her duties towards herself, her partner, any existing children and the foetus.

4. **Moral decisions should not be based on love or on sympathy.** This may appear harsh. A young woman is raped and gets pregnant. She does not want to keep the child as it will remind her of this traumatic event. Situation ethicists would argue that in this situation an abortion is the most agapeistic thing to do. Kant would argue that in ethics, love and sympathy should be set aside. The vital thing is to perform your moral duty. Thus, in discussing abortion, whatever sympathy you have for the rape victim should not be allowed to cloud any ethical decision.

5. **The problem of universalizability** – The basis of the Categorical Imperative is the idea that moral decisions are universally applicable and that all rational people

can agree to these. Kant recognizes that people are not rational. Kant understands human nature, copying a phrase from Plato, to be like warped-wood. This does not mean, though, that human beings should give up searching for moral certainty. The principles of the Categorical Imperative, Kant believes, will help individuals make rational moral choices. The principles are not absolutes; they assist rather than dictate. To test universalizability, we could take the example of a woman who decides, after a scan, that she does not want a daughter. Suppose every woman only wanted a son and decided to abort all female foetuses. The result would be that the human race would die out in time. This would conflict with Kant's principle about the preservation of human life. Therefore abortion fails the test of universalizability.

6. **Treating humanity as an end and not a means to an end** – The case above can also be used to illustrate the idea that we should never treat humanity as a means to an end. Kantians would argue that it is wrong to abort a foetus because of its sex because the woman is treating the foetus as a means to an end, that is, a way to fulfil her desire for a son, rather than an end in itself.

Abortion and Utilitarianism

There is no single view of abortion among utilitarians. This is because utilitarians are divided in their understanding of how to apply the principle of Utility. There are, however, some fundamentals to which all utilitarians hold. The first is that there is no absolute value placed on human life. This is important when it comes to the question of abortion. It allows utilitarians to move on from the problematical issue of when human life begins. The next fundamental that is shared by all utilitarians is that of consequences. The consequences of an action determine whether such an act should take place or not. The third fundamental is that whatever the benefit might be of an action, it should be determined by whether it benefits the maximal number of people possible. These three key aspects unite all utilitarians in their analysis of abortion. As a result Utilitarianism avoids other pitfalls of the abortion debate. These are whether (a) the woman has a right to an abortion and (b) whether the woman alone should be considered as the moral agent or not.

Utilitarians, however, differ over several issues, which means that it is not possible to say whether utilitarians are favourably disposed to abortion or not. The first of these differences arise from the long debate over what the greatest good is. Classical utilitarians thought of this in terms of happiness or pleasure. Today, many modern utilitarians refer to the maximization of welfare rather than happiness. It is difficult to be precise, however, about what welfare means. The general well-being of a society is clearly what is meant but how is that translated into an evaluation of the merits or otherwise of an abortion?

Preference utilitarians refer to what is in the best interests of the people involved but how is it possible to calculate what these are? A woman might argue that it is in her best interest to have an abortion. Her family and the man she had intercourse with might object. Who decides? Is it to be left to lawyers to calculate, as happens in the family division of the High Court, what is in the person's best interests? Does she have no choice?

To think about

List all the people who may be affected by the choice of having an abortion. For each person or group of people, consider the positive and negative effects of (a) having an abortion and (b) not having an abortion. Is it possible to calculate the maximal possible happiness or welfare of an abortion?

Rule utilitarians wish to create a basic rule of thumb to judge all abortions. This has its advantages and its problems. It takes into account the fact that an abortion has a number of consequences. The first is obvious. The foetus is terminated. The second is the effect of the abortion on the pregnant woman. The utilitarian must consider both the physical and psychological effects of the induced termination procedure and the long-term effects of giving birth to an unwanted or severely disabled child. There are also other people who are affected by an abortion. The father-to-be may see the process differently; he is taken into account in Utilitarianism in a way that other moral theories do not. The woman's family may also hold different opinions. But utilitarians, if they are to maximize benefit, must take other people into account. There are the doctors and nurses who perform and assist at the operation. Their welfare is of equal importance. There are the orderlies in the hospital whose job it is to remove the foetal material to the incinerator. Then there are the other users of health services who might argue that, with limited resources in the health service, money spent on abortions could be better spent elsewhere. On the other hand, taxpayers may realize the welfare benefit of abortion. It could be seen as a way of helping to control population in an under-resourced society. Or then again as contributing to a lack of working young people. To create a template for all these different scenarios is, it is argued, virtually impossible. A number of scholars conclude (a) that it is impossible to draw up a rule of thumb in this area and (b) that there is no value in trying to see how an abortion will maximize happiness or welfare.

Act utilitarians see the difficulty involved in drawing up a rule of thumb and they judge that it ought not to be attempted. They prefer to judge each case on its merits. Each abortion is judged on the basis of the maximization of welfare at the time. This has its merits but it has two fundamental problems. They are:

1. By judging an abortion on its individual merits at the time, it is not possible to evaluate the long-term consequences of the action. An abortion may be, here and now, to the benefit of the maximal number of people but you have no way of assessing the long-term damage or benefit to society.

2. Looking at a particular abortion runs the risk of going against the principle at the heart of Utilitarianism. The Hedonic Calculus is about the happiness or welfare of the maximal number of people involved. It should not be bound by individual welfare. By looking at a single abortion, however, the moral agent will choose to evaluate that particular abortion on its individual merits. The maximal welfare benefit will be replaced by the well-being of those people involved in that particular abortion decision. The consequence is that each decision will be different.

In recent years the work of Peter Singer has been influential in discussions about applied morality. He is a Preference utilitarian. He makes the point that abortions may be the preferred option in the case of unwanted pregnancies. He argues that society would benefit if the women who do not want children were able to have an abortion. Those who support Singer's contention also argue that there is a knock-on benefit to society. This is the **theory of replaceability**: general happiness would be advanced by the replacement of an unhealthy foetus with a healthy one.

The strengths of the Singer position are that it takes into account:

1. the general good
2. the special status of the foetus as not yet a person
3. the needs of those affected by abnormalities in the foetus, or pregnancy as a result of rape or underage sexual intercourse
4. that human happiness equates with the termination of pregnancy if the sentient being (the woman) is happier and thereby society is happier.

The weaknesses of the Singer position are seen as being that:

1. It is not possible to give a clear-cut definition of what constitutes a person.
2. The foetus has a right to happiness as well as the woman, and a child with disabilities may produce human happiness as well as a healthy baby.
3. A malformed foetus has as much right to happiness (i.e. birth) as a healthy foetus.

4. The large number of abortions every year sends out the signal that human and potential human life is not important. This contributes to a general decline in behaviour in society. Crimes that devalue human life increase, such as murder and crimes of violence against the person. The murder rate in Great Britain has risen considerably since the legalization of abortion and some people argue that these are linked. It is argued that, if this is the case, abortion is contrary to utilitarian values of the greatest good for the greatest number.

To think about

'Babies bring joy and happiness whether they are healthy or not.' What impact would the health status of a foetus have in a utilitarian consideration of abortion?

The right to a child

Introduction

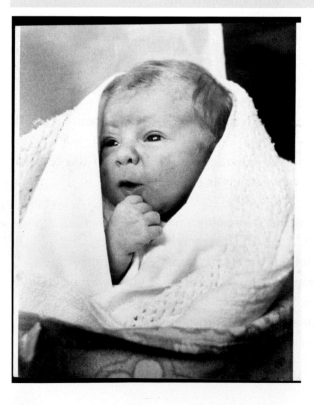

Louise Brown was the world's first baby to be conceived using IVF.

Just before midnight on 25 July 1978 at Oldham and District General Hospital, near Manchester, a 5lb 12oz baby was born to Mrs Lesley Brown. The baby, named Louise, was the world's first so-called **test-tube baby**. The consultant, Patrick Steptoe, who performed the caesarean section that night was part of the team that developed what is properly called **in vitro fertilization (IVF)**. (The name *vitro* comes from the Latin for 'glass'. It refers to the fertilization process that takes place in a glass container.) Today in vitro fertilization is used throughout the world to help women who are unable to conceive naturally to have children.

So-called test-tube babies raise a number of ethical problems. The most important of these is whether people have a right to a child. There are, as well, a number of more practical ethical issues.

The right to a child

You may remember in the opening chapter of this book the nature of human rights was examined. A definition of rights was given from the Chilean human rights philosopher, Cristóbal Orrego. He suggests that a right is:

> . . . *that-what-is-due-to-another because he has a title to that object. (Cristóbal Orrego,* Human Rights & Wrongs: Exceptionless Moral Principles)

This can now be applied to the right to a child. Orrego is saying that a right is something that is due to a person because that individual qualifies for it. The Spanish word for 'title' also means 'qualification'. This interpretation of rights raises the fundamental question of who has the right to a child. Or, using Orrego's understanding of rights, what qualifies someone to have a child? There are two answers to this question.

The first is that a woman is a free agent. Freedom includes a woman's right to use her body however she thinks fit as long as, following the ideas of J.S. Mill in *On Liberty*, by doing so she does not damage the very liberty that allows her to do whatever she wants. For example, this freedom allows a woman to become a prostitute, but it would not allow her to be forced into prostitution. It can be argued the right of freedom of choice ought not to be denied if the technology for IVF is available. In the same way, a woman choosing to be a surrogate mother should not be prevented from exercising her freedom of choice to become a surrogate.

There is another way of looking at the right to a child. This is based on natural rights. Many women have a natural urge to be a mother. They feel it is part of their psychological make-up. Therefore, to deny a woman her inclination for motherhood is against her natural rights. It would be, to illustrate this, like denying a person the right to work. However, the naturalistic fallacy can be used to counter this idea of a natural right to have a child. A woman may, by nature, be motherly but this does not mean that she has the right to have children.

Some human rights philosophers take the position that there are fundamental human rights but that the right to a child is not one of these. Their argument is that IVF treatment is not a right but **a liberty**. A liberty is a privilege given to the individual by society. It can be withdrawn if society thinks it is being abused or is not in the interests

Key terms

freedom of choice – the idea that human beings exercise free will.

naturalistic fallacy – the idea that just because nature acts in a certain way it does not follow that this is how things ought to be.

of, in utilitarian thought, the maximal number of people. Take this example. A boy is born with an outstanding natural talent for football. Should he be allowed to fulfil his talent and play football professionally? This might be desirable, but few people would say that this is his right. Similarly, it could be argued that a woman's urge for a child is a desire rather than an absolute right.

A further question lies in the extent of this right to a child. There has, in recent years, been a growth in the number of older women in their fifties and sixties having IVF treatment. In 2006 a Spanish woman in her sixties gave birth to twins. Does she have a right to a child? This case highlighted the problem in relation to the conflicting rights of the child. In July 2009 this Spanish woman died at the age of 69. She left behind her two-year-old children. It is argued that, using the **universalizability principle**, if a right does not have universal application it should not be considered a right. If it is considered morally wrong for a woman in her sixties or seventies to give birth to a child, because of the subsequent effect on the child, then there is no universal moral right to children. Should this right also be extended to single parents? Should it be extended to same-sex couples?

Extension note

Between a rock and a hard place

On 15 July 2009 the Spanish newspaper the *Diario de Cadiz* reported the death of Maria de Carmen Bousada; she was 69 and had been suffering from cancer for some time. For most of her life she had lived quietly in Cadiz, Spain. Her mother was widowed when Maria was still young. Maria never married and she cared for her ageing parent until her mother died aged 101.

At the age of 66 following the death of her mother, Maria sold her house to raise the $59,000 (£36,000) she would need to pay for fertility treatment. She went to a fertility clinic in Los Angeles, where she lied about her age on the consent form, claiming that she was 55 (the facility's maximum age for single women receiving IVF treatment).

In an interview provided to Associated Press Television News, Maria said 'I think everyone should become a mother at the right time for them'. Maria gave birth to twins, Christian and Pau, in December 2006 in Barcelona. She was 66 years and 358 days old. In January 2007 Maria said in an interview 'Often circumstances put you between a rock and a hard place, and maybe things shouldn't have been done in the way they were done, but that was the only way to achieve the thing I had always dreamed of, and I did it'. The twins were two years old at the death of their mother and will be raised by family members.

Was it morally right for a woman this age to have fertility treatment? Is a child a gift or a right?

In vitro fertilization: other moral issues

There are other moral issues surrounding in vitro fertilization, which relate to the process involved in the fertilization. They include:

- What is the moral status of the fertilized embryos that are not implanted into the woman? This is the spare embryo problem.

When eggs have been fertilized only two or three are implanted back into the woman. The embryos are graded and the best ones chosen for implantation. What happens to the unused embryos that have been fertilized? In the UK this depends on the woman, the partner (if they have one) and any donors. They may wish to have the embryos frozen and made available for later implantation. They may allow the fertilized embryos to be used for medical research, training or donate them for the treatment of other women. Alternatively, they may wish them to be destroyed. If used in medical research all embryos must be destroyed within 14 days of fertilization.

There are several moral issues raised by the disposal of unused embryos. These relate to when a collection of cells becomes a person. This is the same problem as relates to abortion. It also raises the question of how embryos are regarded. The grading of embryos raises the ethical question of whether human fertilized eggs should be treated like eggs in a supermarket. It is argued that human embryos should not be regarded as objects or things.

To think about

Could it be argued that it is better to experiment with the unwanted embryos left over from IVF treatment than to discard them, as waste is immoral?

- What is the moral status of the biological father when he is not the spouse/partner of the mother? This is the donor father problem.

Key terms

spare embryo – during the in vitro fertilization process several embryos will be developed; of these the best will be implanted into the woman. The unused embryos can be frozen for later treatment, donated for research, training or to other patients or they may be destroyed.

donor father – a man who donates his sperm for use in fertility treatment.

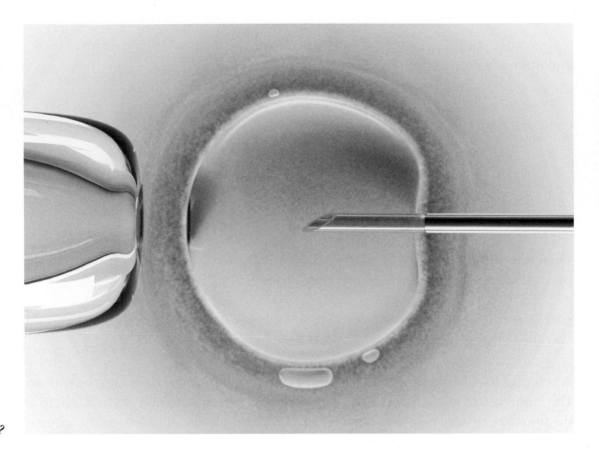

What moral responsibilities do those who donate sperm, eggs or embryos have for their donor-conceived offspring?

In the United Kingdom clinics can only pay expenses such as travel and loss of earnings to the donor as it is considered morally wrong to pay for donor sperm. This is not the case in other countries. Commercialization, some ethicists argue, raises important moral issues about the relationship of the donor to the child. This issue also applies to surrogate mothers, as discussed in the section on the 'money for babies' problem.

A further problem is the right to know. Children born using donor sperm may wish, later in life, to know who their biological father is. Laws regarding this right are complicated. Before April 2005 donors could remain anonymous. Children conceived after April 2005 now have the right to access the identity of their donor father when they are 18 years old. However, donors can still refuse contact with their donor-conceived child. This can be psychologically damaging to the child. Legally, donor fathers are not required to take on any responsibilities for their donor-conceived offspring, but what moral responsibilities does a donor father have? Someone who has donated sperm as a young man may not wish, later in life, to tell his wife and family that he has a son or daughter. He may not wish to take on emotional responsibility for a child he has not seen.

To think about

Do you think it is morally wrong to make money from being a sperm donor or a surrogate mother?

- What moral issues are raised by multiple births? This is the issue of **multiple births**.

In the UK, the number of embryos implanted during IVF treatment is restricted because of the risks associated with multiple births. Women under 40 years of age can have a maximum of two embryos implanted back into their womb, and women over 40 a maximum of three. In some countries larger numbers of fertilized embryos are implanted to increase the chances of success. This can result in multiple births, with as many as eight babies being born as a result of the in vitro fertilization process. This can pose dangerous health risks to the woman and the children. The mother may also have difficulties taking care of a large number of children.

- Who should be permitted to have in vitro fertilization? This issue relates to the **age and sexuality** of the parent-to-be.

The law allows any woman to have fertility treatment. Although in the UK treatment is restricted to those under the age of about 50, this is not the case in many countries. Women in their late fifties and sixties have been known to have children as a result of fertility treatment. This, it is argued, goes against the natural order of things. It has another effect. Parents will be in their late sixties and seventies or deceased when these children reach their teenage years. Some regard this as not being in the best interests of the children.

There is also the question of providing fertility treatment to single women and to lesbian couples. Following a number of legal battles over the refusal of fertility treatment to lesbian couples, the Human Fertilization and Embryology Act 2008 was amended in October 2009. The new legislation has amended the law so that fertility clinics no longer have to consider the 'need for a father' when assessing suitability for fertility treatment. The new legislation means that people will be assessed on their ability to offer 'supportive parenting'. The result is that lesbian couples can no longer be refused fertility treatment on the grounds of sexual orientation. In the eyes of the law all women have an equal right to fertility treatment; the moral question is whether all women and all men have a right to a child.

- Is it morally right for a mother to have a child for a third party? This is the surrogate mother dilemma.

There are various moral issues with surrogacy. The first is the idea that a woman who carries a foetus for nine months enjoys a unique relationship with the child. There have been several cases in America where the surrogate mother has had a change of heart and ignored legal surrogacy agreements. This can lead to long legal battles. In England and Wales surrogacy is not recognized by law, therefore it is not possible to draw up a legally-binding surrogacy agreement. Any disagreement over custody will

Key term

surrogate mother – a woman who bears a child on behalf of another woman. This can be from the implantation of a fertilized egg from the other woman or by using her own egg fertilized by the other woman's partner.

need to be pursued in court. In the two published cases in the UK, the court has ruled in both cases against the surrogate mother.

A deontologist might assert that the surrogate mother has a duty of care towards the child. That duty is natural and any agreement contrary to this damages the nature of moral responsibility in society. If the surrogate is acting as a host for a child that is biologically another couple's, then there are conflicting duties here since the biological mother and father also have a moral responsibility towards the embryo they have produced. Some medical ethicists argue that in this case surrogacy and motherhood are not the same, since the foetus is not biologically the product of the surrogate.

Another issue is whether surrogacy should be allowed in the case of homosexual couples. Some gay men have a natural desire to raise a family but their sexuality is a barrier. They now have the right in law to have a child through a surrogate, subject to the approval of their local social services and National Health Service (NHS) trust. There are still many obstacles, which make it very difficult for a gay couple to get the required permissions. Under changes made in 2009 the birth certificate of a child born by IVF can contain the names of a single woman or two women. These changes did not extend to allowing two men to be named as parents. Present rules complicate the right of two men to have a child by IVF. Yet it is possible in theory. Some clinicians argue that this type of surrogacy should not be allowed. Critics argue that children need a female role model. Against this it is pointed out that children also need a father figure and many families do not have one. Thus, to expect the perfect domestic situation for children conceived by in vitro fertilization and not for those conceived naturally is hypocritical. Social services and the NHS set high hurdles for those couples who want IVF. They have no control over the parents of children born naturally.

- Is it morally right for a surrogate mother to be paid to have a pregnancy? This is the **money for babies** problem.

No woman becomes a surrogate without a cause. This may be because of familial ties, for example a woman who agrees to be a surrogate for her sister. It may be because money is involved. In the UK it is illegal to accept payment for surrogacy. However this is permitted in countries such as America. There are moral issues involved when a woman rents her womb for another's child. They involve whether a part of the human body can be bought and sold in this way. A utilitarian might not find the payment of money a problem, since an infertile couple raising a family serves the general welfare. A religious person might, on the other hand, find the use of parts of the body for money to be a devaluing of human life or against the natural order. Paying surrogate mothers opens up the issue of exploitation.

Cecile Fabre argues that surrogacy should be seen as a job just like that of prostitution. Both involve the use of the body. Her book, *Whose Body is it Anyway?*, looks at the issues from an ethical standpoint. She argues that life is, for most human beings, a good thing both for those born naturally and those by a surrogate mother. Children are not harmed by surrogate mothers or by the natural parents. Thus, she maintains, since no harm is done paid contracts ought to be regarded as ethical. This takes a consequentialist line that a Natural Law philosopher would not necessarily accept.

- Ought not the high cost and high failure rate of fertility treatment make it too expensive to be available on the NHS?

A utilitarian view of the maximization of welfare or happiness raises the issue of welfare cost–benefit analysis. This can be analysed in two ways. The first is the practical question of money. Fertility treatment is expensive. It is also prone to failure. Women may have to go through treatment several times before it is successful. Money in the NHS is limited and therefore **services have to be prioritized**. Some have argued whether provision of a service which is not necessary for a patient's health is a misuse of NHS money. Can expenditure on IVF be justified when many NHS trusts have been criticized, for example, for their care of the elderly. The second issue is the possible psychological effect on the woman of not being able to have a child. This, it is argued, has long-term costs to the NHS. Clinical depression has to be treated and this has to be paid for. As a result it is difficult to give an effective welfare cost–benefit analysis.

A deontologist would necessarily take a different position in which duty is central. This would also have to take account of whether a desire for a child transgresses the Kantian principle that you should never treat another as a means to an end but only as an end in themselves. Some neo-Kantians argue that the desire for a child is not about the needs of the child but rather the benefit of the parent. Steven Kelman, the American economic philosopher, believes that a deontologist must also take into account costs to the health service.

Religious approach

A Christian approach to IVF and surrogacy depends on which ethical approach is followed. The Roman Catholic Church has, since the thirteenth century, relied heavily on the Natural Law ethical framework of Aquinas. From the first successful use of IVF the Roman Catholic Church was concerned about certain issues associated with it. In 1987 the Church published a report called *Donum Vitae*, or the *Instruction on Respect for Human Life in its Origin and on the Dignity of Procreation*. This examined Catholic attitudes to IVF treatment, surrogacy and the use of foetal material in research. Two concerns stand out. They are what happens to the unused fertilized eggs and whether a person has a right to a child or whether it is a gift of God. There are a number of other issues that concern the Roman Catholic Church. One is the effect of IVF on adoptions. The Church's voluntary adoption agencies find it increasingly difficult to place children, especially young people in their teens, with adoptive parents. IVF has not helped this situation. The main issues that the Roman Catholic Church is concerned about are the use or destruction of fertilized eggs and the issue of the right of a person to have a child.

Fertilized eggs

The Church is against the use of foetal material for experiments. It argues that a fertilized egg is the first stage of human life. Life is sacred and to use fertilized eggs and foetal material in experiments goes against **reverence for human life**.

The Church would argue that creating spare embryos is *not* an accidental by-product but rather part of the essence of IVF treatment. Additional eggs are fertilized in case the first attempt to produce a baby goes wrong. There is no guarantee that the second attempt will produce a foetus. Defrosted embryos have a lower chance of being viable, since the process of freezing and defrosting involves possible damage to the embryos, even if they were perfect before freezing. Some additional eggs are not and never would be required, as they are not of a good enough standard to be implanted. Consequently their only use is for experiments and Roman Catholics consider this to be wrong.

The *Donum Vitae* report asserted that governments must act to control the use of foetal material. Whilst seeing the benefit of experiments the report insisted that:

> *The inviolable right to life of every innocent human individual and the rights of the family and of the institution of marriage constitute fundamental moral values. (Congregation for the Doctrine of the Faith, 1987*, Instruction on Respect for Human Life in its Origin and on the Dignity of Procreation Replies to Certain Questions of the Day, *available from www.vatican.va/roman_curia/ congregations/cfaith/documents/rc_con_cfaith_doc_19870222_respect-for-human-life_en.html [accessed 01/06/2010])*

Gift of God

In the same encyclical, a child is considered not as a right but as a blessing: 'Every human being is always to be accepted as a gift and blessing of God' (Congregation for the Doctrine of the Faith, *Instruction on Respect for Human Life in its Origin and on the Dignity of Procreation Replies to Certain Questions of the Day*). The Church has extolled the virtue of **celibacy** both for women and for men. There is virtue in not

Is a child a right or a gift?

having children as there is in having a family. Rights suggest that there is a natural link between being a woman and having children. The Church rejects this because of its support for **chastity** and **virginity**.

Other churches take a slightly different line. Many Protestants, following Protestant Natural Law, argue that self-conservation is part of God's plan for creation. They also place great emphasis on the family. An example they use is the writer to the Ephesians emphasis on the centrality of family life for Christians. The **family is a gift of God**. It is important for Christians to bring up a family, to love God and to serve others. John Calvin, one of the first Protestant reformers, placed emphasis on family life. As a result, IVF is seen as a blessing for those women who cannot have children. At the same time many, though not all, Protestants reject the idea of a family based on single or same-sex (lesbian or gay) parents.

Many Protestants see the use of **foetal material for experiments** as a positive thing. They do not accept that life begins at conception and therefore it is not the destruction of human life. Protestants, however, are keen to stop the development of the foetus outside the womb for experimental purposes. The law, they believe, needs to control what is used, when it is used and to what purpose it is put.

Celia Deane-Drummond, an English theologian and an expert on science and religion, argues that the Christian concept of wisdom should be applied to the issue of IVF and the use of foetal material. Wisdom, she argues, means that scientists should act prudently. Progress in IVF treatment and in stem cell research should only take place in a prudent way. There are concerns about the use of IVF for older women and also the development of **designer and saviour babies** (see pages 165–167). Christian prudence must ensure that there is no absolute right to IVF treatment.

Some libertarian philosophers, in response, argue that it is not possible in a free market to restrict access to IVF treatment to, for example, women under 45. It is unfair to do so since a woman's motherly instinct does not disappear at a specific age. They also point out that there is nothing to prevent older men becoming fathers. Women should have the same rights as men.

Natural Law approach

On the face of it Natural Law ought to be opposed to IVF treatment and to surrogacy. There are a number of reasons for this; not simply because so-called test-tube babies are created unnaturally.

Masturbation

Natural Law theory regards masturbation as an immoral act, since the purpose of the production of sperm is meant to be productive rather than self-indulgent pleasure. Masturbation does not involve the natural teleology of the possible procreation of children. However, it can be argued that masturbation where the sperm produced is collected for use in IVF does have the intent of procreation. Therefore, some scholars argue that masturbation in this circumstance can be morally justified, even within the terms of the Natural Law theory, on the basis of intention.

Others, however, criticize the use of donor **sperm if it has come from a man other than the woman's partner or spouse**. Children born by this method are not biologically related to their father. This is seen as disrupting the family unit and as a consequence is banned in some Catholic countries.

Unnatural pregnancy

Many Natural Law writers are critical of the way in which the foetus is conceived. This is unnatural and therefore contrary to what nature intends. **Surrogacy** is seen as a particular problem, as it involves a woman carrying a child to term for another. There is also the problem of the large number of discarded fertilized eggs, which are necessary if the process is to be successful.

The same argument though can be used about surrogacy as has been made with regard to masturbation. Nature is adaptable and this is part of the process of Natural Law.

Consequently surrogacy can be seen as morally acceptable if its end is, as in the teaching of Aristotle, to achieve what is inbuilt into the blueprint of nature, eudaimonia. Clearly this is the case of the foetuses that make it to birth. The woman is happy, the child is happy and the family content since all have fulfilled their inbuilt *telos*.

Natural Law was, for Aquinas, the method by which God's eternal love and creativity is revealed in the universe. It could be argued that, however unnatural IVF treatment may be, it still conforms to Aquinas' general principle. A woman has a need to reproduce and, by doing so, take part in God's love and creative universal plan. Her inability to do so may be thought of as part of that plan or it may not. Equally IVF may also be considered as part of God's loving creativity.

Later Natural Law theories might be more inclined to regard IVF as part of the natural order of things. As the historian Jonathan Israel points out, during the eighteenth century the Natural Law theory increasingly became less religious in nature. It became concerned with the natural order. He quotes the German scholar, Johann Georg Wachter (1673–1757):

Self-conservation is the law of nature. (Johann Georg Wachter, Origines juris naturalis, *cited in Jonathan I. Israel*, Enlightenment Contested: Philosophy, Modernity, and the Emancipation of Man 1670–1752, *Oxford University Press, 2006)*

As IVF can be seen as working to conserve the species/bloodline it can be seen to work in harmony with the law of nature, rather than running counter to it.

Problem of fertilized eggs

There remains a problem; in order to secure a healthy child it is necessary for several eggs to be fertilized during the IVF process. These fertilized eggs are graded and normally one or two of the best eggs are then put back into the biological mother. The rest of the top grade eggs may be frozen at this stage, just in case the first pregnancy is unsuccessful. Inferior fertilized eggs are at this stage discarded. They may be destroyed or donated for medical research. This discarding of fertilized eggs raises a moral issue; if human life begins at conception then it would be wrong to destroy them or use them in experiments. The law allows for this foetal material to be used for 14 days after fertilization has occurred. This is to prevent such foetal material from being developed to the state of a foetus.

Some Natural Law theorists take the attitude that the **law of unintended consequences** covers this. The **law of double effect** is also relevant. IVF treatment was not designed to create a large number of rejected fertilized eggs. That was an unintended consequence of the procedure.

Kantian approach

One of the problems with a deontological approach to ethics is that there are **competing duties**. Which duty comes first? Is it duty to oneself, duty to your family, your neighbour or to all mankind? Kant believed that moral maxims have universal application and therefore there is no difference between a person's duty to themselves and to others.

The case of IVF treatment raises this problem. Why would someone want a child? A survey in Australia, among women seeking IVF, shows that they have an instinctive desire to reproduce and a sense of duty towards their partner or spouse. A woman may feel incomplete in herself and, in one sense, she has a duty to herself to feel fulfilled. We may also feel a duty to our wider family, to give grandparents the pleasure of having grandchildren. We may also feel a sense of duty to give something back to society. These duties are all morally virtuous and point towards having IVF treatment. But, at this point, issues get more complex.

Kant believed that when love is involved in a moral decision reason is compromised. Most of these specified duties involve the issue of love. To put it simply: we have a sense of duty to our partner, our family, and our society because we love them. This, some argue, clouds reason.

Kant believed in what he called extreme duty. Thus he rejected self-interest as a moral basis to duty. We have other duties and, using Kant's universalizability principle, if one of these is valid then IVF should not be undertaken. Two examples can be noted. First, we have a duty towards other people using the NHS. Could money used for IVF be better spent on treating people with life-threatening medical conditions? As the moral agent we alone must answer this question for ourselves. There is a wider duty. In a world where the human population is predicted to grow by 2.6 billion by 2050, facing over-population and the destruction of the environment, it might be asked whether it is the moral agent's duty *not* to have a child. Although Kantian ethics is not consequentialist, it has to take into account the universal kingdom of ends. Therefore, as Kant imagines it, put a group of rational human beings in a room and give them a blank piece of paper and ask them to make universal moral laws for the good of all that ensure respect for all. It might be argued that, in such a room, the case for or against IVF would be on a knife-edge. Competing duties create problems in deciding whether IVF is morally right or wrong.

The final issue that needs to be addressed in Kantian ethics is the question of the universalizability of IVF treatment. Kantians would argue that if there is one case in which IVF treatment would be wrong then it is always morally wrong. This can be applied to the broader question of IVF being universally available to all women unable to have children. It can also be applied to the question of whether it is morally wrong to destroy fertilized eggs or to use them in experiments.

Utilitarian approach

There is no single utilitarian approach to IVF and to surrogacy. Opinions vary as the theoretical approach varies. The American utilitarian philosopher, Saul Smilansky, takes the view that IVF can be seen as part of a package that maximizes human welfare. While it is true that IVF and surrogacy are expensive it is, he maintains, undeniable that family life and procreation are good for society. This increases welfare. As a result the cost factor is offset against long-term benefits for society.

This raises an important question of how the Hedonic Calculus is to be calculated. Is it based on short-term benefits for the greatest number or on long-term benefits? If we take the example of Bentham's **panopticon** or all-seeing prison (see page 69), where prisoners underwent a tough system of labour, silence and physical punishment, we can see that in the short term the harsh prison regime brought great unhappiness and resulted in prison suicides. Bentham's argument, however, was that it produced **long-term benefits** in the decline of crime, on the one hand, and the rehabilitation of the criminal on the other.

This can be applied to IVF. A utilitarian case against IVF can be made in terms of the expense of the treatment to the NHS. This is a short-term disadvantage. The real question of medical expense is complicated. The inability to have a child may cause depression which is expensive for the NHS to treat. On the other hand, having more children may represent a greater long-term cost for the NHS.

Two other factors may make the utilitarian support IVF. The first is that many see family life as the bedrock of society. This is not to say that alternative lifestyles are not respected. It is simply that there is greater social cohesiveness when family life flourishes. Public policy should be designed around this framework to maximize happiness. As a result IVF and surrogacy are beneficial. One other factor a utilitarian must look at is the effect on the public purse of an **ageing population**. By 2020, it is estimated, there will be a huge increase in those over 65. This is down to the baby boom in the 1950s and to people living longer, due to advances in medicine. There is a cost to government expenditure and a need for younger people of working age to pay for this increase in expenditure. IVF helps to increase the number of young people in society.

Utilitarianism balances the consequences of IVF and surrogacy. It is a consequentialist ethical system. Its weakness is that it does not really know what the long-term effect will be. A Rule utilitarian wants to place IVF within some rule of thumb moral maxim. Thus a Rule utilitarian might argue that, all things being equal, IVF treatment is beneficial to society both in terms of creating happy and meaningful lives and also, through the use of foetal material, by helping to develop cures to genetically related diseases. A Rule utilitarian would be anxious to prevent IVF and surrogacy being used for selfish advantage, as this goes against the principle of social welfare for the maximal number of people.

Practice exam questions

(a) Explain the arguments in favour of the right of all women to have a child.

There are two crucial points to this question. The first is that it does not ask you to argue whether the arguments you set out are right or wrong. You are asked clearly to set out just **one side of the debate**. The second point is that you are asked about **the right of *all* women**. The word *all* is crucial. You could look at the idea of human rights and how some argue that a woman has an **intrinsic right** to have children. You could examine whether the right of a woman to have a child is universal. Those who argue in favour of this believe it should extend to lesbians, single women and to older women. Although this essay does not require criticisms of the theory, it might be useful to set out the problem of **competing rights** and the possible conflict between the woman's right and those of her offspring when, for example, considering the age of the mother.

(b) To what extent is Kantianism a useful method for making decisions about abortion?

You could start this (b) type essay by setting out the strengths and weaknesses of Kantian thought with regard to abortion. On the positive side you might include respect for the **autonomy** of the individual and the **duty to preserve life**. However, you might note that many of the strengths in Kant's theory, when applied to abortion, can also be seen as weaknesses. For example, **universalizability** can be seen as good, since there are no exceptions to the rule, and bad, since it ignores issues such as rape or under-age sex. **The principle of extreme duty** can be seen as good, since a person is obliged to care for children and to develop family life, and bad, since it forces people to endure hardships in life for the sake of duty. The idea that **happiness has no part to play in any ethical decision-making** can be seen as good, as it prevents selfishness, and bad, since, for example, it ignores the plight of a rape victim. In conclusion you could evaluate whether the strengths outweigh the weaknesses or vice versa.

Develop your knowledge

There are a number of books that address the issues of abortion, the right to a child and related medical moral issues including:

Medical Ethics Today: The BMA's handbook of ethics and law, Second edition by British Medical Association Ethics Department (BMJ Publishing Group, 2004)
A Companion to Bioethics by Helga Huhse and Peter Singer (Blackwell, 2009)
Moral Problems in Medicine by Michael Palmer (Lutterworth Press, 2005)
A Companion to Ethics by Peter Singer (ed.) (Blackwell, 1993)
The Cambridge Textbook of Bioethics by Peter Singer and A.M. Viens (Cambridge University Press, 2008)
The Puzzle of Ethics by Peter Vardy and Paul Grosch (Fount, 1999)

7

Euthanasia

Introduction

The term euthanasia comes from two Greek words. The first part of the word is *eu* meaning 'good' or 'well'. It is found in the word eudaimonia which means happiness or a state of contentment. The second Greek word is *thanatos*, meaning 'death'. As a whole, the word euthanasia means literally a **good death**. This though is too simple a description. In medical ethics, euthanasia is an act or practice that brings about the painless death of a person to end their suffering. It is usually, though not always, applied to the death of an individual suffering from a terminal illness or a person that has given up the will to live. Euthanasia can be broadly divided into two categories:

- **active euthanasia** means acting to deliberately bring about the death of the person, for example by administering a lethal injection or an overdose of medication
- **passive euthanasia** means failing to prevent the death of the person when intervention is in the agent's power. Treatment is either withdrawn or not given to the person, for example turning off a life-support machine or withdrawing nutrition.

Euthanasia can be divided into three further types:

- **Voluntary euthanasia** is the intentional ending of a person's life at their request or with their consent. This can also be known as **assisted suicide**. This can include a person who wishes to die but is physically unable to end their life themselves; they may ask for help from a family member or a doctor to end their suffering. It can also include the use of living wills, where a person records their desires regarding future medical treatment in circumstances where they are no longer able to express informed consent. In the majority of cases of assisted suicide, the decision of when, where and how they should die is made by the individual.
- **Non-voluntary euthanasia** is where a person cannot make a decision for themselves or is incapable of making their wishes known and someone else judges it would be kinder to end their life. This can apply to the removal of life support from a patient in a coma, a patient with brain damage or from a very young baby. This is known as non-voluntary euthanasia as it is without the person's express request.

- **Involuntary euthanasia** is when the decision to euthanatize a person is made either against their wishes or without their consent even if the person is capable of consenting.

All three of these types of euthanasia may be either passive or active.

Euthanasia is a controversial issue. Daniel James (centre), a 23-year-old rugby player from Worcester, was left paralysed after an accident in a practice scrum. He later travelled to the Swiss clinic Dignitas to be euthanatized.

Euthanasia is illegal in most countries. This does not mean, however, that it does not take place, even in those countries where it is banned. There is a fine line between euthanasia and allowing a patient to die naturally. Some countries and states allow euthanasia. The first countries to legalize euthanasia were the Netherlands in 2001 and Belgium in 2002. In the late twentieth century, several European countries introduced special provisions in their criminal codes for lenient sentencing and the consideration of extenuating circumstances in prosecutions for euthanasia. In jurisdictions where euthanasia is legal it is not undertaken without safeguards. It is considered important that the relatives have some input into the decision but that they do not control it. This is to prevent any self-interest that might develop if close relatives made the final decision.

Key terms

Sanctity of Life – the sacredness of human life.

Quality of Life – idea that for life to be considered worthwhile a human being has to possess certain attributes, for example sentience, ability to communicate, to reason, to work and enjoy leisure, etc.

Euthanasia raises a number of major moral issues. They include some issues that are similar to those examined in the consideration of abortion in Chapter 6. These include the issues of the Sanctity of Life and the Quality of Life. A further issue lies in the principle of the **right to life**.

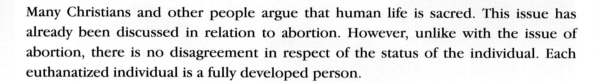

The Sanctity of Life

Many Christians and other people argue that human life is sacred. This issue has already been discussed in relation to abortion. However, unlike with the issue of abortion, there is no disagreement in respect of the status of the individual. Each euthanatized individual is a fully developed person.

In respect of euthanasia the term Sanctity of Life can be applied to argue:

- That **all life is sacred**. The word sacred does not necessarily have a religious connotation; it can mean something that is special or set apart. Philosophically it refers to the fact that without life nothing can exist. Life itself has a unique quality. Christians assert that human life is particularly special. Genesis states that human beings are created in God's image, implying that there is something divine in the nature of humanity. Christians believe in the Incarnation, that Jesus was the embodiment of God the Son in human flesh, and this further illustrates the unique nature of humanity. Since God's nature cannot change it follows that the human quality of God exists for all eternity. This is the position of St Athenasius of Alexandria (293–373) among others. It means that human beings are unique since they have divine attributes.
- That **all lives are sacred**. The second part of the notion of the Sanctity of Life is the sacred nature of the individual's life. Each person is unique.
- **That all lives should be treated as sacred**. The unique nature of human lives means that it is not permissible for another person, however well meaning, to take the life of another. A human being has no right to destroy what God has made special. This means only God can, through natural causes, take the life of what he created. For those who believe that human beings possess divine attributes, to kill a human being is tantamount to killing God.

Key point

Christians and people from other faiths regard human life as special or sacred, since humans alone are made in the image of God. A human being has no right to destroy what God has made special.

There are a number of criticisms of this theory. One of these is that life should not be protected at all costs. In *Life's Dominion*, Ronald Dworkin, the American philosopher of law, asserts that by Sanctity of Life human beings mean two distinct things. They are:

- Life should be preserved.
- Life should be of a high quality.

He goes on to assert that human beings have a natural inclination to believe that their neighbours' lives should not be taken. Equally they want them to live a happy and healthy existence. They do not want their lives to be a living hell. As a result, euthanasia is a way of affirming life. It affirms the eudaimonic quality of being alive, as eudaimonia means contentment and flourishing. A suffering person no longer experiences that high Quality of Life. The individual no longer flourishes and therefore it would be wrong to preserve life at all costs.

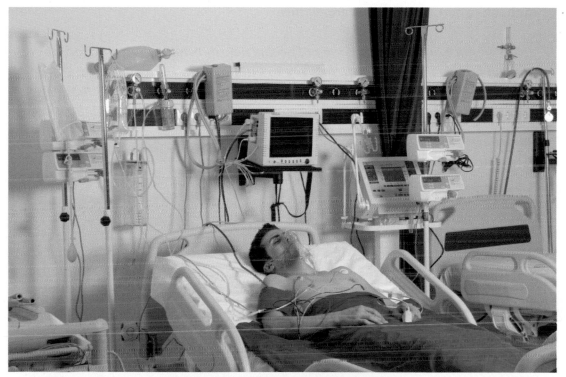

When a person cannot communicate their wishes should we assume that they would want their life preserved at all costs?

Extension note

The hospice movement
Hospitals specifically for the terminally ill existed before the twentieth century, but following World War II there was a renewed recognition of the special needs of dying patients which led to the modern hospice movement. The first hospice, St Christopher's Hospice, was founded in 1967 in London.

Advocates of palliative care challenge the idea that the act of hastening death to end suffering is merciful. They argue that modern science can almost always reduce pain to a tolerable level through medical treatment and psychological counselling can help a patient come to terms with a terminal illness. This leaves few untreatable cases. Additionally, the hospice movement argues that the pro-euthanasia lobby would be wiser to focus its energy and resources on campaigning for better palliative care and the proliferation of hospices for the terminally ill. Hospices aim to provide a sympathetic and reassuring environment dedicated to making patients' last days as pleasant as possible; patients can live out their remaining days in relative comfort. Of course, this argument requires evidence of the success of palliative care, and the number of patients worldwide requesting euthanasia seems to call this into question.

Legalizing euthanasia would have an effect on the palliative care service. Anthony Smith, an expert in palliative care, writes:

Every hospice and hospital knows of people who develop a paranoid fear that the nurses, doctors and medicines are to kill them . . . How difficult it would be to reassure such patients if we did actually kill some people deliberately! (Anthony Smith, 'A right to die', Nucleus, *January 1994, p2–7, available from ethicsforschools.org [accessed 02/06/2010])*

The Quality of Life

Those who argue in favour of euthanasia assert that the key point is the Quality of Life of the individual. If the person is suffering and no longer wants to live, is it morally right for that person's life to be prolonged? Should life be preserved at all costs?

To think about

Who should determine the quality of someone's life? Should the decision lie with the patient, their family or medical professionals? For each group, discuss why they might not be best placed to make this decision.

Perhaps only the patient can judge his or her Quality of Life. An individual has human dignity. Many illnesses that are physically and/or mentally incapacitating may remove a person's dignity. This can be debilitating and emotionally distressing. The patient may feel that their Quality of Life is compromised to such an extent that they want to end their life. Alternatively they may feel the Quality of Life they have is different from what they previously had but it is not reduced enough to make them feel they don't want to live that way. Ultimately, this is an individual personal decision.

It is argued that doctors have a role in judging Quality of Life. They and the social services would have to decide whether the loss of Quality of Life is temporary or permanent. This should prevent people being euthanatized who are temporarily depressed by their situation.

Those who argue against the principle of Quality of Life assert that it is an inexact term and therefore it is difficult to judge. There is a danger that some patients will determine their Quality of Life on the basis of the burden they are placing on their family, rather than their own wishes. They may wish to die to save their carer further suffering. People at the end of their lives are vulnerable. They may wish to end their lives for the benefit of their relatives or friends.

Society may need to be careful about what it allows in such circumstances. Concerns about this were noted in the 1990s; some people feared that if voluntary euthanasia were legalized then people might take that option for this reason. This view was made clear in a statement made by Lord Walton, who chaired a House of Lords Select Committee Report on Medical Ethics. He stated that:

We were also concerned that vulnerable people – the elderly, lonely, sick or distressed – would feel pressure, whether real or imagined, to request early death. (Medical Ethics: Select Committee Report *HL Deb 09 May 1994 vol 554 cc1344-412 available from http://hansard.millbanksystems.com/lords/1994/ may/09/medical-ethics-select-committee-report* [accessed 02/06/2010])

Some people argue that doctors should not be allowed to 'play God' with people's lives. It is argued by some scholars that doctors have a poor record when it comes to the ethical issues surrounding death. In 2000 the charity Age Concern highlighted the practice by some doctors of putting on patients' files 'do not resuscitate'. This was condemned at the time as an unacceptable practice. In America this practice has also led to criticisms that doctors make value judgements on who is worth saving; statistical evidence showed that the elderly, alcoholics, black people, non-English speakers and carriers of HIV were the most likely not to be resuscitated.

Another related issue is our lack of knowledge for making such important decisions; very little is known about the workings of the brain. The case of Rom Houben (see Extension note p150) raises the issue of whether doctors can discern whether a patient is in a persistent vegetative state (PVS) or not. Euthanasia is an irreversible action; the decision must be correct.

Extension note

Rom Houben

In 1983 Rom Houben was involved in a car crash. He was seriously injured and fell into a coma. The doctors declared Houben to be in a persistent vegetative state. In 2006, a new doctor, Steven Laureys, reassessed Houben's condition, claiming that brain scans showed that he was conscious. Using a technique called facilitated communication, Laureys claimed that Houben was able to communicate using a keypad and the help of a therapist. His messages suggested that he was conscious of being trapped within his own body for 23 years. There is though a great deal of controversy over this technique and in February 2010 Laureys retracted a number of claims. It is now widely believed that the messages were not coming from Houben.

Whatever the truth of this case, it does highlight a disturbing idea. How can we know for sure what level of awareness Houben has, or any other patient who is in a similar situation and unable to communicate? What implication does this have for assessing Quality of Life and making decisions about suitable treatment?

The doctor/patient relationship

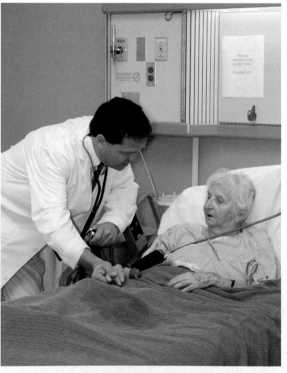

Would the legalization of euthanasia alter the doctor/patient relationship?

The question of who determines the Quality of Life of the patient also, it is argued, affects the relationship between the patient and the doctor. The **Hippocratic oath** is a vital part of the relationship between the doctor and the patient. Written in the fifth century BCE by Hippocrates, a contemporary of Socrates, it is still an important work in medical ethics. It states that the role of the doctor is to save lives and abstain from doing harm. There are those who argue that euthanasia goes against this principle and therefore is unacceptable. Some medical ethicists, on the other hand, argue that the principle of not doing harm must allow doctors to remove support from sick patients when the treatment is worse than the illness or where there is no possible cure and medicine to alleviate the symptoms of the disease only prolongs a person's life of suffering.

Many fear that the role of doctors would undergo a qualitative change if doctors were given, in any sense, the power to kill. According to the British Medical Association:

> *If doctors are authorised to kill or help kill, however carefully circumscribed the situation, they acquire an additional role which the BMA believes is alien to the one of care giver and healer. (Select Committee on the Assisted Dying for the Terminally Ill Bill, Assisted Dying for the Terminally Ill Bill [HL]: Volume II Evidence, House of Lords, 2005)*

Trust between doctor and patient is vital within treatment. This trust could be destroyed if the patient were aware of the doctor's power to kill, irrespective of the actual safeguards and of that doctor's integrity.

The slippery slope argument

Various scholars have used the slippery slope argument to criticize the use of the Quality of Life as a test. This is a view held by a number of groups, such as members of the Roman Catholic Church. It is argued that if euthanasia were made legal, the practice of killing patients would become more habitual, which would not be morally good. The criteria for whether a patient should be killed or saved might change. Some argue that this slippery slope has occurred already. Euthanasia was practised in Hitler's Germany. What began as the euthanatizing of handicapped babies spread into other areas; these included the mentally ill and later the Romany population of Eastern Europe, homosexuals and Jews in the Holocaust. Abuse is inevitable, it is argued, when human life ceases to be sacred. This is one way of looking at the slippery slope argument.

Another aspect of the slippery slope argument is the idea that voluntary euthanasia will lead to non-voluntary euthanasia and then progressively to involuntary euthanasia. In the Netherlands a government report seemed to support this idea. There voluntary euthanasia is legal but the Remmelink Report showed that over half the cases of those euthanatized had *not* given permission for their own deaths.

However, some scholars reject the slippery slope argument on the basis that it is a logical fallacy. They argue there is no reason to assume that if a sensible amount of something is permitted, it will inevitably lead to extremes.

The right to life

Article 2 of the *Convention for the Protection of Human Rights and Fundamental Freedoms*, as amended by *Protocol 13*, guarantees the right to life. This and other articles, such as those guaranteeing Quality of Life, can be used to support euthanasia from a human rights perspective. It is argued that the individual owns his or her body

Key term

slippery slope argument – the theory that a course of action may lead by degrees to something bad happening or a situation getting progressively worse.

and that each person has the right to decide when and how to die. The state should not enter into this matter.

The right to life raises the issue of the individual's **autonomy**. Libertarians maintain, as a development from the work of John Locke, that the individual has an absolute right to his or her body. The state has no right to intrude in this. Bentham, an opponent of human rights, was absolutely certain that nature placed on the individual freedom to determine his or her pain or pleasure. Bentham was an early example of someone who asked to be euthanatized.

The right to life equates to the **right to death**. An individual should be free to determine how and when to die. It is argued that this can be achieved through a living will, a statement setting out how you would like to be treated in the event of not being able to communicate your wishes.

Those who oppose this principle argue that the right to life is concerned with the preservation of life and not its destruction.

Key point

In human rights theory the right of the individual to autonomy implies the right to die.

Christian attitudes to euthanasia

The issue of euthanasia is linked in Christian thought to suicide. Voluntary euthanasia is seen as assisted suicide. The Christian response to one is then related to the other. The Christian faith has traditionally been opposed to suicide. The human body is a creation of God and therefore to kill that body, before its natural lifespan, is regarded as immoral. St Paul, in his first letter to the Corinthians, talks about the body as the temple of the Holy Spirit. Later Paul, in the same letter, speaks about accepting your lot in life. The attitude is one of uncomplaining acceptance. The essence of the message is that life, and with it the body, is a gift of God and whatever condition the individual is in should be accepted with fortitude. There is therefore something intrinsically wrong with destroying that which is God's gift.

The tradition of uncomplaining self-denial is one aspect of Christian ethics that can be related to euthanasia. There is, though, another side to Christian teaching. This is not about self-sacrifice but about self-love and self-worth. Fletcher's *Situation Ethics* makes allowances for euthanasia. The taking of life to show care and love to the victim of suffering is acceptable. Fletcher justifies euthanasia when the suffering of the patient is so great that life becomes unbearable. A distinction can be made between this ethical theory and those that argue in favour of the Quality of Life of the patient. Fletcher's analysis does not emphasize the Quality of Life of the patient; rather emphasis is placed on the need for **agape** when someone is suffering badly. The Quality of Life argument would allow the termination of a mentally disturbed patient if that patient considers his or her life unbearable. Fletcher dismisses this idea. Agape cannot justify the assisted suicide of a person suffering from depression. This is because Fletcher differentiates between physical and psychological suffering. Physical suffering is easier to identify. Psychological suffering is a much harder thing to calculate. A person's emotional state can change. They may wish to be euthanatized when they are emotionally at a low ebb. Would this be an agapeistic thing to do? Fletcher rejects the idea that people with psychological problems ought to be euthanatized. It would, though, be agapeistic in the case of a terminally ill patient. Therefore Fletcher was happy to serve as President of the American Euthanasia Society.

Gregory Pence argues that allowing voluntary euthanasia is a moral thing to do. He argues that in terms of moral values, forcing someone to die a slow suffering death is no different from just forcing someone to die. Both courses of action violate a person's autonomy.

Pence goes as far as to say that suicide is not universally wrong, arguing that Jesus effectively committed suicide by taking on religious authorities in Jerusalem. However, many who say there is a difference between suicide and martyrdom question Pence's view. Jesus did not want to die but had to.

Euthanasia in Natural Law theory

In the Natural Law theory of Aquinas, assisted suicide goes against the **primary precept** of the preservation of life. Another problem is the **role of doctors** in the euthanatizing of a human being. Aristotle, following the tradition of ancient Athens, believed that the role of a doctor is the preservation of human life, not its destruction. Using the Aristotelian model, the function and purpose of a doctor implies the idea of curing. To kill runs contrary to the nature of a doctor in precisely the same way that cowardice is contrary to the role of a soldier. Since Aristotle believed that virtue lies in the fulfilment of the function and purpose of a thing, it follows that euthanasia is not virtuous since killing is contrary to a doctor's role.

There is a further way of looking at euthanasia. It runs counter to the Golden Rule of Jesus. Germain Grisez argues, in *The Way of the Lord Jesus: Difficult Moral Questions*, that it would be wrong to take the life of another since you would not wish it on yourself. He cites the example of a Dutch couple. In the Netherlands euthanasia is legal. The husband suffers from Alzheimer's disease. His spouse is advised by the local doctor to have her husband euthanatized. The woman is unhappy at the thought, as she is a Catholic. The doctor persists and asks the woman whether she would wish to live like her husband. She replies that she would not. Grisez points out that it is illogical to proceed from that reply to euthanasia. Euthanasia is not merely an act of ending suffering. It is the act of taking the life of another.

Continuing the tradition of Aristotle and Aquinas, modern New Natural Law promotes harmony. Here it is not harmony in nature but harmony within the individual. Grisez refers to inner harmony as the integrity and inner peace of a morally mature and well-integrated person. Would such a person euthanatize a vulnerable and frail person because that individual is sick and weak? Would that person not feel remorse and even guilt? Would such sensations not affect a person's ability to become a morally mature individual? However, it could also be asked whether the refusal to help a loved one who wants to die would also lead to feelings of guilt.

Kantian approach to euthanasia

A deontological ethical system, such as that of Kant, prohibits euthanasia on the grounds that the individual has a moral duty to others, such as relatives (and perhaps even dependants). These override specific rights such as the hypothetical right to die. Duty works both ways. A carer has a duty to look after the vulnerable and frail, to ensure that they come to no harm. They are to be treated as an end in themselves. Equally the person cared for has a duty to their carers. This would prevent them asking for an assisted suicide because of the harm it would cause to their carers and to the doctors.

Kant has little time for the idea that people have the right to choose death in order to stop their suffering. This can be taken to its logical conclusion. Many things cause pain. This includes such things as childbirth and sport. Imagine if every time you were in pain you decided to stop that activity. Before long you would have given up most things. A person who wants a family would decide not to have children because the act of childbirth is painful. To be in pain is therefore no sound criterion, in Kantian thought, for euthanasia.

There is, though, a conflict within Kantian thought. Central to Kant's ethical philosophy is the idea of autonomy yet his deontology lays down certain imperatives that have to be followed. This problem is particularly acute with regard to euthanasia. Kant regards human freedom as vitally important yet it has to be set aside when it comes to assisted suicide. He argues that assisted suicide creates a society far removed from the desired *summum bonum*.

Kant's ideas were written at a time when **palliative care** did not really exist. Drugs that can now be used to reduce pain also have the effect of hastening death. Margaret Battin, an American moral philosopher who has studied euthanasia in the Netherlands, argues that Kant would have approved of palliative care even if it hastens death. This is treating a person as an autonomous individual. She also argues that there is really not a great need to legalize euthanasia since palliative care is much better than in the past. Pain can be reduced greatly. Further, she argues that Kant's moral society would be harmed were euthanasia legalized. She raises an important issue that affects patients in America and other countries where healthcare is not free at the point of delivery. This is the issue of insurance. Might insurance companies pressurize patients to be euthanatized if it were legal? This would save them vast amounts of money but it would run contrary to Kant's principle of never treating people as a means to an end but only as an end in themselves. In the UK, where healthcare is free at the point of delivery, the National Health Service (NHS) takes the position of the insurance company in this argument.

Euthanasia and Utilitarianism

Utilitarians differ over the morality of euthanasia. This is not surprising given the different types of Utilitarianism that exist today. Most modern utilitarians, however, oppose involuntary euthanasia. They do so for a variety of reasons. Some oppose involuntary euthanasia because it runs contrary to the notion of human freedom and autonomy, central to the ideas of J.S. Mill. Mill argued that 'the greatest good of the greatest number' only makes sense if human beings are free. If, for example, the majority of humanity were to be slaves then the maximization principle would have no significance, since none would be free to decide. Therefore, freedom or, specifically, human autonomy is a foundational value.

Involuntary euthanasia could be seen as wrong if we take the slippery slope argument. Hospitals are places of care. Doctors are care workers. People need both and both rely on trust. Now imagine if involuntary euthanasia were legal. The sick might fear going to their doctor or to hospital. The resultant spread of disease would run contrary to the greatest good for the greatest number principle.

There are some utilitarians who take a different view. They wish to remove the notion that human life is sacred in order to achieve the maximization principle. This is the position of Peter Singer. The de-sanctification of human life would allow all sentient beings to be part of the welfare calculus, which many modern utilitarians employ. It is argued that keeping people who have a poor Quality of Life alive is costly to society, costly to other sick people and costly to the environment. The amount of money spent on healthcare for terminally ill patients is disproportionate. Money would be saved if such people were euthanatized. The greatest good for the greatest number principle would result, as money poured into caring for the terminally ill would be used for cases where there is a good chance of recovery. Keeping someone alive on a life-support machine can be very expensive; however, giving someone a lethal injection does not cost as much.

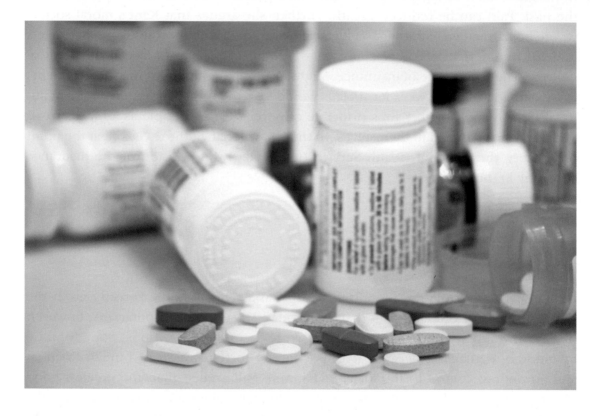

Drugs can be used to preserve life or to hasten death. Should the cost of medical care be considered in the decision to euthanatize a person?

There are other benefits to involuntary euthanasia. One of these is the reduction in the stress caused to relatives and friends of a terminally ill person. Many relatives give up a lot of their life caring for the terminally ill. For some it can be a soul-destroying experience. They give up work or take temporary or part-time jobs. Their lifestyle is affected. Yet, contrary to this, it can be argued that carers get happiness and pleasure looking after the weak and vulnerable. They do it out of a sense of love and duty. Some argue that Singer and others do not analyse the benefits that the very act of caring for the terminally ill has for humanity in general. Additionally, the value placed on all human life, whatever the condition, enhances general welfare principles that exist within modern Utilitarianism. Some argue that a society that values all human life is less likely to commit crimes against the person.

To think about

Drugs used in assisted suicide can cost about £30, but it can take £30,000 to take care of a patient who is terminally ill. Should cost be a primary consideration when it comes to healthcare?

There are several grounds that utilitarians give for allowing non-voluntary and voluntary euthanasia. Some have already been examined in Singer's ideas on involuntary euthanasia. A further reason is the principle of mercy and its utilitarian value.

The principle of mercy, the alleviation of suffering, is an important part of a theory known as **negative Utilitarianism** or **painism**. Painism is the view put forward in 1990 by Richard Ryder that it is pain and not pleasure that determines utility. Thus the **prevention of pain** is the sole moral issue that should influence a moral decision. Ryder rejects all notions of the aggregate of pleasure. He argues that, following the theory of the aggregate of pleasure, gang rape, for example, could be seen as morally right if it maximizes the pleasure of the majority involved. This is clearly wrong. Ryder's example might be extreme but it clearly reveals a weakness in the principle of the aggregate of pleasure. When Ryder talks about pain he means more than just a passing physical discomfort. He means suffering that lasts and ruins human contentment. He argues that this suffering is the only evil. The sole moral objective therefore ought to be the reduction of the suffering of others. This cannot be done on an aggregate basis. It can never be justified to harm one person in order to benefit another.

Ryder's painism raises the issue of the **principle of double effect**. When is it legitimate to euthanatize in order to reduce pain and suffering and when is it not? Ethicists that favour the principle of double effect argue that there is a clear line between deliberately taking life and hastening death by alleviating suffering. Yet some scholars are not so sure. Take the example of a very sick person, who is no longer able to swallow properly and is in constant need of hydration through a tube. This person is slowly dying. At what point is it acceptable, in order to stop suffering, for the hydration to cease? Is the chief motive the prevention of a slow, lingering death, or is it the deliberate termination of that person's life? Perhaps the two motives are wrapped up together? Or perhaps they are, in the end, the same? Who should judge?

Key point

The principle of double effect can allow euthanasia on the basis that ending life is not the principle motivation.

When dealing with euthanasia the importance of Ryder's form of negative Utilitarianism can be seen. The suffering person's life should never be ended on the basis of the relief of pain for the greater number. It is not an aggregate. It should only be used if the suffering of that individual is so great that life no longer becomes worth living. Importantly, Ryder argues that this pain must always be extreme. Ryder also argues that pain is not limited to human beings and that other sentient beings ought to be protected from extreme pain, as well as human beings. This connects human euthanasia to the destruction of other creatures, to save them from further suffering.

Extension note

Mercy or murder? The case of 'Dr Death'

In 1999 Dr Jack Kevorkian, a doctor who ran a hospice in Oakland County in Michigan, America, was charged with the murder of Thomas Youk, a 52-year-old man suffering from a form of motor neuron disease. Kevorkian filmed himself giving a lethal injection to the patient. He then sent a copy of the film to the CBS News programme *60 Minutes*, who broadcast it along with an interview in which Kevorkian dared prosecutors to file charges against him or legalize euthanasia. He was arrested and 'Dr Death', as he was known, was brought to trial for second-degree murder. Kevorkian was well known to the police. He had been arrested on several occasions for assisting the suicide of 130 other people. The film was evidence of what he had been doing.

Kevorkian's defence was that he was performing an act of mercy. The victim's wife and brother supported him. The jury saw it differently. They found him guilty by a unanimous verdict. The trial judge, in her judgement, spoke directly to Kevorkian, saying 'You had the audacity to go on national television, show the world what you did and dare the legal system to stop you. Well, sir, consider yourself stopped.' Kevorkian was sentenced to 10–25 years in prison. He was released on parole in 2007. Since then he has spoken to the press, stating his continued support for euthanasia. His life has been made into a television film entitled *You Don't Know Jack* with Al Pacino playing the role of Kevorkian.

The case of Kevorkian raises the issue of a doctor's motive in performing euthanasia. Was mercy the object? Was money or publicity? There was no evidence that Kevorkian did it for any financial gain; indeed his trial and prison sentence had the opposite effect. Kevorkian, to this day, defends his actions. Others are more critical.

To think about

'Doctors are supposed to save lives, not to end them.' What are the duties of a doctor? Do you think they should be allowed by law to perform euthanasia?

J.S. Mill's views can be used in support of voluntary euthanasia. Mill's theory focused on the need for human freedom and **freedom of choice**. Modern society allows, as Mill hoped, individuals to make choices for themselves. They choose, for example, where they live and, all things being equal, what they buy and where they buy it. Why then should that choice not include when and where they die? Mill gave support for this view in his work *On Liberty*. He wrote:

Over himself, over his own body and mind, the individual is sovereign. (John Stuart Mill, On Liberty, *Penguin Books, 1985)*

There are those who argue that Mill's views are not quite so straightforward. Mill, it should be remembered, was against voluntary slavery and against prostitution as both involve the decision of someone to give up his or her freedom. It can be argued that euthanasia is the ultimate sacrifice of freedom. In Mill's understanding of the natural world, it cannot be claimed that the death of a person sets them free. Death is final.

Yet there is a counter argument based on Mill's support for the death penalty. On 21 April 1868 Mill, who was an MP, made a speech in favour of the death penalty for murder. He quoted an ancient Roman question:

Is it, indeed, so dreadful a thing to die? (Committee, HC Deb 21 April 1868 vol 191 cc1033-63 available from http://hansard.millbanksystems.com/commons/1868/ apr/21/committee#S3V0191P0_18680421_HOC_33 [accessed 02/06/2010])

The position of Mill should not be seen as showing sympathy for those suffering from serious illnesses. In *Whewell on Moral Philosophy* Mill rejects the idea of sympathy as a basis for moral decision-making, calling such beliefs 'extravagant and fantastical' (John Stuart Mill, *Dissertations and Discussions: Political, Philosophical, and Historical*, Longmans, Green, Reader, and Dyer, 1867). Sympathy for a suffering person should not form the basis of a moral system designed for humanity.

Bentham's position is very different to that of Mill. He argued in 1775 against the death penalty and regarded the taking of life as barbaric. This suggests that Bentham was opposed to euthanasia but this would be a wrong assumption. Bentham, on his deathbed, asked for his life to be terminated. Earlier he wrote that the issue of assisted suicide for the suffering creates sympathy for those involved. Yet sympathy is not, for Bentham, a virtue but rather a principle to be condemned. Thus, as with Mill, there are mixed signals being sent out.

Today many utilitarians are in favour of making euthanasia legal in some circumstances. They base this support on the welfare of the individual and the general good of society.

Practice exam questions

(a) Explain how Utilitarianism might be applied to euthanasia.

The starting point to the question could be that there are different solutions to the problem of euthanasia among utilitarians. You might want to look at particular approaches, including those of Bentham, Mill, Singer and the negative utilitarian approach of Ryder. You could mention the maximization of pleasure, happiness or welfare and the way in which euthanasia may be necessary in order to minimize suffering. You could also consider the welfare calculus which looks at the cost of looking after terminally ill patients.

(b) 'Kant's ethical system is not useful for addressing the problem of euthanasia.' Discuss.

In discussing the validity of this quote you might want to examine those areas of Kantian thought that are applicable to euthanasia. You could look at the idea of extreme duty and also apply Kant's rejection of suicide to the issue. You could also look at the three tests of the Categorical Imperative and how they might be applied to euthanasia. You may also wish to examine whether any of these approaches actually addresses fundamental issues such as the Quality of Life and human dignity. Can his ideas be applied to non-voluntary and involuntary euthanasia? In the end you could evaluate whether Kantian ethics is useful for addressing this issue despite its weaknesses.

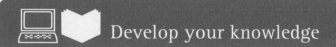

Develop your knowledge

There are several excellent books on euthanasia. These include:

Assisted Suicide and Euthanasia: Christian Moral Perspectives: The Washington Report by Committee on Medical Ethics, Episcopal Diocese of Washington D.C. (Continuum International Publishing Group, 1997)

Life's Dominion: Argument about Abortion and Euthanasia by Ronald Dworkin (HarperCollins, 1995)

Euthanasia Examined: Ethical, Clinical and Legal Perspectives by John Keown (Cambridge University Press, 1995)

A Companion to Ethics by Peter Singer (ed.) (Blackwell, 1993)

The Cambridge Textbook of Bioethics by Peter Singer and A.M. Viens (Cambridge University Press, 2008)

8

Genetic engineering

Key term

DNA – deoxyribonucleic acid, which carries the genetic information of living beings. DNA is the main constituent of chromosomes.

Introduction

Genetic engineering involves the deliberate manipulation, modification or recombination of DNA in order to alter the characteristics of an organism. Today manipulation of DNA allows scientists to produce genetically-modified (GM) plants and animals. It also allows alterations to be made to human DNA.

In recent years there has been an increasing interest in genetic engineering. This is, in part, due to government science funding. Genetic engineering has offered itself as a solution to many of the major problems of the world. The **genetic modification of crops** and the **genetic engineering of animals** for slaughter are seen as important steps in the development of food supplies to feed an ever-increasing human population. The use of genetically-modified embryo tissue is, at the same time, seen as a way of developing new medical techniques which will extend and improve the

Genetic engineering can be used to develop medical techniques; here scientists used human cells to culture a cartilage in the shape of the human ear and then implanted it into the body of the mouse.

Quality of Life of human beings. Such techniques will, it is argued, allow for the eradication of particular medical conditions or genetic disorders such as Parkinson's disease or certain types of cancer.

Genetic modification of crops

Genetics is concerned with genes that are constructed of DNA, the so-called basic building blocks of life. Genetic engineering is concerned with altering the DNA within particular plants or animals in order to create more healthy yields. In the 1970s scientists first discovered the building blocks of genetic material and soon were able to alter the structure of plants. Tomatoes were one of the first modifications. Tomatoes are a fragile fruit, prone to bruising and to mould. Companies paid laboratories money to engineer a tomato that would not rot. The result was a plant that is widely used today in sauces for pasta and baked beans. Soon other crops were being modified, particularly maize, wheat and cotton. Such plants are widely grown in America and elsewhere. Companies pay farmers in the developing world good prices to grow modified crops. It is argued that there are benefits from growing such crops. The major one is the reduction in use of fertilizers, herbicides and pesticides. This is a bonus since the overuse of such products has done damage to the ecosystem. Yet some argue that the negative consequences outweigh the benefits. It is argued that, because of the contractual relationship between the farmers and the multinational corporations, land cannot easily be converted back. This is because (a) farmers become dependent on particular multinational corporations for their income and (b) the soil becomes conditioned by the particular fertilizers and herbicides, which are adapted for genetically-modified crops. Farmers buy into a package. They have to use seed and fertilizers/herbicides that can only be bought from the multinational company. This creates a state of dependency that, it has been argued, is to the long-term disadvantage of farmers in the developing world.

Key point

Many environmentalists claim that genetic engineering undermines the diversity of the ecosystem. GM manufacturers argue that GM crops are needed to ensure that the world's growing population is fed.

Crop yields vary. It used to be thought that GM crops would produce much greater yields than normal crops. Evidence suggests that this is not always the case. GM cotton was supposed to fulfil two distinct yet interconnected jobs – to increase yield and to be resistant to the bollworm. Unfortunately, although it managed to do the latter, after a number of years the yield declined due to the increase of pests other than the bollworm.

Key terms

Green lobby – pressure groups that campaign on ecological issues.

stem cell – a cell at an early stage of development which has the potential to develop into any type of cell, for example a blood cell or a brain cell.

In the United Kingdom GM farming has been allowed only for experimental purposes. It is argued, within the so-called Green lobby, that GM plants damage the natural fauna and flora. It has been argued that certain butterflies and aphids, necessary for the ecosystem, have been destroyed in some parts of the world by GM crops. This is because genetically-modified crops are resistant to particular aphids, which has an effect on the food chain.

Such claims have been disputed but public opinion is generally hostile to the genetic modification of crops for food. It has been described as Frankenstein-food in the media. Public hostility to GM food has led most supermarket chains to ban it from stores. However, some overseas manufactured foods do contain some genetically-modified ingredients. This is particularly true of soya and tomato puree.

To think about

Do you think GM foods are the best solution to problems of worldwide food shortages?

Genetic modification of animals

The idea behind genetically modifying animals is similar to that for GM crops. Animals are genetically modified to be healthier and less prone to disease. They therefore provide better quality food and increased profits for farmers.

The cloning of animals is a development of this modification of the genetic structure of an animal. Cloning is the process of creating a genetically identical copy of an organism. The method can be used to attempt to produce healthy animals that yield high quality meat. The idea is to take a good sheep and clone another from that animal. **Dolly the sheep**, developed in 1997 at the Roslin Institute near Edinburgh by Ian Wilmut and his team, was the first example of this. Such cloning has not always been a great success in terms of producing good quality animals. Many cloned animals have died earlier than expected or developed health issues. Some people argue that cloning is still in its infancy.

The human embryo

In Britain embryo research is legal. Stem cells can be removed from an embryo up to and including the fourteenth day after conception. It is argued that up to 14 days the embryo has little to suggest that it has the properties of a human being. This is currently the view held by the regulatory body, the Human Fertilisation and Embryology Association (HFEA), and by the British Humanist Association. Embryo research is designed to discover the causes and solutions to genetic disorders and diseases, such as Parkinson's disease. An important issue is the creation of human embryos for research (see the right to a child section of Chapter 6 page 131). Robert Edwards, the IVF pioneer, has argued that it is wrong to develop embryos specifically for research. The Australian ethicist Nicole Gerrand, on the other hand, has argued that there is no intrinsic difference between spare embryos and those created deliberately for experiments.

Genetic modification of humans

Despite the claims made by a Korean genetic engineer to have cloned a human being, this is, at this stage, scientifically unlikely for several years. Yet **stem cell research** and the alteration of human genes has increased the possibility that certain diseases may be genetically eradicated. The first alteration of human **somatic cells**, body cells, was done in the early 1990s. Such techniques have led to the potential for designer babies, as well as saviour siblings.

In vitro fertilization (IVF) techniques allow doctors to screen embryos for genetic disorders, selecting healthy embryos to place back in the womb. It may also be possible to alter the genetic make-up of an embryo, replacing faulty sections of DNA with healthy DNA, to eradicate genetic medical conditions. Some people fear that this may lead to the use of genetic technology to modify embryos to have certain desirable attributes, creating what newspapers refer to as 'designer babies'. Do we have the moral right to choose the sex of a foetus or influence its genetic make-up? Is it right, as the expression goes, to 'play God' with embryos?

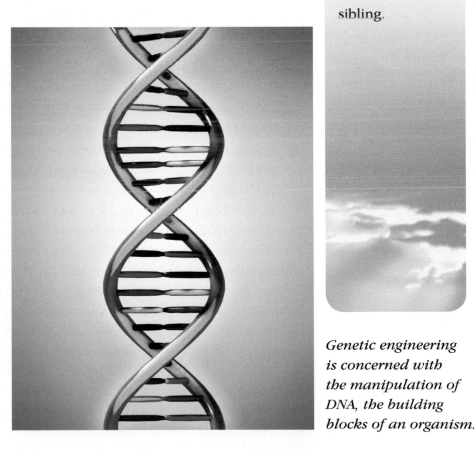

Key terms

designer baby – a baby whose genetic make-up has been selected to ensure the presence or absence of particular genes or characteristics.

saviour sibling – a baby whose genetic make-up has been selected so their stem cells can be used in treatment of a sibling.

Genetic engineering is concerned with the manipulation of DNA, the building blocks of an organism.

165

Most medical practitioners are against the idea of genetically modifying embryos for cosmetic reasons, for example choosing a baby's eye colour. However, they may feel differently about modifying embryos to remove the risk of life-threatening genetic conditions. What does it mean to accuse a doctor of 'playing God'? Are doctors not always interfering with nature, for example when using medicine to treat patients?

Extension note

Saviour siblings

In 2002 the Human Fertility and Embryology Authority (HFEA) published a report entitled *Pre-implantation Tissue Typing,* examining the rules on so-called 'saviour siblings'. The rules laid out in that report were applied to the cases of Zain Hashmi and Charlie Whitaker.

These cases concern two very sick infants. Both suffered from blood abnormalities. Yet here the similarities ended. Zain's illness was life threatening and hereditary. As a result the HFEA allowed Raj and Shahana, Zain's parents, to have another baby, who would be screened for genetic problems and selected as a tissue match for Zain. Several courses of fertility treatment failed to produce a baby. The HFEA rejected the claim of Charlie and his parents. Charlie had a life-threatening illness but this was not hereditary but rather spasmodic, meaning it did not pass from generation to generation. Thus the Whitakers' case for a saviour sibling was rejected. Subsequently the couple travelled to America and had a child there.

The Whitaker case raised questions about what should be allowed and what banned. The HFEA have since laid down certain mandatory guidelines. The first of these is that saviour siblings will not be allowed to help either parent but only to benefit a sibling. They will only be allowed if that sibling has (a) a life-threatening condition and (b) the disease is hereditary in nature. The saviour sibling must not be modified genetically as an embryo or its organs used. The only part of the saviour that can be used is blood from its umbilical cord. Further, the use of a saviour sibling will not be allowed unless (a) all other methods of solving the sibling's disease have been tried and (b) there is no danger to the health of the saviour foetus. The HFEA also put further qualifications on the use of a saviour baby. They are that the parents must agree to (a) counselling before the fertility treatment takes place and (b) take part in follow-up research, to examine the long-term effect on both the saviour and his or her sibling.

Following the report the Fletcher family, from Northern Ireland, were allowed to have fertility treatment in London for a saviour sibling for Joshua, their sick son. Jodie Fletcher became the first saviour baby in the UK. She was born in July 2005.

There has been, since 2005, an increasing number of saviour babies conceived. These saviour babies raise profound ethical issues about the universal right to a child. Is it morally right to engineer a child for a purpose? Some pro-choice clinicians argue that as long as the child is loved it ceases to be important why the baby was born. They also argue that restrictions on saviour babies are absurd; how can any committee judge what illness deserves treatment and what does not? Pro-choice scholars, such as the English ethicist Stephen Wilkinson, also argue that no damage is done to the saviour foetus. It is only the blood from the umbilical cord that is required, a thing that would be in normal circumstances destroyed.

This section should be examined in conjunction with the right to a child section of Chapter 6 (see pages 128–143).

Christian views on genetic engineering

Christian attitudes to genetic research and embryo technology vary. They follow the same lines as those discussed under abortion, the right to a child and euthanasia. Some Christians argue that life is sacred and this includes the life of any human being born with a disability. Roman Catholic Christians follow the tradition of Natural Law philosophy. In various statements Benedict XVI has said embryo research is morally wrong and could lead to a new form of eugenics. Scientists will have the ability to produce the type of child you want. Should they? It is suggested that use of genetic engineering will have the effect of creating designer babies. Scholars such as Karl Popper (1902–1994) refer to the use of eugenics in Nazi Germany to create a 'master race' and to eradicate those members of society who were considered undesirable.

To think about

'It is only a short step from genetic modification of human beings to the creation of a super race.' Do you think this slippery slope argument is valid?

There is also the issue of a lack of knowledge about the genome. It is argued that even though scientists are discovering what DNA does, we still do not know what the long-term effects of modifying genomes will be. Christian Natural Law scholars argue that, in the scheme of Creation, **playing God** is a dangerous and immoral business when the consequences of genetic modification remain unknown.

Key terms

eugenics – science of improving the population by controlled breeding to increase the occurrence of characteristics which are viewed as desirable.

genome – the complete set of genes or genetic material present in a cell or organism.

Key term

immanence – idea that God is present in and sustains every part of the universe.

Some Christians, however, assert that scientists should take part in genetic research. God is a God of love and does not want human beings to suffer. What is more, God has made human beings **stewards of the earth**. A steward exists to improve what he or she is in charge of.

Some of the thinking behind this idea comes from the French Catholic palaeontologist, Pierre Teilhard de Chardin (1881–1955). He held that evolution is still going on and that it will not end until human beings achieve their final *telos*, in being with God. Teilhard drew on his scientific understanding of Darwinism and on Aristotle's Natural Law to argue that human beings and nature will continue to evolve towards God. The American theologian, Philip Hefner, regards genetic engineering as part of this process.

Some Christians argue that the **law of double effect** should be applied to embryo research. A good moral act has the secondary consequence of killing the embryo. Genetic research does not seek to kill the embryo. This is a by-product of the research.

A Liberal Christian view can be found within the ideas of situation ethics. God has given human beings an intelligent brain and thereby has given humanity the ability to develop medicine to eradicate suffering and disease. Genetic engineering is just an advanced form of medical treatment that it is to be welcomed if it enhances **agape** through the eradication of diseases, which cause large numbers of people to suffer and die prematurely. A very similar response can be found in the writings of John Hick, who maintains the importance of the immanence of God in Creation and that such medical treatment can be identified with the ethics of this immanence.

Another Christian position takes up the idea that parental love, the love of God as father for his Creation, leads to research into diseases that affect children and to the creation of saviour siblings. G.W. Harris expresses this idea in a non-theological way. He argues, in *Agent-centered Morality*, that medical efforts to improve the lot of a child is fitting within the **normative thoughts of parental love.** It is virtuous to want the best for your child – in its embryonic form as much as when it is an adult.

Natural Law and genetic engineering

The Roman Catholic view of genetic engineering is based on Natural Law. This is opposed to genetic engineering if it involves the destruction of an embryo. Some modern theorists argue that there are other ways of carrying out genetic research without using embryos. This includes stem cells being extracted from adults or from the umbilical cord of a newborn child. Those involved in stem cell research argue that cells extracted from adults are not of the right quality for research.

Some Natural Law writers argue that it is wrong for scientists to reconstruct human life. Each embryo is created as a unique being and is sacred, irrespective of what that life turns out to be. In an encyclical shortly before his death, Pope John Paul II (1920–2005) put forward the idea that there is something inherently wrong in science creating designer babies. We live in an imperfect world. Imperfection is built into human nature and to use genetic engineering to drive out what is not regarded as normal would be wrong. Each human life is valued in itself.

Further criticisms are that genetic engineering is in its infancy and the long-term consequences of eradicating certain faulty genes are not fully known. Might the cure be worse than the disease? The English contemporary moral philosopher John O'Neill has argued that there is a certain arrogance in the principle that science knows best and that genetic engineering is part of that best. It can be argued that there have to be limits on what science does for the sake of both the world and the world of science. How are we to judge what these limits should be?

There are some Natural Law scholars that do not share this aversion to genetic engineering. They reject the narrow focus of Aristotelian principles of function, leading to a purpose, for an end. They favour a general view of respect for the Sanctity of Life and the dignity of animals. One such scholar is the American philosopher Wesley Wildman. He argues that genetic engineering can be used to help people and animals but that it has its limits. It needs to be firmly controlled by the general principles of Natural Law. There needs to be, what he calls, a **bioethical compass**. This is a system of guiding principles that control genetic engineers and all those involved in any kind of decision-making regarding medical and biological research. He views with approval the expression 'playing God in an appropriate way'. Hefner views human beings as part of the process of Natural Law. The genetic engineer is with God the 'created co-creator'.

Kantian ethics and genetic engineering

Kant's moral philosophy is non-consequentialist and therefore the outcome of genetic engineering cannot be regarded as important. What needs to be considered is whether this procedure fits into the Categorical Imperative or not. This cannot be seen as a simple rule of thumb. Kant did not create his moral philosophy for human beings to obey blindly. Each human being must judge for himself whether the parts of the Categorical Imperative can be used or not. Universalizability is important. Does genetic engineering raise universal moral issues? Imagine a situation where it would be morally wrong to take part in genetic engineering. This may involve using people as a means to an end. However, in most cases of genetic research, human beings are not used, if you view embryos as not being human but only with the potential of humanity. Thus, it may be possible to use Kantian ethics to build up a case for genetic engineering with regard to animals and human beings.

The aim of GM crops and GM animals is to produce a high quality, high yield supply of food to meet the needs of a growing population.

The case of genetic modification of crops, paradoxically, does raise important issues of using people as a means to an end. From a Kantian point of view it could be argued that obligations that farmers have (to use the seed of multinational corporations and their fertilizers and herbicides) raises issues about the use of people for an end. How do the multinationals view their development of GM crops? Are they doing it to save the planet or are they doing it to make a profit? They may of course be doing it for both reasons. Neither matters when it comes to Kant's moral argument. What matters is whether the corporation is exploiting the farmer on the way to meeting its aim. If farmers are being exploited then the production of GM crops is morally wrong, whatever the merit of the case for greater food production is.

The issue of using people as a means to an end could also be applied to the idea of saviour siblings. Has the newborn baby been conceived with the *primary* goal of helping his or her sick sibling? Is the saviour sibling being used as a means to an end rather than an end in itself? It could be argued that this is necessary if the life of the sick sibling is to be preserved. Human beings have a duty to preserve life and therefore two of Kant's ethical principles seem to conflict. On the one hand, the saviour sibling is being used as a means to an end while, on the other, Kant requires human beings to preserve life as a fundamental duty.

Kant would not see a problem with this conflict. What appears to be contradictory is in fact a misunderstanding of the Categorical Imperative and how it is applied. For Kant, the universal law principle is the most important consideration. Human beings have a duty to save life but this cannot contradict the maxim of making what you decide a universal law. Therefore, while the preservation of life is a duty it is important to apply the issue of saviour siblings universally. If we can imagine one situation where it would be wrong to create saviour siblings, then it cannot be a universal law.

Kant implied that human beings often ignore the rational basis of morality as a universal law in favour of a subjective approach. You may not wish your child to die and therefore you wish to create a saviour sibling. Human beings do not look at the big picture but only at particular cases that affect them. As Kant points out in the *Groundwork for the Metaphysics of Morals*, it is the maxim of the universal law that is the key to all moral decisions.

Key point

For Kant the maxim of the universal law is the key to all moral decisions.

Utilitarianism and genetic engineering

Utilitarian ethics views genetic engineering in a positive way. The prevention of disease is seen as a social good in terms of the greatest good for the greatest number. The maximization of welfare means the minimization of pain. Richard Ryder argues that genetic engineering has positive effects by minimizing pain in society. The eradication of disease and disabilities that cause pain is a good thing.

Utilitarians do not place any intrinsic value on the life of an embryo. Therefore they do not see anything wrong with using embryonic material in genetic engineering. This can be justified if certain diseases are eradicated. But what about the long-term consequences of genetic engineering? What does eradicating disability say about the nature of human life – are humans only valuable when they are genetically perfect? There are some utilitarians who, along the lines of Karl Popper, argue that genetic engineering will in the long term create a desire for 'super people'. This may have the consequence of making the majority, who are not blessed with superior athleticism and intelligence, feel inadequate. There is the potential, therefore, for the general welfare of society to be affected. There is a balance to be considered in Utilitarianism. Genetic engineering has the potential to maximize the happiness or welfare of the maximal number of people. It also has the potential to do the reverse.

Peter Singer considers, in the tradition of Bentham, all sentient beings in the equation of maximal happiness or welfare. Animals matter. Singer believes that genetic engineering brings positive results for animals and for society. If diseases were eradicated there would no longer be a need for experiments on animals.

Practice exam questions

(a) Explain how the ethics of the religion you have studied might be applied to genetic engineering.

In examining a religious (Christian) approach to genetic engineering you may want to mention Christian Natural Law theory as well as liberal Christian positions, particularly situation ethics. You may want to take each strand of genetic engineering separately, looking at issues such as genetically-modified crop production and the need to feed the planet, genetically-modified animals, saviour siblings and attempts to eradicate certain genetic diseases. A religious approach to these topics might examine such issues as the love of God and the creative immanence of God, on the one hand, and the preservation of the laws of nature and the problem of designer babies, crops and animals on the other. Different strands of Christian ethics emphasize different sides of the debate.

(b) 'Utilitarianism offers the best approach to the issue of genetic engineering.' Discuss.

In support of the quotation you could look at the principle of Utility, both in terms of the Hedonic Calculus and also of general welfare. You could look at how genetic engineering might be seen as maximizing human happiness, whether it is the example of the eradication of certain diseases or increases in food production. You might also look at the weaknesses of the utilitarian approach. You could argue that it is difficult to predict what the long-term consequences of genetic engineering will be on society, giving brief examples. You could look at other approaches to the issue. You should not dwell on these other theories, except to illustrate how they reveal particular strengths and weaknesses within the utilitarian approach. You could conclude with an evaluation of whether Utilitarianism does or does not offer the best approach.

Develop your knowledge

There are numerous good introductions to genetic engineering. These include:

A Companion to Bioethics by Helga Kuhse and Peter Singer (Blackwell, 2001)

An Introduction to Genetic Engineering by Desmond S.T. Nicholl (Cambridge University Press, 2008)

Remaking Eden: How Genetic Engineering and Cloning will Transform the American Family by Lee M. Silver (Harper, 1998)

The Cambridge Textbook of Bioethics by Peter Singer and A.M. Viens (Cambridge University Press, 2008)

9

Introduction

Since the end of World War II there has only been one year in which a British soldier has not been killed on active service. This is a stark reminder that war is not a thing of the past. The 'war to end all wars', as World War I was known, has come and gone and still the fighting goes on.

Ethical theories about warfare fall into a number of specific categories. They are:

1. Pacifism: the belief that war and violence are unjustifiable and that all disputes should be settled peacefully.
2. Pacificism: belief that war and violence are only justifiable in defence of vulnerable and defenceless people.
3. Just War theory: the belief that to resort to violence or war is justified if it meets certain criteria.
4. Militarism: the belief that a country should maintain a strong military capability and be prepared to use it aggressively to promote or defend its interests.

Origins of the Just War theory

The Just War theory asserts that armed force can be justified only if it meets certain criteria. This approach to war can be traced back to St Ambrose of Milan (339–397) and Augustine.

Ambrose was bishop of Milan and was also a Roman lawyer. His life was steeped in the traditions of ancient Rome and in the Scriptures. He used both to justify his Just War theory. Before Christianity became the religion of the Empire, most Christians abstained from warfare. They took a pacifist position as advocated by the words of Jesus. In Matthew, Jesus says to Peter:

Put your sword back into its place; for all who take the sword will perish by the sword. (Matthew 26:52)

The Church Fathers, up to the time of Ambrose, regarded this passage as a message that only in exceptional circumstances should Christians fight in war. This appears to be the reason why the Roman authorities were particularly brutal to soldiers who converted to Christianity. Tertullian, in his comments on this passage from Matthew, states:

> *But how will a Christian fight? No, how will he serve even in peace, without a sword, which the Lord took away? The Lord, in disarming Peter, disarmed every soldier. (Author's translation of Jacques-Paul Migne,* Patrologia Latina *Volume 1, 1844)*

Ambrose took a different line. He argued that the words of Jesus apply to personal conflict, which means Christians are not justified in fighting in self-defence. Such action would, as Ambrose saw it, stain the love that a Christian has for his neighbour. War is different. It can be justified on moral grounds as the defence of your neighbour. As a result, it is a moral imperative that Christians should fight for the weak and oppressed. What is the point, Ambrose argued, of maintaining your life but seeing people less fortunate than you die? Strangely, when discussing warfare, love is the crucial factor in fighting. Ambrose regards **divine law** as the central feature of Christian morality. Ambrose quotes John's Gospel in which Jesus says to his disciples:

> *'This is my commandment, that you love one another as I have loved you. No one has greater love than this, to lay down one's life for one's friends. You are my friends. . .' (John 15:12–14)*

Key point

The Just War theory asserts that war can only be justified if it meets certain criteria, for example, war must be fought for a just cause and as a last resort.

Pacificism

What Ambrose recommends is Christian pacificism. Christians have a moral duty to fight for the state, which exists to protect the vulnerable. A weak point in his argument is that governments are not always so morally upright. Authorities often exercise power not for the benefit of the weak but for the benefit of the rich and powerful. Ought a Christian to take up arms in such circumstances? Can a soldier decide which cause is just and which is not?

Augustine followed Ambrose's teaching. He separated an individual act of violence or killing from that sanctioned by lawful authority. Augustine put forward two conditions under which war could take place. They were that it had to be sanctioned by **lawful**

Key term

pacificism – belief that war and violence are only justifiable in defence of vulnerable and defenceless people.

authority and that there had to be a **just cause**. Augustine considered that the purpose of war should be to bring peace, even if this involves killing innocent people. He stipulated that war must be waged without love of violence, cruelty and enmity.

Just War terms

The Just War theory divides conflicts up into three parts, of which the last is a later addition. These relate to the period before armed conflict starts, the period of the conflict, and the post-war settlement. These three parts are known by their Latin names. They are:

• *jus ad bellum* – justice of resorting to war
• *jus in bello* – justice of conduct during war
• *jus post bellum* – justice after war.

Jus ad bellum: lawful authority

The Just War theory asserts that war must be declared by a lawful authority. Augustine had no difficulty with regard to lawful authority since, as a Roman citizen, there was only one, the emperor. It is argued that today lawful authority is much more difficult to interpret. There are around two hundred countries in the world, each one being a lawful authority. It is also argued that this concept of a lawful authority prevents citizens rising up against an oppressive regime since the citizens are not a legitimate government. This is seen a defect in the theory.

Jus ad bellum: just cause

Augustine first developed the idea of a just cause. He argued that a war should only be waged for a just reason. He had in mind the Christian virtue of caring for those in need. Therefore a nation has the right to protect its citizens if they are molested or attacked by another state. It also has the right to attack a third party if they are harbouring such enemies. An enemy may also be attacked by another country if the properties of that country's citizens are confiscated.

Several other scholars have since added to Augustine's list. Hugo Grotius asserted that a nation has the right to intervene in the affairs of a neighbour in order to prevent injustice from occurring.

The list of just causes has grown over the years. Today it encompasses a large number of reasons. Those who object to the theory argue that virtually everything could be made to be a just cause; countries can easily make facts fit one or more elements of the just causes. Those opposed to the Just War theory argue that these wide-ranging reasons would lead to warfare everywhere. It is lucky that countries are restrained in using the just cause argument. But are they?

In recent years the principle given by Grotius has been used to invade Iraq and Augustine's argument to invade Afghanistan. The War of Jenkins' Ear is a reminder of how the just cause can be used.

Extension note

Jenkins' ear kills thousands

In March 1738 a strange incident occurred at the Houses of Parliament. A young sea captain arrived at Westminster to lobby the House of Commons. The merchant captain arrived with his shrivelled ear in a jam jar. Captain Robert Jenkins was there to show members of Parliament what the Spanish had done to his ear. Parliament was shocked. Ministers were outraged that a subject of the Crown had been treated so badly by an officer of the Spanish navy in the Caribbean. The nation was incensed by the words of the Spanish officer as he severed Captain Jenkins' ear: 'Go, and tell your king, that I will do the same (to him), if he dares do the same (as you)'.

Was this a just cause for war? The British government thought so and war was declared. It lasted nine years and at the end of it over 20,000 people had lost their lives. It is argued that any threat, whether apparent or real, may constitute a just cause. It is also argued that both sides in a dispute may think that they have just cause.

Jus ad bellum: right intention

Aquinas added a third condition. War must not only be for a just cause and be sanctioned by a lawful authority. It must also be fought with the **right intention**. In the *Summa Theologica* he writes:

> *The right intention of those waging war is required, that is, they must intend to promote the good and to avoid evil. (St Thomas Aquinas and Thomas R. Heath,* Summa Theologiae Vol 35 Consequences of Charity, *Cambridge University Press, 2006)*

This addition fits easily with Aquinas' philosophy. Intention creates a teleological basis for war. It requires knowing what your aims are, how to pursue these and the final result you foresee. Aquinas turns to the **concept of peace** when discussing what these right intentions are. Whatever is done in war must be to ensure peace and harmony in society afterwards. But can war ever produce lasting peace? Wars often create a more dangerous world than that which existed before the conflict. How is it possible to determine whether or not peace will occur?

It has been argued that the war in Afghanistan is a good indication of this problem. The invasion of Afghanistan occurred soon after the September 11 attacks in 2001 which targeted the World Trade Center in New York and the Pentagon. The invasion was rapid and initially effective in forcing the withdrawal of Taliban forces, who the American government accused of giving sanctuary to al-Qaeda, the group responsible for the 9/11 attacks. Yet peace has not been restored to Afghanistan. In 2010 soldiers and Afghani citizens were still being killed in increasing numbers. It might be argued that modern warfare bears no resemblance to medieval wars. Terrorism and insurgency is the nature of war today. Thus procuring peace from any war is extremely unlikely.

The intention of protagonists in any war is hard to judge. The case of the present war in Iraq is a case in point. America and its allies went to war with Iraq on the justification that Iraq was not complying with UN sanctions and was harbouring weapons of mass destruction. However, after invading Iraq, allied forces were not able to find any such weapons. Some commentators argue that the real reason for the invasion was economic. Iraq is an oil-rich country. It was hypothesized that control of the oil supplies was the main intention of the war. This cause would be unjustified in terms of the Just War theory.

Soldiers on patrol in Iraq.

It is not just a practical question of how to judge the intentions of those who instigate war. There is also a more fundamental philosophical issue. Some modern scholars argue against the idea that war has logical causes and intentions. They maintain that most wars are irrational, chaotic events, which start unintentionally. The French philosopher, Voltaire (1694–1778), regarded war as totally irrational. Therefore it is impossible to speak of just causes or good intentions. War shows that human beings are still savage in nature. War can never be morally justified.

Jus ad bellum: last resort

One aspect of the Just War theory, developed by Grotius, is that of war being the last resort. In Grotius' work *The Rights of War and Peace*, written in 1625, he lists the methods that countries should take in preventing war from being declared. They include conferences, negotiations and tribunals, as well as the stranger spectacle of single armed-combat, with one warrior fighting for each country.

Today the **United Nations (UN)** organization has become the most important international broker in disputes between countries. The organization has various means at its disposal to prevent war. Countries will use it as a go-between to find a way to avoid war through peaceful resolution. Through the **Security Council** it can impose diplomatic and economic sanctions to stop aggression by one country against another or between a country's government and its minority groups. UN peacekeeping forces may also be deployed to prevent or curtail war. Today there is a well-developed system of international law and pan-national organizations such as the UN, the European Union (EU) and the North Atlantic Treaty Organization (NATO), all of which try to stop disputes at an early stage. It can be argued that these organizations put the Just War theory into practice by making war a last resort.

However, it can also be argued that the condition of last resort has no relevance today as most disputes are between groups of countries and rogue or failed states. The term **rogue state** refers to a state that, in contemporary usage, is suspected of pursuing weapons of mass destruction and missile programmes and of sponsoring terrorism, or who tries to undermine international law. This can either be direct involvement in terrorism or indirect, by that state being the paymaster of terrorist groups. A **failed state** is a country which is unwilling or unable to deliver core services to its people; it fails to provide territorial control, safety and security, to manage public resources, to deliver basic services or to protect and support its people. There is political, social and economic failure and a perpetual state of anarchy. These countries cannot be dealt with on the basis of rational discussion as there is no government, a corrupt government, or one that lacks sufficient power. At present, Somalia is an example of a failed state. Somalia has been without an effective central government since 1991. It has suffered famine and disease and is ruled by warlords and groups of militia. It is argued that the Just War theory has nothing to say when dealing with such states.

There is a further problem with the last resort argument. This lies in its ability to allow the enemy to prepare for conflict. Modern warfare is very different from the wars of attrition fought in the past. It involves maximum force and minimum time or, rather, that is the theory. The element of surprise is important in modern warfare. You do not tell the enemy when the attack will start. The Allies, after World War II, learnt the lessons of the German invasion of Poland in 1939 and the bombing of the American base at Pearl Harbor in 1941. These were unannounced events. They prevented the Polish and the Americans from preparing for conflict.

Aquinas and Grotius both would have regarded surprise attacks as being immoral and contrary to the Just War theory. Many modern war analysts, however, believe that the last resort condition should be removed from any modern Just War theory. A warning leads to wars lasting far longer and being more destructive than if the war comes without warning and is over quickly. This has moral implications because a longer period of warfare means a greater loss of life and more extensive destruction of a state's infrastructure.

Jus ad bellum: likelihood of success

Grotius added another feature to the Just War theory. He argued that the likelihood of success must be taken into account before declaring war. This is again a problematical position to hold.

Firstly, if there is a just cause and all other avenues have been tried, should war not be the only possible outcome? The case of the Sudetenland illustrates this point. On 1 October 1938 the armies of the Third Reich moved into a part of Czechoslovakia known as the Sudetenland. The occupation of the Sudetenland was sanctioned by the Munich agreement, a settlement agreed by Germany, Great Britain, France and Italy. Neither Britain nor France were prepared for military confrontation with Germany and were keen to avoid it at almost any cost. The Sudetenland was considered small and of no great importance; the surrender of this land was to appease Germany. In Munich, Hitler and the British Prime Minister, Neville Chamberlain, declared their wish to resolve further differences by consultation to assure peace. Within a short time, Hitler's army went on to invade the rest of Czechoslovakia and then to attack Poland, an act that precipitated World War II. Was Chamberlain justified in not fighting in 1938? Grotius' position would ask that the likelihood of success be taken into account when making this decision.

Secondly, is it possible to know what the likely result of a war will be? The war in Vietnam is a case in point. It is argued that the Americans calculated the war would be brief and victory inevitable; they viewed the opposition as an ill-prepared and underequipped band of fighters. Against the might of the American superpower it should have been, as they say, no contest. In fact it proved to be a long drawn-out war with high human cost on both sides. The odds on success are an inexact science, especially in an age of insurgency.

Key term

insurgency – rebels or revolutionaries rising in active revolt.

To think about

Is it right to give in to an enemy when your cause is just but you have little chance of success?

Jus in bello: proportionality

Central to *jus in bello* is the idea of **proportionality**. This stipulates that the damage inflicted upon an enemy must be in proportion to the good that is gained. For example, it would be out of all proportion to bomb a country over a dispute about an acre of land or fishing rights. This may appear far-fetched but it is the case that countries have fought wars over small pieces of land and over fishing rights. For example, Ethiopia recently fought a war against Eritrea over small tracts of land on their common but undesignated border. In the later Middle Ages the German Baltic states fought wars against Denmark over the herring trade while the UK fought the so-called 'Cod Wars' against Iceland (in the 1970s) over fishing rights in the North Atlantic.

The claim is often made that such small pockets of land have strategic importance and to allow the enemy to take control of this territory would be a dishonour to the country. The English theologian Barrie Paskins has nothing good to say for this justification. Wars fought in defence of national honour must be treated with caution, as the importance of individual humans is always greater than that of a country's national honour. Removing the idea of national honour, patriotic pride, forces a state to recognize the worth of the **common link of humanity** between itself and its enemy.

Proportionality can therefore seem morally sound. Yet there is a problem. How is it possible to judge what constitutes a proportional response? The war in the Falklands is a case in point. In 1982 the military dictatorship of Argentina sent troops to the British colony of the Falkland Islands. These islands in the South Atlantic, several hundred miles off the coast of Argentina, were quickly taken and renamed *Las Malvinas*. The islands were inhabited by just under 2000 British people and a few million sheep. Shortly after the islands were captured, Margaret Thatcher, then British prime minister, announced that a convoy of ships would be sent to the South Atlantic to restore the Falkland Islands to British control. Thus began the Falkland Islands War. Hundreds of troops were killed on either side. Was the war proportional? How is it possible to judge proportionality? At one stage during the war a British submarine fired torpedoes at an Argentine warship, the *General Belgrano*. The cruiser, which was an old American warship that had survived the attack on Pearl Harbor, was sunk. 368 lives were lost. At the time many commentators were critical of the decision to sink the vessel. Was this a disproportionate response to the taking of two small islands in the South Atlantic?

The Thiepval Memorial, the Memorial to the Missing of the Somme, remembers the 72,194 British and South African soldiers who died in the Battle of the Somme between 1916–1918, and whose bodies were never found. The memorial includes Harry Hare, uncle of the writer of this book, killed aged 17. In all, over one million soldiers perished in the battle.

There is a further problem with proportionality. The nature of modern warfare is contrary to it. Since soldiers rely on logistics, communications, transport and provisions, modern warfare hits the infrastructure of a state. This will include power stations, railway and road junctions, telecommunications hubs, gas and oil facilities, as well as the enemy's command centres. This tactic of striking hard at the infrastructure of a state with missiles and bombs is what the Americans term '**shock and awe**'. Destruction needs to be quick and severe. The destruction of electricity power stations will disrupt not only the electricity supply but also the water supply and sewage system, by preventing pumps from working. Such destruction will prevent the enemy's army or air force from being able to function properly. This means that victory is achieved by attacking infrastructures and then removing the last remnants of an enemy army or insurgents rather than by a full-scale war. This type of response is very disruptive and disproportionate but it does have the moral advantage of ending the war quickly. The same could be said of the dropping of the atomic bombs on Hiroshima and Nagasaki at the end of World War II. It can be argued that saving lives by ending a war quickly was done at the cost of proportionality.

Jus in bello: civilians in war

Aquinas was clear that civilians are innocent parties in war and therefore they are (a) not to be targeted and (b) to be protected from abuse. Later writers have added another rule. Civilians are not to be used as a **human shield** by either army. Grotius makes the point that civilians should not be accountable for the crimes of their rulers, irrespective of whether or not the people have supported their government. Grotius quotes a statement made by the ancient Greek writer Proculus:

For one bad person a people often suffer. (Hugo Grotius, The Rights of War and Peace *Book II, Liberty Fund, 2005)*

Grotius argues that the people should not suffer for the mistakes of their rulers; the people are like children to their father, the ruler. Would it be right to kill children because of an offence by their father? His answer is morally it would not, yet that is precisely what happens in war.

In 1983 Catholic Bishops of the United States issued a pastoral letter. In the letter they identified groups of people, such as children and hospital patients, who could never be classed as combatants. They followed this with the order that:

The lives of innocent persons may never be taken directly, regardless of the purpose alleged for doing so. (The Challenge of Peace: God's Promise and Our Response – A Pastoral Letter on War and Peace by the National Conference of Catholic Bishops *available from www.usccb.org/sdwp/international/TheChallengeofPeace. pdf [accessed 02/06/2010])*

Violence should be shown towards the aggressors, not towards those who are caught up in conflict through no fault of their own. This command can appear hard to follow, as even with the development of sophisticated weapons, accidents in war happen and it is perhaps inevitable that there will be civilian casualties. Today the military refer to **collateral damage**, the unintentional destruction of innocent people and their property. Many scholars, such as Oliver O'Donovan and Keith Pavlischek, accept that this cannot be avoided but should be kept to a minimum. They argue that civilians should not be deliberately targeted. This means that the carpet-bombing of cities, which caused mass civilian casualties in World War II in Coventry and Dresden, should not take place. However, as the Israeli bombing of Gaza in 2008/2009 demonstrates, the morality of military conduct can be difficult to judge. What some might consider collateral damage could be seen by others as deliberate wanton destruction.

The Just War theory argues that military conduct in war should be above reproach. Civilians are not to be deliberately targeted. Soldiers are to refrain from reprisals and from cruel and inhumane punishment of captured personnel. **Torture** must not be used. At the end of the war, Grotius argues, those captured in battle are to be returned to their families.

Extension note

Ticking bomb in the room next door

Modern warfare is different from in the past, as Oliver O'Donovan argues in *The Just War Revisited*. Wars are today more likely to be fought between an army and insurgents. In this situation some scholars argue that the traditional rules of the Just War theory do not apply. Imagine that there is a ticking bomb in the next room and the only way you can stop the bomb going off is to torture one of the terrorists that you have captured. What do you do?

The consequentialist may argue that torture should, in this situation, be allowed. This is the view put forward by Alan Dershowitz, a law professor at Harvard University. His argument is straightforward. Torture should be legalized in certain specific circumstances or else it will be practised illegally in a great number of situations, where it should not occur. It could be controlled if it were legal.

Other scholars are appalled by this suggestion. The English ethicist, Bob Brecher, puts it this way. Human beings have a duty to protect the dignity of others, as they would themselves. It would be wrong to torture since the body is integral to personal identity. The victim of torture is damaged both physically and mentally. Thus this action in all circumstances is contrary to the duty to respect others.

Jus in bello: weaponry

The *jus in bello* argument developed by Aquinas and Augustine largely assumes that wars take place on battlefields. However, over the centuries, it became clear that a code of ethics was needed to instruct Christians on how to wage war in order to prevent killing civilians and to limit destruction. The development of new technology often forces a reappraisal of how wars should be fought. In the thirteenth century the Second Lateran Council ruled that use of crossbows and siege machines (weapons designed to catapult missiles over city walls) was to be banned in wars between Christians. This was the first reference to use of indiscriminate weapons that affect civilians and the military. The rule was largely ignored, but the issue of indiscriminate weapons continues to be a moral problem. The use of napalm during the Vietnam War by the Americans was widely condemned for the damage it did to innocent civilians. More recently the use of chemical and biological weapons, 'dirty bombs' which contain nuclear or radioactive material not as the explosive element but to spread radiation, improvised explosive devices and plastic landmines have raised the same moral issue that siege machines did in the medieval period.

Children flee from an aerial napalm attack near Trang Bang in Vietnam. The use of indiscriminate weapons such as napalm is widely criticized as their use involves widespread destruction of civilian areas as well as strategic targets.

Chemical and nuclear weapons are particularly dangerous because the long-term effects of their use are still unknown and may continue to harm civilians long after a war has ended.

To think about

Is there such a thing as a morally acceptable piece of weaponry?

Jus post bellum

Today *jus post bellum* is considered as important as justice before and during conflict. Many ethicists argue that a war can only be moral if:

a. its result has been carefully considered

b. that result is proportional to the reasons for the war in the first place

c. the result can be ultimately successful.

The last consideration plays an important part in modern Just War theory. The importance of the success of the final outcome has generally been ignored in earlier forms of the Just War theory. Aquinas hardly mentions the *post bellum* situation (the situation after the war is over). Yet modern experience suggests that 'winning the peace' is the central issue. Saddam Hussein was defeated in Iraq in 2003, but ultimate success would mean establishing stability in post-war Iraq. In a 2006 report entitled *The Ethics of Pushbutton Warfare*, Michael Eyman describes how traditionally probability of success was the key issue in warfare, whereas:

> *Today the situation is different. . . . The problem isn't 'can we do it' but rather will it actually lead to the political outcome that we desire. (Michael D. Eyman, 2006,* The Ethics of Pushbutton Warfare: Self-imposed Constraints on the Technological Freedom to Apply Military Force *available from www.afresearch.org [accessed 02/06/2010])*

Eyman cites many reasons why the final outcome might be a problem after the initial war is over. These include the influence of neighbouring countries, cultural issues, the history of the region, international relationships, self-interest and internal political restraints. Eyman is led to reject much of the Just War theory as a consequence of the problem of *jus post bellum*.

Others have merely added justice after the war to what is just before and during the war. Brian Orend, the Canadian moral philosopher, is the most influential of a group who have developed and applied Grotius' ideas on the Just War. He argues that the Just War theory is in fact the application of human rights in the war situation. He regards the outcome of the war as crucial. He is interested in what he describes as an **ethical exit strategy**. *Jus post bellum*, according to Orend and others, permits:

- The trial of any leaders that have performed or ordered unlawful acts before or during the war. A clear distinction is made between those in authority within a regime and those not. It does not allow a victorious country to change the nature or culture of the country taken. Thus ethnic cleansing or changes to institutional structures would not be allowed.
- The right of the victorious nation to reparations for any damage done in or before the war. This raises, however, the issue of the stability of the defeated country. The victorious powers have to ensure the viability of the defeated state. As such, any reparations cannot be so great that the defeated country remains poor and prone to internal conflict.

There are certain problems with Orend's recipe, one of which he admits. This is, as with *jus ad bellum* and *jus in bello*, whether the Just War theory has any relevance to the new world order in which contention is mainly within countries rather than between them.

To think about

Can the Just War theory be applied to the war against terrorism?

Arguments for and against Just War theory

The Just War theory can be seen to have a number of strengths:

1. It tries to protect the innocent victims of warfare.
2. It encourages combatants to think about the moral implications of their actions.
3. It rejects the view that there are no rules of conduct in war situations.
4. It maintains the central importance of the dignity of each human being.
5. It places moral integrity above the pursuit of naked power.
6. It tries to prevent the excesses of warfare by rejecting the notion of retribution.
7. The culture, traditions and laws of the defeated nation are respected. Therefore, future grievances that might lead to further conflict are avoided.

There are, though, a number of weaknesses to the theory.

1. The question of discrimination between a soldier and a non-combatant is a problem. It is key to *jus in bello*. In the wars of the later part of the twentieth century it is increasingly hard to tell the difference between who is innocent and who is guilty In certain countries all adults, both male and female, are obliged to do military service for a period each year. Are they all combatants, even when they are watching television at home with their children? Many wars are paid for by private businessmen and companies to gain resources, such as diamonds in parts of Africa. Are these paymasters combatants as well as their employees?

2. It is argued that the concepts of war and justice have no place together. They are incompatible. The theologian Walter Wink, in his book *The Powers that be: Theology for a New Millennium*, considers that Augustine's teaching of the Just War theory led Christians on the wrong path. He believes that there can never be just reasons for war. Wink argues that justice is brought about by equality and fairness, something which war can never achieve, so the idea of a Just War is a contradiction in terms.

3. Perhaps the major problem with Just War theory is that it is open to great abuse. It can seem as though people will always be able to justify a war no matter what unjust ulterior motives, such as economic gain, drive them.

4. In limiting the 'just war' to clashes between states it fails to set out clearly what rules are necessary in dealing with civil wars and wars against insurgents.

Key terms

pacifism – the belief that war and violence are unjustifiable and that all disputes should be settled peacefully.

Virtue Ethics – morality based on the good an action produces for the moral agent.

Pacifism

Within the early Church there were many Christians who were pacifists. They were not prepared to fight in war in any circumstances, since the Kingdom of God would be ruled over by the Prince of Peace. Pacifism is the belief that there are no circumstances in which violence is acceptable. Pacifists argue that Christ called on his disciples to turn the other cheek, 'But if anyone strikes you on the right cheek, turn the other also' (Matthew 5:39).

Then Peter came and said to him, 'Lord, if another member of the church sins against me, how often should I forgive? As many as seven times? Jesus said to him, 'Not seven times, but, I tell you, seventy-seven times.' (Matthew 18:21–22)

This, in Jewish terms at the time, was the equivalent to an infinite number. Thus, Christian pacifists argue that it is never acceptable to fight even if attacked. They also argue, and here they agree with many non-Christian pacifists, that violence only creates more violence. A culture of retaliation begins and there is no end to it. Pacifist Virtue Ethics argues that violence, however justified it may be, harms the moral agent. The individual sees aggression and violence as part of the natural order rather than as contrary to how life should be. Violence desensitizes the individual. He or she accepts violent acts as the way life is.

The early Christian pacifist tendency did not last. When the Christian faith became the official religion of the Roman Empire, Christians were called to fight under the banner of Jesus. A clear distinction was made between personal violence and forgiveness, in which Christians were obliged to turn the other cheek, and state violence and retribution. Yet among some Christian scholars, doubts persisted about what many regarded as a double standard.

The **Society of Friends** or Quaker movement rejects the idea that the church should be run by a hierarchy. Its founder, George Fox (1624–1691), was an itinerant preacher during the English Civil War. At first he preached violence but he was imprisoned by both the king's supporters and by Oliver Cromwell. Imprisoned a second time, he realized that violent regime change did not influence people's hearts and minds. It is only by a Christian example of love and peace that real change will occur. During the two world wars Quakers refused to fight and were conscripted to work as medical auxiliaries. In 1947 the Society of Friends won the Nobel Prize for Peace for their beliefs and actions.

Modern Quakers subscribe to the Peace Declaration, signed by George Fox and eleven of his supporters when Charles II returned from exile in 1660. Today Quaker organizations are active in promoting non-violent conflict resolution. There are Quaker United Nations Offices (QUNOs) in Geneva and New York, working with the United

Nations on peace building, disarmament and human rights and refugee programmes. Quaker Peace and Social Witness (QPSW) run the Ecumenical Accompaniment Programme in Palestine and Israel (EAPPI) in collaboration with other church and church-related organizations. They place volunteers to work alongside people on both sides of the conflict, to monitor abuses of human rights and to offer protection by their presence. The **Peace Testimony**, as the Peace Declaration is now known, is also interpreted to include actions that bring peace to civil society, such as work among criminals and ex-offenders. Many Quakers see the Peace Testimony as authorizing civil disobedience (non-violent protest) in countries that are run by tyrannical regimes.

Key point

Pacifism is the belief that war and violence are never justified.

Various Christian writers have taken up this idea that peace and love brings real change. For example, Dorothy Day (1897–1980) co-founded the Catholic Worker Movement in 1933 in America and Canada. During World War II the movement advocated absolute pacifism following the principles in the Sermon on the Mount. War was viewed as a sin against love and against life. However, this pacifist stance was developed during the rise of Fascism in Europe. Many, such as George Orwell (1903–1950) in *Pacifism and the War*, argued that to be a pacifist during Hitler's rule was like being a collaborator with Nazi ideology. As Orwell put it:

Pacifism is objectively pro-Fascist. . . . If you hamper the war-effort of one side you automatically help that of the other. (George Orwell, The Complete Works of George Orwell, *Martin Secker and Warburg, 1998)*

Was Orwell right? Is taking no action an action in itself? Can a pacifist stance be seen as condoning actions because it does not fight against them? The strengths of pacifism are its absolute values in its commitment to non-violence and the worth of human life. Its weakness is that in a world where violent conflict is a reality, a pacifist stance can be seen as condoning immoral actions when it does not fight against them.

Pacifists do not condone war under any circumstances.

Natural Law theory and war and peace

Both the Catholic Aquinas and the Protestant Grotius argued in favour of a Just War theory on the basis of Natural Law. A Natural Law approach to the issue of warfare would consider the motives and means of conflict. There is order and balance in nature and therefore wars have to be proportionate. Justice and virtue are inbuilt into the scheme of things and therefore wars have to be for a right cause and virtuous. The Just War theory is Natural Law in action in warfare.

Natural Law in peace is an equally complex idea. Aquinas wrote on the power of monarchs. Peace could only be assured if the natural balance between Church and state was maintained. Order in society brought peace and harmony. Harmony brought with it the interaction of social classes. When classes worked harmoniously peace was assured. When they did not chaos resulted. A peaceful society is therefore based on the ideals of order, harmony and balance.

Kantian approach to war and peace

Kant's ethical views on war and peace are developed in his *Principles of Politics* and *On Perpetual Peace*. Both are notable in that they dwell on practical issues. For example, Kant is against wars that are about the property rights of rulers. Equally he opposed the existence of **standing armies**, professional armies that exist in times of peace as well as war. Interestingly, both works ignore issues such as the Categorical Imperative. Kant seems concerned with relations between states and not with personal moral decision-making.

Two crucial aspects of his moral philosophy, however, do play an important role in his discussion of war and peace. They are **human autonomy** and **duty**. Kant believed in the freedom and autonomy of every rational person. He knew though that most rulers opposed that freedom and autonomy. These rulers treat people as means to an end. Rulers should not behave in this way but they do. This analysis of the politics of his time created a problem for Kant. On the one hand conflict is inevitable for human autonomy to exist while, on the other hand, war is unjust.

These contradictions led Kant to imagine that it is possible for reason, rather than force, to triumph over tyranny. Yet he recognized that warfare is inevitable until a rational, democratic and moral society has been created. He believed that kings and princes fight wars for territorial advantage, while democratic states ruled by rational citizens would choose to live in peace. This idea has been developed in recent years by the philosopher John Rawls (1921–2002) and others. It also has its doubters. Some argue that America and other Western democracies are not exactly states dedicated to the pursuit of peace and international harmony.

To think about

'Democracies love peace; dictatorships prefer violence.' Is this a fair assessment of the world today?

People should be **pacific**, peace-lovers, though not pacifists since there are certain situations where it is dutiful to protect the innocent. Duty is the other important term in Kant's discussion of war and peace. Kant saw one positive feature of war. This is that it produces acts of heroism, acts of unimaginable selfless giving. In warfare people do the most extraordinary things. They do not do it out of love, which as a moral motive Kant condemns. They do it out of a sense of duty. Soldiers in battle together act out of a sense of duty toward their regiment or corps. They may despise the soldier next to them but when he is wounded they will go out of their way to save him from certain death. For Kant, philosophically, war brings out this aspect of the moral law that, he believes, exists in nature.

Kant noted the duty of soldiers to protect the innocent in warfare and to defend their comrades. It might be argued that these duties conflict. A soldier, in defence of another member of his battalion, might need to destroy a house where non-combatants are living. Kant saw no contradiction. For Kant the maxim of the universal law is the key to all moral decisions.

To think about

'A soldier should always obey the orders of his commanding officer; it is his duty.' Is this morally right?

There is a problem with Kant here. A soldier is not a free moral agent. He has to obey the commands of his superiors. Kant does not argue that a soldier should disobey orders if he thinks that they conflict with the maxim of the universal law. The reverse is, in fact, the case. He asserts that a soldier must obey orders; it is his duty. It would, he adds, be 'very harmful' if he did not.

This apparent contradiction in Kant's thought, some scholars argue, highlights a problem with his ethics. This problem is that when Kantian theory is applied to practical situations contradictions appear. Kant's solution to these contradictions was an appeal to the *summum bonum*, when the perfect moral law will be revealed. Kant saw no problem with these apparent moral contradictions. Many modern thinkers, however, are not so sure. They argue that Kant's ethical system is of little use when dealing with practical moral issues, such as war and peace.

There are other deep contradictions in Kant's view of war and peace. He praised warfare for bringing change while at the same time insisting on the need for perpetual peace and that war is unjust. Some argue that Kant's deontological moral philosophy is teleological and consequentialist when it comes to warfare. He rejects the consequences of moral actions while, at the same time, arguing that conflict changes society for the better.

Some scholars see the importance of peace and the support of peaceful resolution as a strength of Kantian thought. At the height of the French revolutionary wars in Europe, Kant recommended a federation of states dedicated to peace. This would be similar to what is now the United Nations and would remove the need for war. A confederation of states would not be under the control of one person. It would work towards the universal kingdom of ends.

Utilitarian approach to war and peace

There is no single approach to war in Utilitarianism. Commentators on utilitarian attitudes to war generally assume that the principle of the 'greatest good of the greatest number' can be easily applied to warfare. Therefore a war is morally good if its result brings about the happiness, pleasure or welfare of the maximal number of people. However, the Hedonic Calculus cannot be easily applied. There are some Act utilitarians who hold that each war must be judged in terms of the maximization of welfare but most utilitarians regard this case-by-case use of the Hedonic Calculus as too difficult. How, for example, is it possible to judge the outcome of the present war with Iraq or the present conflict in Afghanistan? There are too many uncertainties.

Modern utilitarians, for the most part, reject the simple use of the Hedonic Calculus. They turn instead to a form of Rule utilitarianism. The philosophers Richard Brandt and Richard Hare see the general welfare of the maximal number of people in war as being served by two levels of rules. These may be described as first and second order. The first level rules are the general conventions that govern *jus in bello*. These conform to the **Geneva Convention** and the **Hague Convention** and to many of the principles of the Just War theory. The second level rules are concerned with turning these general principles into particular examples and situations. Thus treating non-combatants as innocent victims of war, a first level principle, will lead to not using civilians as human shields. Hare and Brandt both ascribe to a belief in international law and, with it, a court to try actions that run counter to their principles. This has similarities with Bentham's **pannomion**, his idea for the creation of international law and with it an international army.

Modern utilitarian views on warfare have their strengths:

- War is seen in terms of the general welfare of humanity. Wars that are destructive to the welfare of the maximal number of people are to be avoided at all costs. Therefore, by implication, nuclear and chemical weapons are not to be used.

- Welfare is both universal and specific. Jeffrey Whitman, an American soldier and ethicist, makes the point that welfare principles should be applied to soldiers in battle as well as to civilians. The effect of warfare on soldiers and their subsequent behaviour must be examined in any calculation of welfare. He quotes J.S. Mill in arguing that general moral principles do not always work well in particular situations because of 'universal idiocy'. This idiocy must be factored into any calculation on the benefits of fighting a war. It is not only that some soldiers will behave immorally in battle. Post-war stress will lead a percentage into crime when they leave the armed forces. In 2009 in America and the United Kingdom about one in ten of all prisoners were former members of the armed services.

- Utilitarians regard the *post bellum* effect as vital. This has often been ignored by other theories. There is no point fighting a war if it does lasting harm to the maximal number of people.

Rule Utilitarianism, though, does have its weaknesses. In 1940 the United Kingdom continued fighting Hitler's Germany after the fall of France. Was the resulting death of fifty million people a price worth paying? Clearly even Rule Utilitarianism, with its emphasis on consequences as well as on the rules of engagement, has a problem in calculating what is a price worth paying in warfare.

Practice exam questions

(a) Explain Kant's ethical approach to war and peace.

You could start this essay with a discussion of Kant's attitudes to war and peace as set out in his *Precepts of Politics*, especially in *On Perpetual Peace*. You might also wish to look more broadly at the **importance of duty** and at Kant's views on **human autonomy**. You might wish to mention Kant's ambivalent attitude to war. He commends it for producing **acts of courage** and bravery while considering it at the same time **unjust**. You could explain how he addresses and, some would argue, fails to resolve the inconsistencies in his thought. You may want to mention Kant's recommendation of a federation of states dedicated to peace.

(b) 'Utilitarianism offers little help when considering the ethics of war and peace.' Discuss.

In considering this question you could look at how Utilitarianism can be usefully applied to the issue of war and peace. This might include a look at the ideas of Bentham and Mill as well as those of modern Act, Rule and Preference Utilitarianism. In support of the statement you might want to discuss weaknesses of a utilitarian approach, such as the difficulty of **calculating long-term effects**. Give convincing illustrations to support your ideas where necessary. Whatever position you take should be supported by evidence.

 Develop your knowledge

There are many books that address the issue of war and peace, including:

The Ethics of War by A.J. Coates (Manchester University Press, 1997)
First Among Friends: George Fox & the Creation of Quakerism by H. Larry Ingle (Oxford University Press, 1996)
The Ethics of War: Shared Problems in Different Traditions by Richard Sorabji (ed.) and David Rodin (ed.) (Ashgate Publishing Limited, 2006)
Arguing about War by Michael Walzer (Yale University Press, 2004)

A2

10

Meta-ethics

Introduction

Key terms

epistemology – the theory of knowledge, including the origin of knowledge, the roles of experience and reason in generating knowledge and the validity of knowledge.

ethical naturalism – belief that moral laws can be verified through observation of the natural world.

You will remember that meta-ethics was briefly examined at the start of your AS course. It is now time to look at this part of ethics in more detail. Meta-ethics is not concerned with particular moral theories, as normative ethics is, or how these theories can be applied to ethical issues. It is concerned with what we mean by morality. Meta-ethics covers a variety of epistemological questions. They are:

- What do we mean by 'good' and 'bad' and 'right' and 'wrong'?
- Do such concepts have an existence independent of human feelings?
- How is it possible to discover whether they do or not?
- If they do, what do we mean by them?

Moral philosophers answer these questions in different ways. This depends on the position they hold regarding the fundamental question: What is truth?

Philosophers argue even today about the nature of truth. How they answer that question affects the moral questions of meta-ethics. Some, as the writers of the Gospels did, believe that truth is God-given. There are, for them, absolute moral norms. Theologically these scholars are **fideists**; they believe by faith alone. In morality, fideists follow the Divine Command theory.

Others reject this view and argue that truth lies in empirical data, in sensory perceptions. They take a naturalist position; the natural world is the source of all truth. David Hume (1711–1776), the father of modern empiricism, argues that truth lies in beliefs that human beings have about the natural world. However, these must be verified through observation and experience of nature. Ethical naturalism asserts that, through observation of nature, words like 'good' can be reduced to some fundamental value. As a result, utilitarians can reduce the word 'good' to the fundamental value of pleasure or welfare.

G.E. Moore argued that we know this buttercup is yellow because we recognize the colour yellow when we see it, even though we cannot define what 'yellow' is. In the same way, he argued, we recognize goodness when we see it.

Key point

According to ethical naturalism, the statement 'murder is bad' can be verified by observing the act of murder and its consequences. For intuitionism, no such analysis is needed; we know murder is bad through our intuition.

To think about

Do human beings have an innate sense of what is right and wrong?

Intuitionists believe that there are **foundational moral principles**, from which moral laws develop. Ross called these foundational principles **prima facie**, meaning that on the face of it they are self-evidently true. The foundational principles are listed as:

1. beneficence (being generous or good to others)
2. faithfulness in relationships
3. gratitude for favours done to you
4. justice
5. non-maleficence (not being hurtful to others)
6. promise-keeping
7. self-improvement.

How is it possible to discover what these core values are? The intuitionist argues that they are self-evident. Those opposed to the theory, however, dispute whether human beings have certain innate moral values. A recent academic study in the UK demonstrated, for example, that the legal belief in a jury having a broadly similar understanding of the moral concept of honesty might be far from true. Among those questioned less than half thought it dishonest for a carer to persuade an old person to change his or her will in favour of the carer. Perhaps there are no intrinsic moral values?

To think about

Are certain foundational moral principles intuitive or are they products of the way human beings are brought up?

Strengths and weaknesses of intuitionism

It can be argued that strengths of the intuitionist approach are:

1. Intuitionism is **non-naturalistic**. Morality is not dependent on the material world. Ethical principles are independent of actual events. One benefit of this separation of the natural world from morality is that this theory is **not guilty of the naturalistic fallacy**.
2. It explains why different **societies share moral values**, such as 'murder is wrong'.
3. It does justice to the fact that human beings have an **innate moral sense**, quite independent of personal experience or circumstance.
4. It **does not require a God** as the source of absolute ethical principles.

Various criticisms of the intuitionist approach have been made. They are:

1. **How do we know that we can trust our intuition?** Two people faced with the same moral dilemma could have differing intuitions about what to do. How could we decide which intuition is correct?

2. There is **no link in intuitionism between what is right and what a person ought to do**. The philosopher, J.L. Mackie (1917–1981), saw this as an important criticism. He argues that morality is not just about what a person believes intuitively is right but it is about doing something about it. Intuitionism states what the foundational principles are but does not expect the moral agent to follow these ethical values.

3. Intuitionists **do not explain why intuition is universally applicable to ethics**. It is argued that there is no intrinsic reason why human intuition should be taken as the basis of moral judgements. People have intuitions that it will rain tomorrow but the weather forecast is not based on these intuitions. There are other human instincts that are as common as an intuitive sense of right or wrong. A feeling of pain or pleasure is an example, as is the guilt complex. Many scholars argue that Moore never adequately explained why one particular human experience should form the sole basis for morality.

4. Moral intuitionists **do not take seriously the differences in morality that exist from one society to another**. It could be argued that our intuitions are learnt from the cultures that we live in, so our intuitions would differ from society to society.

Emotivism

Emotivism is a non-cognitive ethical theory. It developed out of the logical positivism that developed in Vienna in the early years of the twentieth century. A group of philosophers, scientists and mathematicians, known as the Vienna Circle, developed a new philosophy. They rejected the absolutism and naturalism of the past and built on the foundations of empiricism. From 1922 until 1938 the Vienna Circle brought about a revolution in philosophy in the same way as expressionism, in the same city, was doing in art. The most important members of the movement were Rudolf Carnap (1891–1970) and Moritz Schlick (1882–1936). Loosely attached to the Circle were a number of foreign philosophers. These included the British philosopher Ludwig Wittgenstein and later A.J. Ayer.

Logical positivists believed that the only absolute truths were based on science. Philosophy had to become scientific rather than romantic. This was accompanied by an interest in the minutiae of language; the importance of philosophy was in its ability to analyse words and arguments logically. The Vienna Circle regarded its job as the analysis of words, sentences and arguments to create philosophy for the age of science and technology. Sentences convey information. This information needs to be analysed and verified otherwise discussion becomes meaningless. Statements, propositions, have to be based on factual information. They also have to be **logically coherent**. The logical positivists believed that without these two principles any statement was not only wrong; it was also meaningless.

The logical positivists therefore created a system that evaluated statements. This was their verification principle. For statements to be true they had either to be analytic or

Key terms

logical positivism – the belief that the only meaningful philosophical problems are those which can be solved by logical analysis.

verification principle – statements are only valid if they can be verified or deduced from empirical data.

synthetic in nature. In an **analytic statement** we can logically deduce from the words if it is true. A **synthetic statement** is one that can be verified by analysing facts.

Extension note

Analytic and synthetic statements

Immanuel Kant developed the concept of analytic and synthetic statements. Prior to Kant, Gottfried Leibniz spoke of **truths of reason** and **truths of fact**. By this Leibniz meant that some truths could be logically deduced from the very word (truths of reason), while others are deduced through sensory experiences (truths of fact).

An **analytic statement**, as the term suggests, does not need to be proved through experience. We can logically deduce from the words in the sentence that it is true. Analytic statements can be mathematical statements or **simple syllogisms**. Here is an example of a simple syllogism.

All bachelors (a) are single men (b).

This statement cannot be false since the meaning of *(a)* is explained by *(b)*.

A **synthetic statement** is one that can be verified from analysing facts, for example 'John is a bachelor'.

If we are certain that both these analytic and synthetic statements are true, we can make the following statements:

All bachelors are single men.
John is a bachelor.
Therefore John is single.

Since it can be verified that John exists and that this particular John is a bachelor, it has to be true that he is single.

The logical positivists then analysed religious and moral language. They reached the conclusion that talk of God and goodness could not be verified, and therefore ethical statements are meaningless. Carnap in *The Logical Structure of the World*, attacked the premise upon which religion and morality are based. Carnap rejected the idea that there is a divide between body and soul, mind and matter, and (in morality) the divide between what is and what ought to be. Life is physical; there is no place for the metaphysical.

The Vienna Circle knew it had no need of God but it was painfully aware that moral goodness could not be as easily removed. They tried but failed to undermine morality. Wittgenstein was one of the first to realize the legitimacy of ethical claims. Human beings

Key terms

analytic statement – a statement that only requires the words within it to verify whether it is true or false. For example, 'all bachelors are single men' requires simply an understanding of the meaning of the word bachelor to verify the statement.

synthetic statement – a statement that requires external information, usually empirical data, to verify whether it is true or false. For example, 'the Battle of Hastings took place in 1066' requires empirical information from contemporary documents and archaeological evidence to verify the statement.

Ludwig Wittgenstein (1889–1951) was one of the leading proponents of linguistic philosophy. He was an associate of the Vienna Circle. He later rejected the simplicity of the Vienna Circle's dismissal of ethical and religious language.

Key term

emotivism – the idea that moral judgements are expressions of the moral agent's feelings rather than statements of fact.

need morals yet they are unverifiable. A moral system has to exist but this creates an apparent contradiction. Morality is necessary but it is not verifiable.

Sir Alfred Ayer

Sir Alfred Ayer's (1910–1989) solution to the problem of the unverifiable nature of moral language is known as emotivism. It is sometimes called the **Hurrah–Boo theory** since it argues that morals are determined by people's feelings and opinions. Ayer said that when we use ethical language we are expressing our emotions about an issue. So when we say something is morally good we are saying 'hurrah' to it. Similarly when we say something is wrong we are saying 'boo' to it.

For Ayer, the claim 'murder is wrong' is not based on some objective moral absolute or principle. We are simply saying 'I don't like murder', or when applied to the wider community, 'if murder became legal then I believe society would not survive'. The statement 'murder is wrong', Ayer argues, cannot be reduced to either an analytic or synthetic statement. Therefore it is not possible to justify the view that murder is either right or wrong. All the individual can say is that he or she does not like murder. Simply put: 'murder stinks!'

Ayer develops this idea in *Language, Truth and Logic*. Here he argues that ethical statements are designed to get a response from the reader or hearer. He calls these responses:

> *. . .ejaculations or commands which are designed to provoke the reader to action of a certain sort. (A.J. Ayer, 'A Critique of Ethics',* Ethical Theory, *Russ Shafer-Landau (Ed.), Blackwell Publishing, 2007)*

Ayer's ideas are based on logical positivism. He rejects the idea that ethical statements have any objective meaning, as they are unverifiable. Yet, during World War II, Ayer began to have doubts about the unverifiable nature of ethical statements. In 1946 he completed a new edition of *Language, Truth and Logic*. This edition included a long appendix that went back on some of his earlier claims. Importantly, Ayer claimed that many ethical statements contain elements of fact. As a result, some ethical statements are descriptive and therefore verifiable while others are not. The statement 'stealing is wrong' is a matter of opinion and therefore non-verifiable. On the other hand, a statement such as 'you know that when you stole from that person you did wrong' is capable of verification through the experience of the person who stole. This subtle yet important difference in Ayer's thought allowed him to maintain his emotivist ethical position while, at the same time, accepting that there are facts in ethics. Ayer (like Wittgenstein and Hare) had experienced the enormity of the evils of World War II and wanted, therefore, to give more authority to ethical statements.

To think about

If ethical statements are just expressions of our emotions, does this mean that the words 'good' and 'bad' are meaningless?

Charles L. Stevenson

In his book *Ethics and Language* the American philosopher Charles L. Stevenson (1908–1979) agrees with Ayer that ethical statements express an emotional response. He argues that it is possible for people to differ in the way they respond, even though they have the same end in mind. This can be illustrated. Two people hold similar views about whether a war is right or wrong. They do so on the basis of a gut reaction to the events. Yet they have radically different methods for ending the conflict. One wants the troops to be withdrawn immediately while the other argues for a planned withdrawal. Ayer's views begin and end with an expression of revulsion. Stevenson believes it is necessary to go further.

Stevenson's views allow emotivism to move beyond a mere shouting match of opinions, which he argues is precisely what Ayer's philosophy involves. This change allows Stevenson to analyse ethical propositions in a way that Ayer does not. Stevenson also believes that ethical statements contain elements of persuasion. They do not simply reflect a person's feelings. They also present a moral claim. When a person says 'murder is wrong' they do not just mean 'murder stinks'. They also imply that the person to whom you are speaking should feel that it is wrong as well. Moral statements do not only express feelings of pleasure or outrage. They also expect the recipient of the statement to share those feelings.

Strengths and weaknesses of emotivism

Emotivism is not without its strengths and weaknesses. The strengths are that it:

1. accepts the importance of the **scientific approach to language**. Words have particular meanings. In order to understand them they have empirically to be verified. It rejects therefore the abstract use of words of previous philosophical discussion.

2. allows the **development of a complex and sophisticated discussion of moral language**. This is demonstrated by the analysis of the statement 'murder is wrong'. It prevents ethicists regarding such statements as self-evidently true.
3. assumes that **ethical statements are not the same as empirically verifiable facts**, which seems to many to be self-evident.
4. stresses the importance of each **individual's moral feelings**.

However, there are problems associated with emotivism:

1. Ethical statements are not judged on the basis of the emotional response they invoke in the hearer. They are judged on the **claims they make**. Therefore, as the British philosopher G.J. Warnock (1923–1995) points out, to claim 'murder is wrong' is to make a factual statement which can be discussed and debated. If this were not the case then as emotions changed so would morality, causing an extreme form of relativism and subjectivism.
2. The fact that moral statements often carry a tremendous weight of public and private emotions **does not mean that these are moral**. It is possible to feel one is right about something and yet be considered to be very wrong.
3. Just because you may have an emotion that something is wrong **does not logically mean that other people should agree**. There is a disconnection between, for example, the statement that 'murder is wrong' and the implicit conclusion that other people should not do it. Schlick saw this disconnection even before Ayer had completed his book.
4. It could be argued that **language is not simply about verifiability**. Sentences should not be seen as the linguistic equivalent of arithmetical sums. Language is much richer and much more opaque than scientific experiments or mathematical numbers.

Prescriptivism

Richard Hare was one of the most original moral philosophers of the twentieth century. He moved beyond the idea that ethical statements are merely expressions of our feelings, to say that moral language is prescriptive and tells us how we ought to act.

He developed an ethical theory known as prescriptivism. It is an ethical system that prescribes what a person should do and, like a doctor's prescription, it will vary from person to person. Consequently, when a person says 'You shall not murder' this is not just an expression of personal revulsion at the thought of killing. It also means that everyone should follow this moral truth. This is the **universalizability principle**, that when an individual prefers one thing rather than something else this implies that this preference would be good for anybody. If x prefers to care for a sick person rather than go to the pub, this implies that were x to be sick then he or she would wish someone to care for x in similar circumstances.

Extension note

Hare, Singapore and prescriptivism

Hare makes the Golden Rule of Christianity: 'In everything do to others as you would have them do to you' (Matthew 7:12) the basis of his prescriptivism. He argues that if such moral preferences are universal it follows that they should be obeyed. Yet Hare concedes that not everyone has the critical ability or time to calculate what he or she should do in a particular situation. Some human beings need moral laws to guide them. They have limited critical powers to turn preferences into actions. Those with more critical powers can use moral laws as rules of thumb, to be used or not used in accordance with their critical appraisal of moral preferences.

Hare had good reasons to believe in the universal nature of morals. He served in the army during World War II and spent three years as a prisoner of war in Changi prison and building the Burma-Thailand railway. The brutality of Japanese treatment of prisoners of war affected his attitude to morality. It was this experience that led him to develop a secular form of the Christian Golden Rule.

Prescriptivism asserts four basic ideas. They are:

1. that moral sentiment is not sufficient. The individual's morality must involve doing what is morally required.
2. that ethical action has to be consistent. It is important in all situations to practise a consistent morality.
3. that moral belief must be kept in harmony with others.
4. that the moral agent cannot be hypocritical.

Key point

According to emotivism, when we would say 'murder is bad' we are expressing our feelings towards murder. According to prescriptivism, this statement is telling us how we ought to act.

Key terms

eudaimonia – Greek for happiness, flourishing or a state of contentment.

Golden Mean – the situation when something works efficiently by avoiding extremes of excess and deficiency.

heart and the lungs must work in tandem. The heart cannot fulfil its function if the lungs hyperventilate. This is not *arete* and the patient may die. The good functioning of organs is harmonic and leads, Aristotle argues, to eudaimonia.

In his work *Organon*, Aristotle discusses this harmonic relationship in terms of the organs of the body. Elsewhere it is applied to other things. Society, for example, is seen like the organs of the body. Each group in society has a natural function, from slaves through to the rulers. Each has its own responsibility. The *arete* of a slave is to perform his or her duties to the satisfaction of the master. The *arete* of the ruler is to guide the state and ensure the harmonious interaction of the various groups in society.

Aristotle's ethical concept of **virtue** has its origins in the way he saw society. People do not exist in isolation, they live in societies. Each group and each person fulfils a function, for a purpose and to an end within society. For Aristotle, what is meant by *arete* will differ from one person to another and from one group to another. Virtue will differ because the role of one person differs from the role of another. Yet, since all are human beings, there is also a virtue that is common to all. This involves the need for each person and group of people to live in harmony with others.

The Golden Mean

Aristotle believed that virtue was to be found in what has come to be called the Golden Mean. It can be most easily understood as striking a balance between excess and deficiency. The Golden Mean is a lack of extremity that achieves the best function of whatever is being examined. The Golden Mean is there to ensure that it works well and it works in harmony with the rest. Here is a simple illustration. Take a water tap. This tap exists to provide water. That is its function. Its purpose might be to provide drinking water to quench your thirst. One day you go to the tap and a huge gush of water flows out, drenching your clothes. On this day the tap is not virtuous. The next day, after you have fixed it, you turn on the tap and there is a shrill sound but no water. Again the tap is not virtuous as it has not fulfilled its function. Finally, on the third day and after a plumber has been called, a good supply of water comes out and it is now a virtuous tap, functioning at its best.

This illustration can be applied to human beings who, like the tap, have a soul grounded in Aristotle's teleology of function, purpose and end.

For example, the Golden Mean of a soldier is courage. If he or she lacks courage they are a coward; if they have an excess of courage they become foolhardy. When they are able to strike a balance and act courageously, then they function best as a soldier.

The chart below shows the way Aristotle applied the Golden Mean to two groups in ancient Greek society. It also illustrates how it can be applied to two groups today.

Group	Deficiency	Golden Mean	Excess
Ancient Greece – slaves	Laziness	Hard working	Exhaustion
Ancient Greece – soldiers	Cowardice	Courage	Foolhardiness
Modern-day UK – bankers	Miserliness	Prudence	Recklessness
Modern-day UK – sportspeople	Laziness	Dedication	Exhaustion

Aristotle believed that human beings have certain virtues that are common to all, since all are human and all exist within society. Each human being, however, has a specific role in society that means that he or she has a particular virtue that conforms to his or her job or social position. The Golden Mean of a soldier is different from that of a slave. A soldier has to be courageous but a slave must not be. In terms of modern professions we could say that the virtue of a banker would be prudence, the mean between being a miser and being reckless. The Golden Mean of a sportsperson would be dedication to his or her sport, without working the body too hard or too little.

Key point

Aristotle believed that virtue was to be found in the Golden Mean, which involves striking a balance between excess and deficiency.

Eudaimonia

Aristotle's idea of the Golden Mean leads on to the concept of eudaimonia. When animate objects find their Golden Mean they achieve eudaimonia, which Aristotle viewed as the contentment attained when something achieves its purpose. For example, a sportsperson is happy when he or she is doing what that individual is designed for. That sportsperson is unhappy when he or she is injured. Eudaimonia is the end or *telos* of all things and all human beings.

At first it might seem that Aristotle's idea of virtue and eudaimonia lacks any moral basis. It is just concerned with the fulfilment of a purpose. Therefore, an eudaimonic bricklayer is one that builds a wall well and an eudaimonic farmer is one that produces prize tomatoes or beans. Yet there is a moral point that should not be lost. Human beings live in communities and eudaimonia is designed not only to achieve personal fulfilment, contentment or happiness; it is designed to fulfil the happiness of society, which brings peace and harmony.

the environment or by neurological impulses this does not mean that the individual will conform to these causal traits. Hume called this ability the liberty of spontaneity.

Hard determinists, however, argue that there is no such thing as spontaneity. What appears to be a spontaneous response is predetermined.

The issue of a lack of moral responsibility creates problems, such as:

- Is it possible to convict one person on the grounds of being morally culpable but not another person? Nigel Eastman and Colin Campbell, two scientists with an interest in the law, argue that while the law wants scientific evidence that an offender is predetermined to behave in a certain way, science is unable to give concrete answers to these questions. They argue that neuroscience is an inexact science. Consequently, it is wrong to argue that one person is not guilty of murder because that person was not morally responsible for his or her actions, while another person is, when committing an identical crime.
- If human behaviour is determined, on what grounds ought a person to be imprisoned for an offence? The usual determinist answer to this question is the protection of the public. Yet it might be argued that many people ought, if this were the case, to be locked up for the whole of their life – there would be no point in varying jail sentences.
- Some argue that a lack of moral responsibility allows for a nihilist interpretation of morality. Can anything be considered good or bad if the perpetrator of the action has no control over what he or she does?

Practice exam question

'Human beings are responsible for their moral actions.' Discuss.

You could start by examining what is meant by being responsible for a moral action. You could structure your essay in such a way that you look at the three strands of the argument about free will, soft determinism and hard determinism. This will probably start with hard determinism. You can look at three different viewpoints based on religious determinism (predestination), the nature argument (based on genetics) and the nurture argument (the influence of society and upbringing). You will need to ask whether a hard determinist view means that human beings are not responsible for their actions. You may then wish to look at libertarianism next, in order to present a position that is radically different from that of hard determinism. You will then examine soft determinism and how it seeks to address the weaknesses in both hard determinism and libertarianism. When discussing each of these three positions you will need to look at how these theories address the issue of moral responsibility. You will want to illustrate your arguments by referring to the thoughts of particular scholars.

Develop your knowledge

There are a number of books which examine free will and determinism, including:

Free Will by Graham McFee (Acumen Publishing Ltd, 2000)
A Companion to Ethics by Peter Singer (ed.) (Blackwell, 1993)
An Essay on Free Will by Peter van Inwagen (Clarendon Press, 1983)

socio-economic forces. Fromm also believed in the Freudian sense of guilt. This produces the worst of both worlds. People's attitudes are predetermined by when they are born and the class in which they grow up. Their anxieties are economic and social. Yet, at the same time, they have guilt about the benefits that come from their place in history.

Therefore a middle-class person will want the wealth needed to buy a house in a leafy suburb yet will feel guilt about these desires. What is worse, both the desire for wealth and the consequential guilt are inbuilt into the individual. This leads to an odd situation, in which the individual lives a happy, economically prosperous life but has no inner contentment. The link between happiness and contentment, found in Aristotle, is broken. Marxists describe this as a feeling of **self-alienation**.

Fromm's view of the conscience underwent a change before his death. Like many left-wing writers in the 1960s, Fromm began to develop the idea of hope and individual liberation from alienation. Fromm wrote:

> *Man is the only creature endowed with conscience. His conscience is the voice that calls him back to himself. (Erich Fromm,* Man for Himself, *Taylor and Francis, 2003)*

Fromm is arguing that the conscience alone allows human beings to rise above the alienation of modern society. This conscience is based on **biophilia**, which is love of and for life. Love is identified as 'care, responsibility, respect and knowledge'.

There is a theoretical problem with Fromm's views. Fromm argues that human beings are predetermined creatures. This determinism sits uncomfortably with Fromm's view that life offers hope. How is it possible to rise above alienation if everyone is determined to be alienated? Fromm argued that to be set free it is necessary to be conscientious, which means being a person of conscience.

Critics of this view are not convinced. They argue that Fromm analysed the situation but did not establish the cure. Scholars also question whether the conscience works to give hope, joy and love. The French philosopher Michel Foucault (1926–1984) argued that the conscience acts to condemn the individual and not to liberate. He points to the link between the conscience and the guilt complex.

There is another more practical problem with Fromm's view of biophilia and the conscience. How is a conscience based on love of and for life to be used? Fromm gives enough information to suggest that an application of the biophilia conscience is possible. A love of life should be applied to all moral decisions. This would mean businesses treating their employees as partners. It would mean not destroying the ecosystem. Fromm's conscience is designed to enhance Quality of Life and to empower every individual.

Conscience in the work of Piaget and Kohlberg

The Swiss psychologist Jean Piaget (1896–1980) maintained that all human beings do not have the same conscience. Imagine your moral character is a train journey. You begin life at Station A and you will end your life at Station C. Piaget argued that there are broadly two types of people. The first take the train but get off at Station B. They do not complete their moral journey; their development has been stunted. The rest reach the terminus at Station C. While they were en route their character and their moral sense has been allowed to develop fully. Those who left at Station B were incapable of developing beyond the early stages of their journey through life.

Piaget described two types of conscience, based on whether or not the person has a fully developed character. The first type of conscience is known as heteronomous morality. This develops from the early years until the age of nine or ten. This type of moral sense is other-based. The child does not decide his or her own moral stance. This is decided for that individual by parents or whoever controls that person's moral upbringing. Moral conscience is based on the observance of rules. This runs hand in hand with punishment when rules are not observed. Piaget argued that some people never develop beyond this stage. Their life is dominated by the need to obey quite precise rules of behaviour. They may look to a God who is their ruler and judge.

The majority of human beings, however, do not get off at Station B. They continue to develop morally. Piaget maintained that such people have autonomous morality. They are mature enough to decide what is morally good for them and what is not. Morality is a matter of self-discipline and not external discipline. Piaget argued that this process starts around the age of ten.

Key terms

heteronomous morality – morality determined by others, such as parents and society.

autonomous morality – morality determined by the self.

For Piaget, early development and relationships play an important role in the development of a moral conscience.

Key term

stewardship – the responsibility to manage or look after another's property. In Christianity, the God-given responsibility to care for the world.

Human beings have a special position in Creation. Man goes on to name all the creatures of the earth, as Genesis 2 states:

So out of the ground the LORD God formed every animal of the field and every bird of the air, and brought them to the man to see what he would call them; and whatever the man called each living creature, that was its name. (Genesis 2:19)

The giving of a name signifies control, power over the creature named. God has, in this act, given humanity control of the earth and its creatures. Human beings are given dominion (authority) over nature in Genesis 1:26. It is a function that they are given because human beings are unique. Most Christians share this understanding of the nature of humanity. Pope John Paul II, in a homily on World Peace Day 1990, put it this way:

Adam and Eve's call to share in the unfolding of God's plan of creation brought into play those abilities and gifts which distinguish the human being from all other creatures. (Message of his holiness Pope John Paul II for the celebration of the World Day of Peace, 1 January 1990, available from www.vatican.va/holy_ father/john_paul_ii/messages/peace/documents/hf_jp-ii_mes_19891208_xxiii-world-day-for-peace_en.html [accessed 04/06/2010])

To think about

If you believe that God gave humans authority over the earth and its creatures what implications or problems might this mean for our relationship with the environment?

Dominion and stewardship

Dominion brings with it **responsibility** and this is an important part of a Christian understanding of environmental ethics. Christians believe they have a **duty of care** for the environment because God created it for them. Sir John Houghton, the Christian, scientist and author of *Global Warming,* asks whether the universe was created with human beings in mind. He argues that the answer to this question is a humbling experience. God made the world for humanity and therefore the planet needs to be treated by human beings with respect and dedication.

Stewardship is the term Christians use to express the idea that God has put human beings in charge of the earth, and that we therefore have an obligation to look after it properly. In Genesis 2:15 Adam is required to look after the Garden of Eden. Later in Genesis there is the story of the patriarch Joseph (see Extension Note page 259–260).

Christians see these as examples of how God intends human beings to look after the world that he has created for them.

Christians believe that God made humans stewards of the earth. As a result they have a duty of care to the environment. For some Christians this means that humans are obliged to take responsibility for ecological problems such as global warming.

Key point

Christians believe that God created humanity to be the stewards of the earth. This means that humans have a responsibility to look after it properly.

Extension note

God's husbandry and good husbandry

The Bible is full of examples of good stewardship of the earth. Both the Old and New Testaments reflect the idea that God made the world for humanity and that individual human beings have a moral responsibility to look after the planet. Farming, both arable and livestock, is seen as an honourable profession. Farmers take part in the process of creation. Husbandry, the care, cultivation and breeding of animals and crops, is a virtue since it imitates the act of God in Creation.

The Old Testament illustrates this care for the earth in the story of Joseph. Joseph was a younger son of Jacob. Most of his brothers despised him because he was a

Key term

eschaton – the end of the world, the final event in the divine plan.

spoilt child. They plotted together and sold him into slavery. However, he eventually rose to a position of importance, becoming the pharaoh's chief adviser. As chief minister Joseph took care of the environment. He insisted that grain should not be wasted but placed in storehouses. He knew that the years of plenty would not last. Eventually after seven years of good harvests there was famine in Egypt and throughout the world. In the story God's hand is at work in what Joseph does. Joseph conforms to God's will by taking care of the environment for the benefit of all people (Genesis 41: 37/57).

Can humans save the planet?

The New Testament, following a tradition that can be found in the Old Testament book of Daniel, accepts that one day the world will come to an end. This belief in the eschaton, the end of days, has affected the way many Christians see the ecological problems of today. The destructive power of humanity and its inability to put things right has been noted for a number of decades. Political leaders gather to debate the issue of the effect of global warming but little change occurs. The United Nations Climate Change Conference 2009 in Copenhagen made minor progress to take the world beyond what was agreed at the Kyoto summit of 1997. Some Christians argue that this inability of human beings to do what is necessary points to the inevitable destruction of the world.

Martin Luther believed that Judgement Day would be preceded by a **complete destruction of the earth**. This is how some Protestants see the ecological problems of today. In America this idea is to be found within members of the conservative Protestant churches. They believe that the world will end in a great flourish. These Protestants quote passages from the book of Revelation which describes the events of the Apocalypse: Christians, dead and living, rising up to heaven (known as the Rapture), the destruction of the world, the Second Coming of Christ and God's final victory at the battle of Armageddon.

While most Christians do not share the literalism of this picture of Judgement Day it continues to have an effect on attitudes to environmental ethics. For some Christians this means that all is in God's hand. Nothing human beings can do about the environment has any relevance.

Yet an increasing number of Christians have become more environmentally concerned. They link environmental issues to God's justice. Christians are called to imitate Jesus and therefore they must be just. It would be unjust for those in the developed economies to exploit the natural resources of developing countries, thereby ruining the lives of the world's poorest people. Christians have a duty of care to protect the planet and to help the less fortunate. In 2008 a group of leaders of the Southern Baptist Church in America began a campaign to change the hearts and minds of Americans over global warming. Richard Cizik, a former executive of the National Association of Evangelicals, also in America, stated that:

> . . . *to harm our world by environmental degradation, is an offense against God. (Richard Cizik,* The Great Warming Interview *available from www. thegreatwarming.com/revrichardcizik.html [accessed 03/06/2010])*

Strengths and weaknesses of a Christian approach

Christian views on environmental issues concentrate on two main ideas. They are that God created the world out of his love and that human beings have a duty of care (stewardship) to the earth. These two ideas mean that ecological issues are treated seriously and that the world is not to be exploited in an unsustainable way.

Christians also link ecological issues to world poverty and social justice. Exploitation of the planet is seen as socially unjust. This can be seen in the Amazon rainforest where soya production has ruined large areas of the forest and, as a consequence, destroyed the livelihood of indigenous peoples.

These Christian attitudes to ecology show that a primary strength lies in its anthropocentric nature. Humans are at the centre and are responsible for what happens to the environment. Yet this strength can be also seen as a weakness. Some ecologists reject the notion that human beings are stewards of the earth. This idea, they believe, sets human beings apart as superior to Creation, rather than seeing humanity as one part of the created order. The dominion given by God to Adam and Eve is seen as the cause of the destruction of the planet. It gives human beings a belief that they can do whatever they like with Creation.

James Lovelock and others argue that there is another fundamental error in Christian views. Christians see the world not only anthropocentrically but also in a theocentric way. They believe that because God is ultimately in control, all will be well in the end. This limits human responsibility. The earth can be exploited because God will make 'all things new'. Lovelock argues that this theocentric understanding must be removed.

The environment and Natural Law theory

One understanding of Natural Law theory offers a possible way out of the problem of anthropocentricity mentioned above. Vladimir Lossky (1904–1958) took a different view of humanity's place in Creation. Human beings are part of Creation. They are like the heart of the body. The heart may be of great importance but it cannot function if

Key term

anthropocentrism – regarding humankind as the central or most important element in existence.

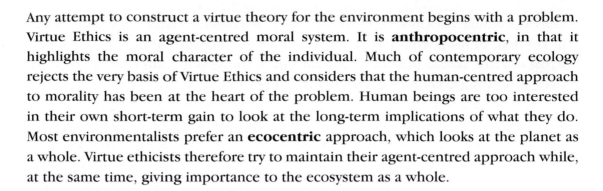

Virtue Ethics and the environment

Any attempt to construct a virtue theory for the environment begins with a problem. Virtue Ethics is an agent-centred moral system. It is **anthropocentric**, in that it highlights the moral character of the individual. Much of contemporary ecology rejects the very basis of Virtue Ethics and considers that the human-centred approach to morality has been at the heart of the problem. Human beings are too interested in their own short-term gain to look at the long-term implications of what they do. Most environmentalists prefer an **ecocentric** approach, which looks at the planet as a whole. Virtue ethicists therefore try to maintain their agent-centred approach while, at the same time, giving importance to the ecosystem as a whole.

Virtue ethicists have another problem. There are, in reality, a variety of approaches to Virtue Ethics. The approaches of Aristotle and Aquinas are fundamentally different from the two essential forms of modern virtue theory. Contemporary Virtue Ethics looks far more at the character of the moral agent and less at the end result of a person's actions. This creates a problem when it comes to environmental ethics. Green morality is about the results of an action rather than the **moral character** of the person who carries out the changes.

Yet, despite these criticisms, various Virtue Ethics theorists have developed a moral approach to the environment, based on the virtues and on individual character. Their argument is that ecological change will only occur if hearts and minds are won over to environmental causes. Therefore character traits are important in order to make people morally aware.

Modern Virtue Ethics seeks to make the moral agent virtuous in one of two ways. The first is by examining the virtues and instilling these in the individual. The other is changing the environment so that the individual will be virtuous. One theory looks at **character traits** while the other is teleological, looking at the outcome that produces virtue. On the face of it a teleological-based approach to virtue theory offers the best way of dealing with the moral problems of the environment because, as stated, Green issues are about results. Many Virtue ethicists consider that the *telos* of environmentalism ought to be sustainability.

Character traits of a virtuous environmentalist

Ecological sustainability brings with it certain character traits, virtues, which human beings will need in abundance in order to protect the earth. The Dutch Virtue ethicist Louke van Wensveen highlights the need for the ecosystem to be sustained by human

self-control. She notes in *Dirty Virtues: The Emergence of Ecological Virtue Ethics* that there are good character traits and bad ones connected with environmentalism. Good character traits include such things as care, loving life, respect for creatures, thrift rather than destructive self-indulgence, and inner peace and tranquillity. All of these traits bring respect for and harmony with the environment.

These traits need to be tested or else the whole Green lobby will be morally **counterfeit**, as she puts it. Suppose a decision was made that, in order to save the planet, a community of indigenous people in the rainforest should be moved into a shanty town miles away from their source of livelihood. Such an image is not far from the truth. In the nineteenth and early twentieth centuries Native American peoples were moved hundreds of miles and resettled in the Indian Territory (now Oklahoma). They were moved to ensure that trade opportunities could be exploited, for example cheap wheat could be produced on the prairies to feed Europe and America. Many Native Americans died during the resettlement. It might have been a seemingly virtuous act sustaining the human race with cheap food but it was done at an unacceptable price. This was a **harmful virtue**.

Today, van Wensveen argues, there is the possibility that similar errors will occur. There was, in the 1970s, the forced sterilization of lower caste men in India to restrict population growth there. Van Wensveen lays down four tests for any virtuous act to ensure sustainability. They are:

- **Repression test** – will people be repressed by any environmental reform?
- **Alienation test** – will environmental change cause the alienation of the people?
- **Guilt test** – is any environmental change being done out of a sense of guilt for past mistakes?
- **Fetishism test** – is any environmental change being made because it is the fashion of the moment?

The American Virtue ethicists Philip Cafaro and Joshua Colt Gambrel have cooperated to produce a better understanding of what character traits are needed to create a sustainable planet and what traits need to be controlled. Cafaro lists four traits that cause human beings to destroy the environment. They are **gluttony, arrogance, greed** and **apathy**. Set against these modern vices they list those virtues that are, what they call, **morally responsive virtues**. One virtue, above all, is required. This is **simplicity**. Human beings today extol complexity. People rely on more and more sophisticated machinery, for example, we are always upgrading our mobile phones to the latest model. Ronald Sandler, another American Virtue ethicist, in *Character and Environment* asserts that the planet will survive only if the human character extols virtue.

Virtue Ethics has a number of strengths when applied to the environment. One of these is its belief that human beings should regard sustainability as a fundamental goal to which they should aim. However, it could be argued that sustainability is not particularly virtuous since it is clearly in human self-interest to save the planet. Another important benefit of Virtue Ethics is its rejection of human arrogance and greed, yet it is possible to argue, as deep ecologists do, that the anthropocentric nature of Virtue Ethics is itself arrogant. It presumes that human beings control the planet.

One particular problem with Virtue Ethics is the way it is not merely anthropocentric but centred on a particular moral agent. This individualism is beneficial when dealing with personal moral issues but is harder to defend when dealing with global problems. How is it possible to apply virtue to a global situation? Van Wensveen attempts to solve this problem by looking at the bases on which environmental decisions are based. Her theory may be described as Rule Virtue Ethics, as it gives universally applicable rules that should be used when making environmental decisions. This avoids the problem of individualism. It also resolves another problem that exists in Virtue Ethics, that is, how does one moral agent's virtuous state relate to another person's? Global problems must address this issue as worldwide solutions are required.

Kantian ethics and the environment

A number of Kantian beliefs can be applied to support environmentalism:

1. **Nature works rationally**. Kant's use of the term irrational is not accidental. Kant believed that nature is enlightened; it works rationally and can only fully be understood through reason. Some scholars, for example Thomas Wagenbaur, see the rational foundation of nature as one of the strengths of a Kantian approach to ecology.

2. **Nature liberates human beings**. Kant sees the natural world as being logical and purposeful. Human beings fit into this natural environment. What is the purpose of nature? Kant gives the answer that nature's purpose is the revealing of autonomy, freedom. This can be seen as another strength of Kantian ideas about the environment. Kant sees an inter-relationship between human beings and creation. Both work in harmony to produce a world where freedom rules.

3. **Cruelty to animals is irrational and should be avoided**. In *Duty to Animals and Spirits* Kant set out his view that respect for animals is important. A person who beats his dog is likely to do it to his children. He is a brute, devoid of that rational understanding that makes a moral being. Kant argued that animals exist to be used by humanity. Their meat exists to be eaten and their skin to be used (he was the son of a saddler). Yet with this privilege comes responsibility to treat animals kindly. Kant put this in an interesting way:

When he [Adam] first said to the sheep 'the fleece which you wear was given to you by nature not for your own use, but mine' and took it from the sheep to wear it himself, he became aware of a prerogative which, by his nature, he enjoyed over all animals. (Immanuel Kant, Political Writings, H.S. Reiss (Ed.), Cambridge University Press, 2003)

This right carries with it a duty of care.

To think about

Do you think that animals exist for our use?

4. **Nature should not be exploited**. Human beings have a duty to themselves to survive and thus the destructive exploitation of the environment is immoral since it would damage the chances of the human race surviving.

5. **Nature must not be treated as a means to an end but only as an end in itself**. This means that any harmful or cruel act against other creatures or the environment is to be condemned as both immoral and also irrational.

6. **Nature is intrinsically beautiful**. Kant links the aesthetic beauty of the environment to moral goodness. To destroy beauty is illogical since it is something that rational people, when meeting to decide moral laws, would consider a vital part of human existence. This idea can be used to argue that biodiversity and places of outstanding natural beauty should not be damaged for profit motives.

There are though some problems with Kantian views on the environment. It is an anthropocentric approach. All things seem to exist for the benefit of humanity. Therefore, for example, the ecosystem is beautiful because it is seen to be so by human beings and animals are made to be of benefit for humanity. These ideas can create human arrogance. Human arrogance leads, it is argued by Naess and others, to the exploitation of the environment. Kant states that the fleece of a sheep exists simply to benefit human life. It might equally be argued that the tusks of elephants exist to provide ivory for human beings.

Key term

sentient-centred – concerned with all sentient animals and not just humans.

A further issue is that Kantian ethical theory is theoretical rather than practical. Kant himself realized the problem. In Chapter 3 on Kantian ethics it was mentioned that Kant states the principle 'never lie'. Yet Kant recognized that this was not always possible. He argued that never lying is a moral principle but that human beings can stray from doing what is right. They may wish to protect someone by lying. Kant recognized that human beings are morally frail; they do not always do what they should. This disparity between theory and life is a weakness, it is argued, in Kantian thought. It would allow people to recognize that human beings should care for the environment, without doing anything about it.

Utilitarianism and the environment

Utilitarian attitudes to the environment differ widely. This division has existed from the beginning. Jeremy Bentham was a proud gardener, who spent many hours growing prize cucumbers and other vegetables. Naturalism was crucial to Benthamite ethics. Pleasure was to be preferred to pain because that is how it was in nature.

For Mill, nature is not nice! Mill pointed out that in nature, gardens untended by human hands quickly turn into wildernesses controlled by a monoculture of weeds. Humanity brings order out of chaos and human hands enhance biodiversity. Kew Gardens without human care would be marshes along the riverside, as once they were.

Bentham is sentient-centred in his view of the maximization of pleasure. Animals matter. Mill, in contrast, is totally **anthropocentric** in his attitudes. What gave Mill optimism was that human beings would rise above the natural environment. Mill condemns all ethical and religious systems based on the observation and copying of the natural world. He comments:

> . . . *nearly all the things which men are hanged or imprisoned for doing to one another, are nature's every day performances . . . No one, either religious or irreligious, believes that the hurtful agencies of nature, considered as a whole, promotes good purposes, in any other way than by inciting human rational creatures to rise up and struggle against them.* (*John Stuart Mill,* Nature; The Utility of Religion; and Theism)

Modern Utilitarianism: a continuing divide

Bentham's and Mill's views about the natural world extend into modern utilitarian attitudes to the environment. Utilitarianism is a consequentialist moral system that today can mean the maximization of human happiness or welfare. But whose welfare is being maximized? Some modern utilitarians agree with Mill that the concept of maximization is concerned principally with human beings. Animals should be treated, as Mill believed, with dignity but this is because the denial of this would produce harmful effects on human beings. For example, dog fighting is, in Mill's terms, morally wrong since by causing unnecessary suffering to animals those involved degrade themselves.

Bentham's approach is different and is followed by several leading contemporary utilitarians, including Peter Singer. They argue that all sentient animals should be considered equally when discussing environmental matters. Bentham famously said with reference to animals: 'the question is not, Can they *reason*? nor, Can they *talk*? but, Can they *suffer*?' (Jeremy Bentham, *An Introduction to the Principles of Morals and Legislation*, Elibron Classics, 2005). Clearly, if sentient animals are taken into account, this has an enormous effect on decisions relating to the ecosystem. Would a hydroelectric dam be built, for example, in the jungle of Borneo if, as a result, a large number of wild sentient animals were to be drowned? Yet, on the other hand, human beings depend on electricity, and electricity generated by environmentally 'clean' means is to be preferred to burning fossil fuels to generate electricity.

> ## Key point
>
> For utilitarians such as Bentham and Singer, all sentient creatures have the same ethical value. Both animals and humans have the capacity to suffer, and they should be taken equally into account in any ethical consideration.

There are other differences apart from that of anthropocentricity. There is an increasing divide between what are known, in environmental ethics, as qualitative and quantitative utilitarians. Qualitative Utilitarianism is a development of Mill's concept of higher pleasure put into the context of human or sentient welfare. Simply put: what sort of environment is required to maximize the Quality of Life of human or all sentient creatures? Quantitative Utilitarianism is a development of Bentham's ideas concerning the greatest good of the greatest number. In contemporary terms quantitative utilitarians look for an environment that will maximize the welfare benefits for the maximal number of people and sentient creatures.

The difficulty of calculating welfare is a criticism that is often made of Utilitarianism as an ethical approach. What kind of timescale should be considered when dealing with ecological projects? What may be environmentally friendly in the short term may not be in the long term. In environmental ethics should the needs of future generations be included in the calculation of welfare for the greatest number?

Key terms

qualitative Utilitarianism – an analysis of actions or moral rules that takes into account the quality of happiness or welfare produced.

quantitative Utilitarianism – an analysis of actions or moral rules that takes into account the quantity of happiness or welfare produced.

Business ethics

Key terms

globalism – viewing the world on a global basis rather than in terms of nations.

globalisation – the process by which businesses or other organizations develop international influence or start operating on an international scale.

In examining the relationship between business and the environment, two issues are central: globalism and globalisation. These issues are separate but inter-related.

Globalism is concerned with the way in which particular political, moral and economic values become the norm for different societies around the world. It is about an attitude in which the needs of the world as a whole supersede the needs of individual nations. This has an effect on cultural diversity. Local customs, values and even the differences between races and nationalities become blurred.

Globalisation, by contrast, describes the practical methods by which global values are transferred into the economies of countries throughout the world.

Extension note

Detached parts and the creation of a world state

Where do you live? Do you have a sense of identity with that place? What is it that makes you feel a Londoner, a moonraker (an inhabitant of Wiltshire) or an Ulsterman? Most people feel a sense of identity with the land of their birth and some would die for it. Yet, increasingly, this sense of identity has become less and less precise. Are you Scottish, English, Welsh or Irish? Or are you British? Or are you a European or a citizen of the world?

A detached part was a part of one county that was completely surrounded by another county and quite separate from the rest of its county. They were an anomaly of land ownership or of tribal groupings, dating back either to the Anglo-Saxons or Normans. These anomalies were everywhere from East Dunbartonshire, in Scotland, to Steep, now in Hampshire. Planners and governments do not like anomalies; they prefer simplicity. Pockets of land were merged to make them easier to manage. New counties were formed out of the anomalies, such as the West Midlands and Humberside. The Yorkshiremen of Hull lost their identity and the people of Dudley ceased being from Worcestershire and became West Midlanders.

This movement to bigger and better structures of government is not just a British phenomenon. It is universal. Small town government gives way to regional authorities. Environmentalists speak of a lack of identity between the land and the people.

During the nineteenth century various philosophers and theologians argued in favour of a world government. Barriers between people would be broken down. The German theologian Ernst Troelsch imagined the creation of a civilized world with a single government. Kant spoke about a world of perpetual peace with a single rational state. Troelsch thought it achievable; Kant did not.

Globalism is the movement for a single universal identity. Globalisation is the removal of socio-economic barriers that prevent the creation of this new world order. Yet this progress from detached parts, in some cases no bigger than a square mile, to a world super-state is hard to achieve. Old loyalties die hard.

Key point

Globalism is the movement for a single universal identity. Globalisation is the removal of the socio-economic barriers that prevent the creation of this new world order.

Business and the environment: the problem of growth

Economic growth is a double-edged sword. It can bring enormous benefits such as greater prosperity. It means that all but the poorest in society can expect to live longer and to have a higher standard of living than our grandparents' generation. Yet the constant pursuit of economic growth also has detrimental effects. One of these is the harm that it does to the environment.

Environmental damage is a natural consequence of the growth of business and industry. This has always been the case. In the late eighteenth century Abraham Darby developed the iron and steel industry in the Ironbridge Gorge in Shropshire on the banks of the river Severn. Today this is a UNESCO World Heritage site, visited by thousands of people each year. The Severn is beautifully clear and trees line the riverbanks. Above this idyllic scene is the Iron Bridge, the world's first. Yet two hundred years ago industrial furnaces bellowed out the stench of polluting gases, prematurely killing those people who breathed in the air.

Human societies need industrial growth but this can bring devastating ecological harm. The natural habitat is destroyed as factories are built. Growth leads to energy demands and to the building of more and more power stations. Pollution is rife. It is said that in 1850 in Sheffield, which was then the centre of the world's steel making industry, the sun was never seen. Pollution hovered over the city all year round.

The Iron Bridge in Shropshire was once a site of heavy industry. Today it is a UNESCO World Heritage site.

The devastation of the environment in the West, during the **Industrial Revolution**, is today being played out on a bigger scale in the emerging economies. China has one of the world's fastest growing economies, with accompanying increases in pollution. In 2010 reports state that more than 200 million Chinese people do not have access to safe drinking water.

Yet some scholars remain quietly confident that the environmental impact caused by industrial growth will not result in long-term damage to the environment. They look to the example of Great Britain, the first nation in the world to industrialize, to illustrate how the exploits of commerce and industry only provide temporary damage. The example of Ironbridge can be cited. What was once an industrial scar has today become a tourist attraction.

The Kuznets Curve

Environmentalists want concrete evidence that growth is not harmful in the long term. In 1991 two environmental economists, Gene Grossman and Alan Krueger, set out to prove that economic growth does not have a long-term effect on the environment. They used what is known as the **Environmental Kuznets Curve**. The graph shows that as people get wealthier so they buy and use things that are better for the environment. They also gain habits, about recycling and tourism for example, which deliver reduced damage to the planet. Grossman and Krueger argued that, in the early years of development, damage is great but later, as people become richer, the damaged environment is restored.

Grossman and Krueger's views found favour in high places. The World Bank openly stated that:

The view that greater economic activity inevitably hurts the environment is based on static assumptions about technology, tastes and environmental investments. (World Bank, World Development Report 1992: Development and the Environment, *Oxford University Press, 1992)*

During the 1990s this view was central to the policy of the World Bank in giving large sums of money for commercial, business and infrastructure projects in the developing nations. By 2000 the Kuznets Curve was criticized for being based on doubtful assumptions. A new view of the relationship of business and industrial growth and the environment developed. This was based on the **principle of sustainability**. In 2000 David Pearce and Edward Barbier published *Blueprint for a Sustainable Economy*. This set out a new way of looking at the British economy. It was based on two ideas that were, at the time, seen as being novel when applied together. They were sustainable economic growth within a cruelty-free environment. Yet some environmental economists asked a fundamental question. They asked whether the term '**Green growth**', as sustainability is sometimes known, is a contradiction in terms.

To think about

Do you think 'Green growth' is possible? Do we have a responsibility to look after our environment, or is it more important that we achieve a better standard of living, whatever the environmental cost?

Multinational companies face many ethical dilemmas as they consider the impact of their business practices on the local workforce and environment. Eric Neumayer, a leading environmental economist, in 2010 laid out how companies can assess sustainability. His list of five indicators is a mix of economic, environmental and philosophical indicators. These add up to what he calls sustainability. They are:

- National accounts – whether a project is worth the cost financially.
- Aggregate welfare – the modern utilitarian principle that what is good is that which produces welfare for the maximal number of people.
- Natural capital – whether any development produces benefits for nature over and above the damage it may do to the environment.
- Ecosystem health – whether the ecosystem of the area remains healthy.
- Human-environment interaction – whether it improves the relationship between the local people affected by a project and their environment.

Key term

trade union – a group of trades or professions formed to protect their rights and interests.

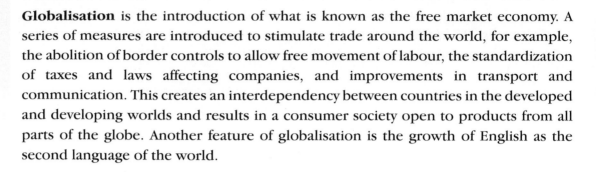

Globalisation

Globalisation is the introduction of what is known as the free market economy. A series of measures are introduced to stimulate trade around the world, for example, the abolition of border controls to allow free movement of labour, the standardization of taxes and laws affecting companies, and improvements in transport and communication. This creates an interdependency between countries in the developed and developing worlds and results in a consumer society open to products from all parts of the globe. Another feature of globalisation is the growth of English as the second language of the world.

Certain features, however, stand in the way of this new global market. Ties of loyalty to country, birthplace and religion prevent a fully integrated global society. Governments are unwilling to give away national power to international organizations. The relative failure of the United Nations Climate Change Conference 2009 in Copenhagen illustrated how national interests can run contrary to global needs.

The new world order, it is argued, can create problems as well as opportunities. Today clothes, carpets, iron and steel are all produced more cheaply in developing countries such as China and Brazil. This results in fewer jobs in the manufacturing sector in developed countries such as the UK and America. Joblessness, as founder of Kid's Company, Camila Batmanghelidjh, argues, is one of the key reasons why many young people feel alienated from society. Globalisation creates an underclass of people who feel **disenfranchised**, or alienated from society.

There has been an increasing growth in the idea of relativism, in terms of morality and the nature of society. People increasingly see themselves as members of specific groups rather than as members of their local or national community. It is argued that, in an odd way, as human beings become part of a global community they become more divided.

Relationship between employers and employees

It is generally agreed today that there has to be a balance struck in business between the aspirations, rights and interests of the worker and those of the company where that individual works. In many sectors of the economy trade unions exist to protect workers' rights. Today's laws on the rights of workers in the UK ensure safety at work, conditions of employment and the right of a worker to join a trade union or other association. Equal opportunities and rights to protect workers from discrimination on the basis of race, religion, gender and sexual orientation are part of the legal framework within which businesses work.

Although some ethical problems have largely disappeared as a result of changes in law and attitudes, new issues have arisen. Some have to do with mass migration and the question of 'British workers for British jobs'. This expression refers to two different ideas. The first is the way in which production of industrial goods and also certain work in the service sector has moved to parts of the developing world. The other meaning has to do with the migration of cheap labour to work in Britain. The consequences of the global economy, it is argued, affect jobs in the United Kingdom.

Various solutions have been put forward to address these issues. These include limiting the numbers of migrant workers, restricting what jobs they can do and even restricting them to certain parts of the country. All of these solutions raise the ethical issue of the treatment of immigrants. What responsibility does a society have for migrant labour? Does a government have a primary moral responsibility to its indigenous population? Christian traditions, following Old Testament custom, place hospitality to foreigners as morally important. Utilitarian ethics might, though, consider the importance of the greatest good for the maximal number. This may mean that, in a recession, jobs would be limited to EU citizens, except where there is a skills shortage. However, this raises the issue of which maximal number is being referred to? Is it the population of the UK or the EU or the world? This is one problem with applying Utilitarianism to this issue. A Virtue ethicist might argue that the concept of British jobs for British workers leads the moral agent to seeing foreigners as different. This would not inspire those character traits that will develop the good (moral) life.

Modern human rights theories have been vitally important in the development of relations between business and workers. Traditional moral approaches, such as Kantian ethics or Utilitarianism, have been criticized for not ensuring good treatment for workers.

To think about

Would you say that the right to join a trade union is a fundamental human right?

Whistle blowing

Another moral aspect of the relationship between the worker and the employer is the issue of whistle blowing. This is where an employer has the perception that either illegal or immoral activities are being pursued by the company for whom he or she

system and coinage. Dishonesty was easy when there were no common standards. Consequently honesty and trust were vital to business and they still are. Leviticus 19, in the Old Testament, lays down certain laws for merchants. Weights and measures must be accurate. The Bible states:

You shall not cheat in measuring length, weight, or quantity. You shall have honest balances, honest weights, an honest ephah [dry measure], and an honest hin [liquid measure]: I am the LORD your God, who brought you out of the land of Egypt. You shall keep all my statutes and all my ordinances, and observe them. (Leviticus 19:36–37)

Business malpractice profanes God's name and his people. Earlier in the same chapter the writer of the law refers to the treatment of workers. They were obviously being maltreated at the time. Hirers are told 'you shall not keep for yourself the wages of a labourer until morning' (Leviticus 19:13).

Another aspect of the relationship between the worker and the employer is **social justice**. Employers must not exploit their workers by reducing them to poverty. Both Amos and Hosea attack the rich of their day for reducing their own people to a state of poverty.

Work is considered, in Christian thought, to be intrinsically beneficial. Adam laboured in the Garden of Eden before the Fall and cultivated the ground after it. The medieval monks lived by the principle 'to work is to pray'. The Protestant work ethic makes a virtue out of hard work. However, the accumulation of wealth for its own sake is not intrinsically good, as Jesus teaches in the Gospels.

Christian attitudes to globalisation vary. Christians talk about catholicity and **oecumene**, meaning the universal nature of the Christian faith, so there is a natural sense that anything that breaks down divisions between people is morally good. Globalisation is viewed as a moral objective, because it enhances this sense of the family of all people on earth.

Christians have a duty of care to all humanity. Globalisation is therefore seen as a tool for ensuring that God's love is applied in the world. This can be demonstrated through a commitment to the relief of poverty. Many Christians believe that globalisation offers an economic route to the abolition of poverty through the interdependence of developed nations with the emerging economies of the Far East and Africa.

In 1981 the economist Amartya Sen noted that hunger and starvation is not caused by a lack of food but rather by a lack of money to pay for it. Globalisation fits in, many Christians argue, with a desire not to provide food aid but to make people richer, so that they can buy the food they need. Many Christian charities reject the traditional form of charity. Christian Aid, for example, has been at the forefront of the policy of helping people to help themselves.

Yet, despite the benefits of globalisation, many Christians argue that progress comes at too high a price. They argue that globalisation leads to multinational corporations exploiting workers and the environment for financial gain. Globalisation leads to the closure of factories in the developed world and the building of new ones in developing countries, where labour costs are lower and employment rights are significantly worse. The American theologian, John B. Cobb, suggests that globalisation exploits the poor and 'destroys human communities and devastates the natural world' (John B. Cobb, 'The Theological Stake in Globalization' available from www.religion-online. org/showarticle.asp?title=1095 [accessed 04/06/2010]).

For Christians globalisation raises fundamental questions. Is it a step towards a fairer world, from which poorer nations will benefit, or is it simply another form of exploitation? Some Christians believe that economic injustice can only be solved globally while others look to individual projects in villages and towns around the world.

This points to a wider issue. It is argued that there is no such thing as a single Christian response to globalisation and business economics. There are rather a whole series of responses, many of which are influenced by secular philosophies. In business ethics many Christians' attitudes to the global market are determined by economic realities rather than the Gospel. Some scholars argue that the situation in the biblical period was very different to today. Others assert that the teachings of Jesus are still vitally important.

Natural Law and business

There are a number of different ways of looking at Natural Law in regard to business ethics. The New Natural Law theory examines the nature of business in terms of the *telos* of virtue and human prospering. Therefore certain industries will be considered to be contrary to the achievement of this *telos*. This would include industries that make money out of the exploitation of others. The sex trade or the arms industry might be considered to run contrary to what, in nature, human society and therefore business is about.

New Natural Law philosophers, such as Germain Grisez, have looked at the issue of corporate finance and examined whether its function, purpose and end is virtuous. Aquinas was opposed to usury (lending money at unreasonably high rates of interest) as it ran counter to the primary precepts within his theory of Natural Law. The exploitation of others, through high interest rates, runs counter to the principle of a harmonious society in which all the organs of society fulfil an integrated and interconnected function.

The image of the parts of a body working in harmony can also be used to illustrate how a business should work in Natural Law. The end of a business is to produce profit and the final end is happiness, contentment. A business must also fulfil the happiness of all its constituent parts: the staff, the management, the board and the consumers. These are the organs of the business and if they fail to work together the result is ultimately death.

Catholic notions of Natural Law in business led to the idea of natural rights, God-given, which protect workers and consumers to ensure that the business is virtuous. The encyclical *Rerum Novarum* of 1891 set out the principle that there should be rights to protect the vulnerable in the workplace. It supported the rights of workers to form trade unions.

Natural Law theory has a number of strengths when dealing with business issues. The most important of these is the concept of human prospering as the ultimate end of human beings. This is seen in terms of moral, as well as economic, betterment. The two are connected in New Natural Law theory. A further strength of the Natural Law theory is the concept that work should be uplifting. This means that the workplace ought to be a moral environment. Natural Law also considers what sort of work is moral and what is not.

Those who reject Natural Law theory argue that the whole basis of Natural Law is flawed and cannot therefore be applied to business ethics. Work has no intrinsic moral basis. It is simply a way of earning a living. Therefore, to argue that work ought to be uplifting is flawed. It is impossible to create a society where every job is inspiring.

Virtue Ethics and business

Virtue ethicists believe that the good or moral life occurs by attaining and holding on to certain virtuous character traits. Manuel Velasquez, an American philosopher who has developed Virtue Ethics in terms of business, lists those qualities that an executive of a company should have. These traits are courage, compassion, fairness, faithfulness, generosity, honesty, integrity, prudence and self-control. A manager and employer will integrate these in his or her life and they will be part of the policies of an ethical company in its day-to-day dealings.

Velasquez points out that those in charge of a company are powerful individuals. This power can and often is abused by executives. Virtue Ethics is the only ethical theory that dwells on the moral status of those who make decisions. Virtue ethicists argue that a virtuous executive will make virtuous decisions. A virtuous managing director ought to have equal regard for those who work for the company, as for the stockholders. There is a moral mean to be met between those who make the product and those who invest so that it can be made.

The weakness of a Virtue Ethics approach, it can be argued, is that it does not take into account the profit motive that underlies all businesses in a capitalist economy. Investors take risks with their money and they would prefer a company determined to make profits rather than one run by a virtuous person. The fundamental goal in modern Virtue Ethics is not profits; but the principle of human flourishing.

To think about

How could Virtue Ethics be useful for making business decisions?

Kantian ethics and business

According to Kant, employers and employees have a duty to each other.

There are a number of Kantian ideas that make it a useful approach to business ethics. These include the importance of treating people as an end in themselves rather than as a means to an end. This is important in business, where the exploitation of employees remains a moral problem. Equally Kant stresses the importance of duty. Workers have a sense of duty towards their employers and equally employers have a duty towards those who work for them. In his **taxonomy of duties**, Kant stressed that human beings have a duty to themselves to avoid being slavish to others. Workers have a duty to themselves to see that their **autonomy** is respected. A further part of his taxonomy that has relevance to business is his view that the making of money for its own sake is ethically wrong. Avarice is considered to be contrary to a person's duty as a moral being (see Taxonomy of duties pages 55–56). The human being who is greedy

Key term

universaliz-ability – the principle that moral values are universal and therefore universally applicable.

is likely to be irrational in nature and led by their emotions. Greed is wrong, since it leads businesses to do immoral things in the pursuit of their goal. Kant also lists lying as wrong, as it runs contrary to the principle of universalizability. Companies must be totally honest about their dealings.

Kant imagined that in time rational people would construct a world moral system, the universal kingdom of ends. Some argue that globalisation is the first step towards this state of perpetual peace that Kant envisaged for this world order. However, as Joanna Rozpedowski points out, globalisation is fundamentally different from Kant's view of the new world order. The fundamental problem is that globalisation starts from a utilitarian premise. It is grounded on practical economic matters and does not start from a priori moral truths.

To think about

Does globalisation benefit people or is it the magnification of worldwide greed?

The idea that globalisation leads to the idea of a world super state, in which perpetual peace reigns supreme, is seen as a utopian dream. It is unrealistic to expect the global economy to be more ethical than the national or local economic structures of the past.

A further weakness is the problem of conflicting duties. An employer has a duty to his or her employees but also duties to the shareholders and to the customers. These duties often conflict. Additionally, it is argued that when a sense of duty to the environment is factored in, this creates contradictions in the overall policies of any company. To whom is the employer ultimately responsible? Is it the workers in the factory, the people buying what is produced there, or those who provide the capital? What about consideration of the impact of the factory on the environment? Clearly the needs of each party are very different.

Business and Utilitarianism

The idea of the maximization of **welfare** is crucial in modern Utilitarianism. Workers' rights are to be sustained and developed if the overall welfare of society is enhanced. They are to be limited if social welfare is affected detrimentally. A welfare utilitarian is likely to assert the right to join a union and to go on strike within the principle of general welfare. The welfare utilitarian, however, is likely to argue that coordinated strikes will have a detrimental effect on the maximal number of people. Indeed, there would be no reason for coordinated strikes unless it was designed to maximize its effect on the general population.

Globalisation has also divided utilitarians. This is caused by differences of opinion concerning whether globalisation will achieve a utilitarian purpose of maximizing human happiness or welfare. Some utilitarians argue that the net benefits of globalisation will outweigh the deficit. Benefits occur in the developing economies, such as China and India, where rapid industrialization and modernization programmes will ensure prosperity. The maximal number of people will benefit, as these countries become increasingly the factory of the world.

Other utilitarians argue that the advantages of globalisation are outweighed by the disadvantages to welfare or to human happiness. Utilitarian environmentalists note such aspects as deforestation and the destruction of environmental diversity resulting from the mass production of cheap food in the developing economies for the developed world. They note the destruction of marine life to provide food and oil for the global economy. Mass tourism, another consequence of globalisation, affects the environment by destroying fragile nature habitats, such as coral reefs.

Utilitarianism has played an important part in the development of the modern Western economy, yet utilitarians do not agree on the benefits of this economic model. This division within Utilitarianism can be seen as a fundamental weakness. Until the period following World War I, utilitarians based their views on the need for the economy to maximize happiness in society. Scholars developed an economic model for society based on the maximization of welfare for the maximal number of people, which contributed to the creation of the welfare state. Since the 1970s, however, the model has gradually changed. Today globalisation is based on privatization and big multinationals. It is important to ask whether either of these economic models, based on utilitarian principles, have delivered what they said they would.

Practice exam question

'Virtue Ethics offers the best approach to the morality of business.' Discuss.

You could start this essay with a description of the various types of Virtue Ethics, particularly those parts of the theories that relate to business. You could look at character traits and how these may relate to business. You might also want to look at other forms of Virtue Ethics that consider, for example, motives. Once you have looked at these you could examine what may be perceived as weaknesses within Virtue Ethics, for example the criticism that it centres on individuals and therefore is difficult to apply to companies and to business in general. You could illustrate your essay with examples of how Virtue Ethics can be applied to particular business issues and what alternatives to these problems there are.

Develop your knowledge

There are many books on environmental ethics. Some of the most recent include:

The Ethics of Climate Change: Right and Wrong in a Warming World by James Garvey (Continuum International Publishing Group, 2008)

A Companion to Environmental Philosophy by Dale Jamieson (Ed.) (Blackwell, 2003)

Ethics and the Environment: An Introduction by Dale Jamieson (Cambridge University Press, 2008)

Of the books on business ethics, two that can be recommended are:

Business Ethics by Andrew Crane and Dirk Matten (Oxford University Press, 2003)

A Companion to Business Ethics by Robert E. Frederick (Ed.) (Blackwell, 2002)

Sexual ethics

Premarital and extramarital sex

Key terms

premarital sex – sex before marriage.

extramarital sex – sexual act between a married person and someone other than their marriage partner.

Later in this chapter on sexual ethics we consider the issues of contraception and homosexuality. This first section addresses three fundamental questions:

1. Is sexual intercourse outside of marriage, premarital sex and extramarital sex, morally wrong?
2. Is sexual activity morally acceptable only within the context of a loving and caring relationship?
3. Is sex such a big deal? Should it just be considered as a natural bodily function of no great importance?

To think about

'Sexual intercourse has nothing to do with love, relationships or having children. It is about pleasure – pure and simple.' Discuss.

Sex and relationships in Christian thought

The Bible

The Bible is the starting point for a Christian understanding of sexual intercourse and human relationships. However, biblical writers give differing views.

The Old Testament begins with the abundance of procreation. God, according to the Creation story in Genesis 1, causes the world to give birth to an abundance of creatures, so great that the land and seas can hardly contain them. Procreation is seen as a gift of God, as an aspect of his goodness in which human beings are called to share. Later in the book of Genesis, the angel of the Lord appears to Abraham and tells him:

> *I will indeed bless you, and I will make your offspring as numerous as the stars of heaven and as the sand that is on the seashore. (Genesis 22:17)*

God's promise and covenant with Abraham was based on the idea that the gift of God is to be found above all in childbirth.

In ancient Jewish law sexual intercourse became inseparable from marriage, as the contractual nature of the marriage relationship regulated the issue of inheritance. Women were expected to be virgins when they married. This rule meant that a man could know that his children were his, in order for him to pass on his birthright. It was virtually impossible for a young woman who had already had sex to marry. This fact explains the law in Exodus 22 which states that a man who has intercourse with a virgin is required to pay a dowry to the girl's father and to marry her. If the girl's father refused to give her away, the dowry would allow the girl to live with her parents, as she was never likely to marry.

Inheritance also appears to be the reason for the Old Testament condemnation of adultery. The Torah places adultery with theft and after murder as a serious offence. The link with theft is deliberate. Adultery was seen as the theft of a wife by another man. Its seriousness meant that the penalty for adultery was capital: death by stoning. The reason for this was twofold. First, adultery would create uncertainty about the legitimacy of any son. Consequently the husband would not know whether the son who inherited the estate was his own offspring or not. The other reason has to do with the status of the wife. She was considered her husband's property and therefore having sex with her was theft of the most important thing that a man owned.

The teaching of Paul

Jesus made very few references to sexual matters. Early Christians, therefore, took guidance on sexual ethics from the teachings of Paul. Writing to the Corinthian church, a place known for its sexual licence, Paul urges Christians to regard the body as a beautiful gift of God. The word **body** did not have as straightforward a meaning for Paul as it does today. It did not just mean the physical form. It can be thought of as your whole personality, which includes your physical form and your character, your consciousness and how your perceive yourself. In a letter discussing sexual desire and prostitution, Paul wrote:

> *The body is meant not for fornication but for the Lord, and the Lord for the body. . . . Do you not know that your bodies are members of Christ? Should I therefore*

take the members of Christ and make them members of a prostitute? Never!
(1 Corinthians 6:13, 15)

Paul goes on to talk about the importance of marriage. Sex outside of marriage is regarded as wrong. Paul sees the sex industry of Corinth in terms of its effect on people. It corrupts the character (the body). He asserts:

Or do you not know that your body is a temple of the Holy Spirit within you,
which you have from God, and that you are not your own? (1 Corinthians 6:19)

The human personality is designed to reveal God's nature and not to become affected by sexual lust. This idea explains Paul's teaching on celibacy. He argues neither for it nor against it, but asserts that if a person's sexual desires cannot be controlled then it is best for that person to remain celibate.

Sex and relationships in later Christian thought

Biblical writers emphasize the contractual relationship between a man and his wife and between his family and hers. Love is regarded as important yet it is a secondary consideration. This reflects the state of affairs in the ancient world. The role of women was generally seen as inferior to that of men. Women did not participate in the political process and while they had influence they did not have power. This situation began to change in the nineteenth century. This is reflected in the development of Christian theology from the reign of Queen Victoria onwards. Liberal theology accepts the equality of men and women in any relationship. It also puts great importance on love as the cement that binds a marriage together. This emphasis on love can be seen not only in situation ethics but also in other types of radical theology that developed in the 1960s.

Love dominates modern Christian understandings of sexual intercourse. The contractual obligations of marriage have been replaced by the centrality of agape. The love between Christ and his Church is used to illustrate the loving and caring relationship a husband ought to have with his wife. The word 'cherish', in the Book of Common Prayer marriage service, is emphasized while the word 'obey' has been written out of modern Christian vows.

The emphasis on love in liberal theology freed sexual relationships from what was seen as the straitjacket of marriage. Increasingly marriage was seen as a bonus rather than a necessity. Sexual intercourse was permitted outside marriage. The American liberal theologian, Harvey Cox, argues that what is important is a relationship of love: whether the couple are married does not matter. Indeed, marriage was seen as an impediment, restricting true love.

Key term

celibacy – abstaining from marriage and sexual relations.

> ## Key point
>
> A liberal Christian response to sexual morality puts love (agape) at the centre of relationships. Sexual intercourse should take place within a loving relationship. This does not necessarily need to be a married relationship.

Cox implies that relationships are fluid yet many people desire a long-term commitment. This may or may not be as a married couple. Cox suggests that in a world of fluid relationships, extramarital sex is inevitable. Yet traditionalists argue that this leads to the destruction of stable relationships. Cox responds to these criticisms by arguing that extramarital sex is a symptom that a relationship has broken down. The couple should recognize this and, in love and charity, move on.

True Love Waits®

Fundamentalist Christians take a less liberal path. They regard love as important yet the Old Testament emphasis on a contractual relationship is also valued highly. That contract is permanent and sexual relationships ought not to be undertaken outside of marriage. In 1993 the principle of True Love Waits® was created as part of Christian sex education. This pledged Baptists not to have sexual intercourse until after marriage. In 1993 this was through a verbal pledge and signing a commitment card. Later, **chastity rings** were introduced for young people to wear to show that they are not prepared to have premarital sex.

An organization was created in 1996, known as the Silver Ring Thing (SRT), which educates young people to remain virgins until marriage. This movement was part of an evangelical campaign against escalating numbers of teenage pregnancies and to spread the message of abstinence. Members wear a ring bearing a reference to Paul's first letter to the Thessalonians:

> *For this is the will of God, your sanctification: that you abstain from fornication; that each one of you knows how to control your own body in holiness and honour. (1 Thessalonians 4:3–4)*

Members of the Silver Ring Thing wear rings to show their pledge to maintain their virginity until marriage.

Modern Roman Catholicism also stresses the importance of virginity before marriage, though it recognizes human weakness. Benedict XVI in his first encyclical, *The Love that Satisfies* (2007), recognized the desire of many for premarital sex. He criticized the sin, as he saw it, while showing forgiveness to individuals. Catholic teaching is grounded in two fundamental principles: Natural Law and the sanctity of the sacrament of marriage.

Sex and relationships in Natural Law theory

Aquinas' view of Natural Law forms the basis for much of the teaching of the Roman Catholic Church. Aquinas developed his ideas at a time, similar to today, when the nuclear family largely existed on paper rather than in reality. Aquinas used his Christian and Aristotelian principles to develop the idea of the moral importance of sexual intercourse only within the marital state. This was a very different idea from that which existed a century earlier. Aquinas' concept of sexuality was intrinsically connected to procreation and not about sexual pleasure. It became accepted because, in part, it brought social cohesiveness in a divided world and, in part, because it had a firm basis in Christianity.

In the *Summa Theologica* Aquinas asserts that the function, purpose and end of sexual intercourse is the procreation of children. Any sexual act that prevents the possibility of childbirth is immoral, since it runs contrary to nature. As a result, anal sex, bestiality and masturbation are all equally intrinsically wrong as they prevent human life being conceived. Such acts thereby became unnatural.

Aquinas commented on other sexual activity that was common in his lifetime. Rape and incest were not unusual and neither was adultery. Aquinas argued that such acts are contrary to right reason. They are unnatural, not because they prevent the potentiality of childbirth, but rather they conflict with the good of society and respect for the other person involved. The key to Aquinas' understanding of Natural Law and sexual relationships is the creation of a harmonious and therefore virtuous society.

Strengths and weaknesses of Christian approaches to sexual relationships

Christian approaches to sexual relationships are remarkably diverse. Four distinct approaches have been examined here – the biblical foundation, liberal theology, evangelical views and Natural Law theory. Each different tradition has its own strengths and weaknesses.

Fundamentalist Christians argue that premarital sex is always wrong. The strength of taking this moral position is the emphasis it places on the importance of marriage, and the importance of self-discipline and self-control. Liberal Christian writers argue that this teaching ignores loving and caring relationships outside of marriage. It also ignores homosexual relationships. Fundamentalist Christians, in response, argue that they are being true to the Gospel and that they have a responsibility to preach what they consider the truth rather than conforming to today's moral norms.

A liberal Christian response to sexual morality regards love (agape) as the primary goal of any relationship. Other Christians argue that the creation of children and the need to maintain a strong and enduring family life are equally important in the consideration of sexual morality.

Some Christians believe that sexual intercourse belongs within the commitment of marriage.

Non-religious scholars argue that there is a fundamental flaw in all Christian responses to sexual ethics. Religious ethical systems are, to a greater or lesser degree, theocentric, that is having God as a central focus. These writers argue that a theocentric position creates a sexual ethic that is inhumane and therefore immoral. Homosexuals are forbidden by their faith from having sexual intercourse, even within the context of a loving and stable relationship, as this is contrary to God's norm for human beings as expressed in the Scriptures. In *The Poverty of Theistic Morality* the American scholar Adolf Grunbaum argues that Christian sexual ethics is based on the narrow views of old men who claim that this is what God wants.

Sex and relationships in Kantian ethics

Kant believed that you should never treat people as a means to an end but only as an end in themselves. Kant used this aspect of the Categorical Imperative to assert that sexual intercourse is morally unsound. He does this by arguing that any person who desires sex is not fundamentally interested in the welfare of the partner. What interests those having sex is not the other person but the fulfilment of a strong sex drive.

There is, though, a contrary view within Kant's moral philosophy. This emphasizes the need for human beings to preserve life. This is one of the individual's primary duties. It leads not only to Kant attacking suicide but also to him regarding masturbation as a greater evil than suicide. While suicide destroys a life which already exists, masturbation does not allow human life. It is therefore contrary to Kant's taxonomy of duties.

Human life cannot be preserved without sexual intercourse yet, at the same time, Kant regarded sex as morally degrading. Marriage is another problem that he had difficulty resolving. Kant wanted marriage to be something higher than bodily desires, but this is what he felt it was. He wrote, in graphic terms, that marriage is a:

Lifelong possession of each other's sexual attributes. (Immanuel Kant, The Metaphysics of Morals, *Mary Gregor (ed.), Cambridge University Press, 1996)*

He sees prostitution and the way in which the rich have mistresses as being precisely the opposite of what he wants for human beings. Prostitutes have a contract with their clients that destroys human autonomy; it makes the prostitute a thing to be used. He also believed that marriage had the potential to be the same. He thought that men might use their wives merely to produce children and that this ought not to be the case. Kant believed in the autonomy of every person and this included married women.

Kant's *summum bonum* may be considered to be the solution to the contradictions in his thought. It is left to the afterlife for the age of reason to be achieved, when human beings will rise above their sexual needs. Moral society will then exist since reason will triumph over the needs of the flesh.

Kant's view of sexual relationships outside of marriage was affected by his view of (a) sex and (b) marriage. He regarded both as imperfect, yet he saw that sex was necessary for the human race to survive, and that marriage was the best method of regulating sexual intercourse and the creation of offspring. Marriage could be abused, but sexual relationships outside of marriage, he believed, created a worse situation. It led to women being treated as things rather than as partners. Kant spoke of marriage as being designed for 'merry conversation', by which he meant companionship. He regarded relationships outside of marriage as temporary affairs, based on sexual relationships rather than true companionship. As such sexual relationships outside of marriage were morally flawed.

To think about

'Kant's views on sexual relationships are contradictory. He just did not understand that human beings are animals.' Discuss.

Sex and relationships in Utilitarianism

Bentham

> ## Extension note
>
> #### Discovery, sex and Tahiti
>
> During the eighteenth century, Europeans continued to explore and then conquer the world. In 1772 John Hawkesworth wrote about the exploits of two British naval captains, Captain Wallis and Captain Cook, and their travels to the Pacific Islands. Hawkesworth's book became a best seller. It told of naked people, living a simple life and openly enjoying sex and, unlike the European, having no shame in what they were doing. It was, as if, these British sailors had stepped back into the Garden of Eden. Europeans were captivated by the stories of the Pacific Islanders. For Europeans, Tahiti became a mythical place of strange creatures and even stranger inhabitants.
>
> After reading about this far-off place the young Bentham reflected about the nature of human beings and the difference between European Christian sexual morality and that of the Pacific Islands. While England was hanging men for homosexual acts, Tahitians were happy having homosexual and heterosexual intercourse in public without any sense of guilt or shame. As Pamela Cheek points out, in *Sexual Antipodes: Enlightenment Globalization and the Placing of Sex*, these discoveries led Bentham and others to question who was the brute. It led him to divide sexual morality into offences against the self, for which there ought to be no penalty, and offences against society, which the law ought to regulate. Bentham's views on sexual relationships were very liberal for his time. Mill, though, regarded Bentham's views as too liberal. Mill called the Pacific Islanders 'barbarians'.

The central feature of Utilitarianism is the principle of the greatest good/happiness/pleasure or welfare for the greatest number. In any examination of utilitarian attitudes to sexual relationships this is the starting point.

Bentham's view of sexual relationships is strikingly modern for his time. Famously he approved of gay relationships, which gave harm to no one and pleasure to many. He also believed that pornography and prostitution should be lawful for similar reasons. He regarded sex as a basic human need that exists to give pleasure, however transitory that may be.

Bentham distinguished **offences against the self** from **offences against society**. Homosexuality, pornography and prostitution are classed as offences against the self. They affect the individuals concerned; they do not affect the wider population. What a person reads, pays for or does in the privacy of the home has no bearing on his or her next-door neighbour, let alone someone living on the other side of the country. Heterosexual Bentham may not have liked homosexuality but he did not see it as a social matter. On the other hand, sexual intercourse that produces a criminal class is a social problem. From a utilitarian point of view childbirth can be good for the maximal number of people in society or it can be bad. It depends on the family life of those involved. Bentham was concerned about those he regarded as the idle, criminally minded poor and their capacity to produce unwanted offspring.

Benthamites, however, regarded the need to reduce poverty and control unwanted births as crucial for the reduction of lawlessness, poverty and disease. It ensured the greatest good for the greatest number. This thinking would justify the forced sterilization of Romany offenders in post-war Sweden and in other parts of Europe.

Mill

Mill's Rule Utilitarianism starts from a different perspective. Human freedom, for Mill, is necessary for human beings to be happy. Therefore without liberty utilitarian values are not possible. Mill's view of sexual relationships is guided by the need for freedom. Importantly, this freedom is equal for men and women. It means that a woman has a right to decide for herself if and when she wants sexual intercourse. This may be within or outside of marriage. The liberty of the woman is vital, as is that of the man. Mill regarded sexual intercourse as a necessary but lower pleasure. Marriage was essentially about friendship and companionship, which were higher pleasures.

Sexual intercourse outside of marriage should not be unlawful. Following Bentham, Mill regarded prostitution as a fact of life, a personal matter between the prostitute and the client. Personal freedom should not be restrained by society. However, Mill, writing with his wife Harriet Taylor (1807–1858), examined the issue of reputation. They argued that it would be wrong, for example, for a husband to cause embarrassment to his wife's reputation by visiting brothels and, more generally, treating her with contempt. They considered that a wife should have the right to leave her husband in such circumstances, at a time when this was not legal. Mill did not consider premarital and extramarital sex as wrong. What was wrong was the exploitation of women, which he believed was more likely outside of marriage than within it.

The issue of embarrassment and the way in which that limits individual freedom also affects Mill's other views about sexual relationships. For example, sexual intercourse ought to be illegal in a busy public place since the general public would be offended.

Key terms

positive autonomy – positive effects of personal freedom, for example, ability to make personal decisions about marriage, partnership, love etc.

negative autonomy – harmful effects of personal freedom, for example, ability to cause harm to the self through drug addiction or sexually transmitted infections.

However, Mill argued that there was nothing wrong with sexual intercourse taking place in a field where the general public was unlikely to go. Pornography and prostitution fitted this same standard. It should not be illegal but it should not occur where it might embarrass or cause offence.

Sex and relationships in modern Utilitarianism

Modern utilitarian approaches to sexual relationships develop the issues raised by Bentham and Mill. Alan Wertheimer, in *Consent to Sexual Relations*, points out that the position that Mill holds disregards the negative effects of autonomy. He argues that positive autonomy, Mill's position, ignores the way in which freedom can be exploited by pimps and by the traffic in sex. Negative autonomy recognizes that freedom may, paradoxically, involve lack of liberty.

The autonomy of the individual is set against the welfare utility of society. Argument often centres on negative and positive autonomy, on the one hand, and offences against the self and against society on the other. There are utilitarians that wish to control certain activities for the welfare benefit of the maximal number of people. Thus, someone who is HIV positive or has AIDS should be prevented from having unprotected sex, for the general good of society. Equally, on grounds of sexually transmitted infections, brothels should be strictly regulated and unprotected sex not allowed. This will protect society. Such laws also recognize the negative effect of personal autonomy.

There are though some utilitarians who, following Mill's view of positive autonomy, argue that such steps impose impossible limits on personal freedom.

To think about

'The sex industry is like any other business. Selling porn is no worse than selling tobacco.' Discuss.

Peter Singer, the Preference utilitarian, argues that human beings should be free to do what they like to whomever they like as long as that other person is not harmed in the process. Singer, following Mill, is concerned with positive harm. Negative harm is, it is argued, impossible to evaluate. How, for example, is it possible to evaluate whether a prostitute is harmed by their ability to sell his or her body for sex? It is obvious if that person is forced into the sex industry but it is less clear if that person decides that this is what they wish to do in life. Equally the effects of premarital sex and extramarital sex must be calculated on the basis of positive harm. A utilitarian view would therefore not see extramarital sex as wrong in itself; however, it would consider the harm that an adulterous relationship would create in terms of the hurt caused and the consequences for a marriage.

Key point

A utilitarian view of sexual ethics argues for the liberty of consenting adults to do what gives them pleasure, as long as it does not cause harm to others or to society.

Sex and relationships in Virtue Ethics

The starting point in Virtue Ethics is the virtuous state of the moral agent. However, how this impinges on sexual ethics is a matter of some argument within Virtue Ethics. Virtue ethicists agree that central to sexual relationships is the idea of a stable commitment between partners. They argue that sexual activity joins two people into an emotional and physical union. It should not be treated lightly as just a bodily sensation. It has a wider effect on the individuals concerned. Therefore, Virtue ethicists regard prostitution as morally wrong since it does not lead to a stable and loving relationship. Further, pornography can also be regarded as morally wrong as it treats the other person as simply an object of no great consequence. However, it is not the harm that it does to the porn star that is the major worry. It is rather the effect that it has on the person looking at the pornographic film or magazine. They lack virtue by treating others as objects.

Sexual relationships should take place within a stable and loving relationship. The question is whether this means that premarital and extramarital sex are acceptable within the context of a stable relationship. With regard to premarital sex there are two Virtue Ethics answers. The first of these asserts that a stable and loving relationship can exist outside of marriage. What is important is whether the couple love each other and whether they are in a long-term relationship. However, many Virtue ethicists argue that such a relationship is not possible outside of marriage. They argue that the legal bonds of marriage lead to the emergence of caring and stable relationships. This second position follows Aristotle's view that marriage creates the conditions in which virtuous love can flourish. Extramarital sex is harder to justify in Virtue Ethics.

Virtue Ethics has a number of strengths when dealing with sexual relationships. These include, it is argued, the importance given to the moral integrity of those involved and also the way in which these moral virtues can be applied to homosexual as well as heterosexual relationships. Some scholars argue that Virtue Ethics is too perfect. There is a need to accept the imperfection of human relationships. It can also be argued that marital bonds and stable relationships are not intrinsically good in themselves. Many people get exploited in relationships. There is no intrinsic moral difference between having sex within a stable relationship and having casual sexual intercourse.

Contraception

Contraception in Christian thought

There is no single view on contraception among Christians. There are stark differences of opinion not only between different Christian denominations but also within them. In ancient and medieval times the use of contraception was rare. Today it is widespread. The writers of the Bible and early Christian writers did not live at a time when contraception was preventative; rather it worked by causing a very early miscarriage. Contraception was therefore seen as morally bad since it had the same effect as an abortion.

Today, however, many Christians no longer regard contraception as morally wrong. Indeed, many regard it as the most moral thing to do in certain situations. From the 1930s the Church of England and other Anglican Churches worldwide saw the need for contraception to prevent unwanted pregnancies. Even before that, Anglican clergy in London's East End had argued in favour of contraception as a way of relieving the poverty of the labouring classes. The plight of the many children who live in extreme poverty in the cities of Latin America and the Indian subcontinent underlines, it is argued, the need for effective birth control in the developing world. The Protestant and Orthodox Churches today hold similar positions to that of the Church of England. God is love and therefore does not wish people to give birth to unwanted children. Nor, it is argued, does God wish to see human beings die from the effects of unprotected sex. Yet many religious people feel that the widespread use of contraception frees human beings from moral responsibility. Evangelical Protestants argue that the widespread use of contraception sends out the wrong message.

Contraception and Natural Law theory

The teaching of the Roman Catholic Church is opposed to artificial contraception. In 1969 in a wide-ranging encyclical entitled *Humanae Vitae*, Pope Paul VI reaffirmed the traditional Natural Law stance of the Church. He argued that the use of condoms creates a physical barrier to prevent childbirth; this is unnatural. Roman Catholics assert the importance of allowing the potential to create human life in intercourse. This is what sex is primarily designed for, the creation of life. Yet the attitude of Paul VI, although fundamentally a continuation of Aquinas' views, was criticized within the Roman Catholic Church. The leading theologian of the Second Vatican Council, Hans Kung, pointed out certain inconsistencies. Paul VI allowed for the rhythm method of birth control. This method requires the woman to work out the natural rhythm of her monthly cycle, recording changes in her body temperature to discover when she is ovulating and to avoid sex at that time. It is designed to prevent conception in a natural way. This suggests for some contemporary Catholic scholars an inconsistency in the approach. Either sexual intercourse is primarily about reproduction or it is not.

Within the Catholic tradition criticisms have been made over its strict adherence to Natural Law theory. It is argued that the ban on contraception does not address two other issues. The first is the importance of the conscience in contemporary Catholic teaching. Pope Benedict XVI has reinforced the traditional stance of the Church yet many Catholics in North America and Western Europe follow their own personal conscience, ignoring the ban despite Church tradition. Birth rates among Catholics and Protestants are remarkably similar in these areas.

There is a further issue, which developed in the late twentieth century. Some Catholics use the principle of **double effect** to argue that it is morally acceptable to use condoms to prevent HIV and AIDS, even though it also prevents the birth of a child.

Contraception in Kantian ethics

The difficulties that exist in Kant's views about sexual relationships also exist in what might be perceived as an interpretation of his views on contraception. On one side of the argument is the view that procreation is an intrinsic duty of the human race. Human beings must preserve life; therefore, contraception would seem to be morally wrong. Yet Kant does not say that it is the duty of every human being to reproduce nor does he say that every act of intercourse ought to result in a child. His condemnation of masturbation, however, does seem to imply that any sexual act should have the potential to create human life.

There are some grounds to suggest that Kant might have approved of contraception. The argument lies in his view that human beings should never be treated as a means to an end. In the eighteenth and nineteenth centuries women were regarded generally as the property of their husbands. Such a view meant that they had little control of when they had sexual intercourse and, as a consequence, little choice in producing a family. Kant, who had a high regard for the autonomy of every rational human being, did not share the view that women were property. Clearly, therefore, Kant would have regarded it as morally wrong for a woman to be forced to have children in precisely the same way that he considered it immoral for a woman to be made to have an abortion.

Contraception and Utilitarianism

The early history of utilitarian attitudes to contraception was centred on the rights of women in marriage to have control over their own lives. Generally in Victorian Britain women were under the authority of their father or husband. Women did not have rights and this extended to when and where they had sexual intercourse. The husband controlled sex in marriage and fathers prevented it outside of marriage. In reality this control did not work for everyone yet the penalties for either refusing to have sex with your husband or for having premarital sex were quite serious. Women were often beaten by their husbands and could be admitted to mental asylums for being 'frigid' or suffering from 'nymphomania'.

Contraception gives women control over their lives. It prevents unwanted pregnancies and theoretically it can stop a woman being forced to have a family. J.S. Mill was the first utilitarian to campaign in favour of contraception. Mill was arrested for distributing obscene literature, material that showed how to use contraception. He was influenced by Annie Besant (1847–1933) who campaigned for the legalization of contraception and for women's rights. Mill saw that the greatest good of the greatest number would not be possible if women were denied liberty.

This idea of the merits of contraception for the greater good is still the utilitarian position. The Cambridge Welfare utilitarians, who followed Sidgwick, campaigned in the 1920s and 1930s for the legalization of contraception. Today issues relating to population growth, to unwanted children and child trafficking, and to AIDS lead contemporary utilitarians to continue to campaign in favour of birth control.

Extension note

Annie Besant

Annie Besant was a social reformer and political campaigner in the late nineteenth and early twentieth centuries. She was a prominent campaigner for women's rights and for Indian nationalism.

In 1867, Annie married Frank Besant, a clergyman, and they had two children. However, the marriage was not a happy one and, in 1873, Annie's increasingly anti-religious views led to a legal separation. She became a prominent member of the Fabian Society and of the National Secular Society. She became an associate of Charles Bradlaugh, the editor of the periodical *National Reformer*, for whom Besant wrote articles on women's rights and marriage.

In 1877 Besant and Bradlaugh published a pamphlet on contraception and as a result were tried for obscenity. The trial divided the nation. Charles Darwin wrote letters attacking the idea of contraception. He argued that it prevented, as he put it, the 'perfecting' of the human race through natural selection. Some classes were more likely to use contraceptives than others. In the trial Annie quoted from J.S. Mill to argue that the widespread use of contraception would lead to fewer unwanted pregnancies, to less poverty and a reduction of crime. All these factors would maximize human happiness.

Besant and Bradlaugh were sentenced to six months in jail. The sentence was subsequently overturned on appeal. Released from prison, Annie later emigrated to India and died in Madras in 1933. She did not live to see Indian independence nor a woman's right to control sex in marriage. India became independent in 1947 but it was not until 1992 that it became an offence under UK law for a husband to force his wife to have sexual intercourse.

To think about

'Contraception is neither morally good nor bad. It is just necessary.' Do you agree?

Contraception and Virtue Ethics

There is no clear-cut answer among Virtue ethicists concerning the morality of contraception. Some Virtue ethicists start from the Aquinas' Natural Law position and argue that what is virtuous lies in human reproduction and the loving and caring relationship that exists within a family. This is the position held by Rosalind Hursthouse. It is argued that contraception leads to casual sex, which is inherently immoral as it treats the other person as a means to personal satisfaction. A virtuous person, it is argued, would wish to have relationships that value the other person.

There are other ways of looking at contraception. Michael Slote emphasizes the caring nature of a virtuous person. He defines three types of care as being central to what makes the individual virtuous. These are:
- care for yourself
- care for family and friends
- care for humanity.

It can be argued that all three types of care emphasize the need to use contraceptives. If you care for yourself you will not wish to die or be sick through sexually transmitted infections. If you care for your family and friends you would wish to reproduce only those who are going to be wanted and brought up in a loving and caring environment. You have therefore a duty to bring into the world only those you are able to look after. Finally, your desire to care for all humanity will take into account the growth of the world's population and the consequential damage done to the environment. You would not, as a virtuous person, wish to add to this. You would also wish, through your charitable giving, to help the developing countries control their population growth. This would in turn have beneficial effects on disease and poverty in developing countries.

There are those, however, who argue that this is a simplistic view of care, based on a consequentialist form of Virtue Ethics. Therefore, for example, some would see the Chinese one-child policy as an illustration of care for humanity and others would regard it as inhumane and therefore not virtuous.

The difficulty in giving a hard and fast answer to the morality of contraception highlights a major flaw in Virtue Ethics as an ethical approach. As the approach depends on the virtuous nature of the individual, each case and each situation becomes unique. For instance, it would be morally virtuous for a person not to wish to infect his or her partner with AIDS/HIV, while it would not be virtuous for a person to use contraception as an aid to sleeping around.

Homosexuality

Introduction

The term homosexual refers to gay and lesbian people: any person that has a sexual preference for someone of the same sex. In the late nineteenth century people with homosexual tendencies were regarded in America as mentally unstable and in the United Kingdom as criminals. Gay sexual relationships were illegal in Great Britain until the late 1960s, when the law was changed to permit gay men to have sexual relationships in the privacy of their own home. At that stage the law determined the age of consent for a gay male as 21. Later changes in the law have lowered the age of consent to 16. Lesbian sexual relationships have never been illegal in the United Kingdom.

Homosexuality and Christian thought

Christians continue to be divided over the issue of homosexuality. Most Christians take their beliefs from the Bible and the traditions of the Church and use their own reason. The emphasis that they place on each of these three sources of authority will influence their view on homosexuality.

Homosexuality and biblical teaching

There are only a few references to homosexuality in the Old Testament. There is an obvious attack on homosexuality in Leviticus:

> *If a man lies with a male as with a woman, both of them have committed an abomination. (Leviticus 20:13)*

The only references to homosexuality in the Old Testament, relate exclusively to gay male relationships. They are condemned. There is no biblical reference to lesbian relationships, even though they existed in the ancient Middle East.

The New Testament has even fewer references to homosexuality. Jesus does not mention homosexuality at all. It doesn't appear in the Sermon on the Mount, which contains Jesus' most important moral teachings.

Liberal Christian views

Liberal Christians, both Protestant and Catholic, take a different viewpoint on the issue of homosexuality. They use the idea of *telos* to attack the basic conclusion of Catholic teaching that homosexual acts are sinful. Their argument is that the *telos* of eudaimonia can only be fulfilled in a stable and loving relationship. God would not wish any human being to suffer a life which is unfulfilled.

Liberal Christians point also to the way biblical passages against homosexuality are used. They point out that Paul, who attacks 'homosexual perversions' is the same man who recommends the institution of slavery and tells women to be silent in church. They argue that few if any traditionalist Christians would accept Paul's view on women and on slavery, so why accept his views on homosexuality? The former archbishop of Cape Town, Desmond Tutu, argues that homosexuals should be treated equally to heterosexuals because they are not to blame for how they were created:

> There is no longer Jew or Greek . . . there is no longer male and female; for all of you are one in Christ Jesus. (Galatians 3:28)

The former bishop of Edinburgh, Richard Holloway, asserts that Christians are called to break down barriers, to be social campaigners for the Gospel of love. He states that far from being in the vanguard of change the Church has often been trying to defend ideas that society has already abandoned.

Liberal Christians take some of their ideas from situation ethics. Fletcher's concept of agape inspired a generation of Episcopalians to take up the mantle of social reform. Bishop Gene Robinson, who is openly gay, regards love as the central theme of God's moral law. He believes that Christians have a duty to practise God's fundamental law – the Golden Rule of Jesus. Situation ethics judges every case on the litmus test of agape. For Robinson, agape reflects itself in commitment to your partner. Therefore sexual intercourse should be judged in terms of the type of relationship that an individual has. Sex is morally wrong if it is promiscuous or for money. Homosexual acts should be judged morally on the same criteria as those of heterosexuals.

Christianity in America is very strong but it is also very divided. On one side are the traditionalists and fundamentalists. Opposed to them are the liberal churches. The Episcopal Church, the American equivalent of the Church of England, historically bridges the divide between traditionalists and liberals. Therefore conflict over homosexuality is strongest within the Episcopalian Church. The appointment of Gene

Robinson as Bishop of New Hampshire has created serious divisions, with some more traditional parishes and dioceses setting up their own church structure.

Christian attitudes to homosexuality, in conclusion, vary enormously. The traditionalist approach, which condemns what it considers the sin of homosexual acts but not the sinner, is the most widely held. This can be found in both the teachings of Protestant and Roman Catholic churches. There are, though, many Christians who dissent from this view. They argue that God is love and would not wish for a group in society to be prevented from doing something that brings no harm to others. They regard love and mutual respect as foundation stones of the Christian faith. The issue continues to be a source of conflict among Christians.

Gay Pride is an annual celebration of lesbian, gay, bisexual and transgendered identity. The rainbow flag is a symbol of the diversity of society.

Homosexuality and Natural Law

Catholic teachings on homosexuality are based on Natural Law. God created male and female to become one flesh, as Genesis puts it, and to reproduce. The act of sexual intercourse has as its *telos* the birth of a child. Homosexual acts can never reproduce and therefore gay sex can never conform to the intention of procreation. Homosexual intercourse is therefore morally wrong. While gay men and women may love each other, the Roman Catholic Church maintains that any sexual act is morally wrong since it can never fulfil its *telos*.

Roman Catholic teaching is therefore quite clear and is based on Scripture and Natural Law. The Catholic Church teaches that such acts are always violations of divine and Natural Law. Yet, in recent years, there has been a softening of Catholic attitudes to homosexuals. While homosexual acts are still forbidden, Catholics are encouraged to understand the gay or lesbian person. In a *Letter to the bishops of the Church on the pastoral care of homosexual persons*, Pope John Paul II argued that the sin should be condemned but not the sinner.

Homosexuality and Kantian ethics

Kant argued that homosexuality is wrong. He did so for a number of reasons. His direct comments on the subject suggest that the power of the Natural Law theory (sexual intercourse that does not have the potentiality for human life is immoral) was still a great influence on him. He wrote that homosexuality was a **crimine carnis** (a crime of the flesh) and that it degrades human beings below the level of animals.

Kant regarded all sexual activity outside of marriage as a means to an end rather than an end in itself. This includes homosexuality, which was legal at the time in his native Prussia. His reason for rejecting any extramarital sexual relationships is that marriage is a permanent commitment while extramarital affairs are unstable.

It can be fairly asked how Kant would have reacted to homosexuality today, in a world of civil partnerships and gay marriages. Some argue that he would have had a different attitude to homosexuality within the legal framework of marriage. Alan Soble, in *Kant and Sexual Perversion*, doubts this. The reason for this is that homosexuality fails to cross the hurdle of an aspect of the Categorical Imperative. This is:

> *Act only on that maxim whereby which you can at the same time will that it become a universal law. (Immanuel Kant,* Groundwork for the Metaphysics of Morals*)*

You may remember that it is on this basis that Kant condemns suicide. Now suppose you believe that there is nothing morally bad about homosexuality. You would, using Kant's method, look at a single case and then apply it to all cases. You would in doing so note a big problem. If everyone were to become homosexual the population of the world would decline to zero. The human race would have committed mass suicide. As a result, Kant maintains that homosexuality is morally bad.

Kant's views on homosexuality are open to criticism. Writing in *The World as Will and Representation* the German philosopher, Arthur Schopenhauer (1788–1860), considered what he called the **paradox** of homosexuality. He attacked Kant's views on homosexuality by asserting that it is a means of preventing greater evils. What is the greater evil that homosexuality prevents? It is the birth of unwanted children.

Others note that Kant was a celibate; he never married. Now, if Kant's own rule was applied to **celibacy** then, as with homosexuality, the whole human race would disappear. Does this mean that all human beings have a duty to marry and reproduce? In a world of overpopulation this may seem an immoral suggestion. Modern philosophers have therefore found it hard to create a strong case for using Kant's ideas when dealing with homosexuality. They often appear contradictory.

Homosexuality and Utilitarianism

The utilitarian approach to homosexuality is very different from that of Kant. Contemporary utilitarians argue that there is nothing wrong with homosexuality. In 2009 Peter Singer produced an article entitled 'Homosexuality is not immoral'. This looks at both the morality of gay relationships and also at the legal situation. Countries should not outlaw an activity that is morally neutral. No sexual activity is moral or immoral in itself; it depends on its effects. This consequentialist view states that whatever sexual activity provides the greatest pleasure or social welfare is the right one. A utilitarian would ensure that there are safeguards as there are with heterosexual acts. These safeguards would restrict activities to the privacy of the home or hotel room, so as not to offend others. People though should be free to do whatever they wish as long as it does not maximize harm or pain.

In early-nineteenth-century England homosexuality was commonly seen as morally evil and homosexual acts were sometimes punished harshly when juries were free to decide what was right and what was wrong. The mob often ruled. Homosexuals were regularly hanged. This was the situation when Jeremy Bentham wrote his *Essay on Paederasty* (the term paederasty means sex between a man and a boy; in the eighteenth century it was used as a general term for anal sex). His work is the first known defence of the homosexual act. It was written in 1785, but not published until after his death. Bentham argues from a utilitarian perspective. He argues that homosexual practices do not harm society and do not lead to the break-up of family life. Therefore, on utilitarian grounds homosexual activity is to be allowed even if, as was the case, Bentham disapproved of it. The law should only enter the bedroom when what occurs there does harm to society. Bentham compared the English situation with ancient Rome, where homosexuality was legal. He argued that Roman society was not affected detrimentally by homosexuality.

Mill supports the basic rationale of Bentham's message. In *On Liberty* he makes the point that some things are morally neutral but when performed in public would be in bad taste. Sexual acts fall in this category. Thus the law ought to ban homosexual acts in a public place but not in the privacy of your own home. It is a case of public decency.

The utilitarian approach has been attacked since Bentham's essay. The following criticisms have been made:

1. There is no such thing as public or private morality. What happens in the privacy of the bedroom has a relevance to society at large. Patrick Devlin (1905–1992), a prominent lawyer of the late twentieth century, argued that homosexuality should continue to warrant a prison sentence. Writing in 1959 he argued that it was impossible to distinguish between what was performed in a public place and what was done in private. He argued that many moral wrongs take place in the home, for example a woman may be beaten by her husband, but it would be wrong to legalize them.

2. The philosopher H.L.A. Hart (1907–1992) argued that there were two different theories of law. He calls these **legal paternalism** and **legal moralism**. He argues that the law should not interfere in the morals of individuals (legal moralism) but that it should interfere to protect the vulnerable (legal paternalism). He regards homosexual acts as applicable here. He argues that young and vulnerable people need the protection of the law when it comes to homosexuality.

Homosexuality and Virtue Ethics

There is no such thing as a single view on homosexuality among Virtue ethicists. Disagreements exist between those who emphasize the Natural Law origins of Virtue Ethics and those who do not. Those who rely on the teleological approach of Natural Law to develop a virtue framework regard homosexuality as being contrary to the conduct of a virtuous person. One argument is that an intrinsic virtue of humanity is the desire to reproduce and thereby to ensure that life goes on. Another virtuous state is that which is found in a loving and caring relationship, within the family. Such ideas can be found in the work of Germain Grisez and Rosalind Hursthouse. This view of Virtue Ethics rejects the idea that it is possible for homosexual couples to have the same reproductive and family life as that of heterosexuals. However, this view does not take into account the possibility for same-sex couples to create a family using modern fertility treatment.

There is another side to Virtue Ethics, which is concerned primarily with character traits. Some scholars argue that virtuous character traits can be found in the lives of homosexuals and therefore there is nothing incompatible between the virtuous life and being gay. What is more, as the American philosopher C.W. Von Bergen points out, there is nothing particularly virtuous in many married family situations. Some Virtue ethicists point to the temporary nature of many gay relationships as an example of how the gay lifestyle goes against the virtuous life. However, this can equally be applied to non-marital sexual partnerships.

How is it possible to assert, on the one hand, that the character of the moral agent is the most important criterion for what is ethical and then to criticize homosexual acts as immoral? The division within Virtue Ethics raises important questions about this ethical theory and its links to Natural Law. Some scholars argue that Virtue Ethics is subjective in nature and therefore what is meant by virtue can be interpreted in a variety of ways; some will condemn homosexual relationships while others will not. Another weakness is the view that while some homosexual relationships meet the criteria of a virtuous state – that they should be long-lasting, loving and caring – they are still condemned because the relationship is considered unnatural. There is the suggestion that some Virtue ethicists move the goalposts. Von Bergen's criticism of this position points the way to the acceptance of homosexual relationships by some Virtue ethicists.

Practice exam question

'Kantian ethics offers little help when discussing matters of sexual relationships.' Discuss.

A starting point for this essay might be that Kant sets out a view of sexual relationships that accepts its passionate nature. You may want to address the complexities in Kantian thought. You could look at the Categorical Imperative, particularly the idea that a person should never treat another as a means to an end. You could use this in discussing prostitution and casual sex. The importance of duty could be considered, including the idea of the permanence of relationships. Other areas that could be tackled include trust in relationships and the issues of homosexual relationships and contraception idea. In evaluating the question you may wish to argue that there are some aspects of Kantian morality that are useful and some that are not. You may wish to consider whether or not the weaknesses in his approach undermine the whole of his view of sexual relationships.

Develop your knowledge

There are numerous good introductions to sexual ethics, including:

Philosophy and Sex by Robert B. Baker, Kathleen J. Wininger and Frederick A. Elliston (Prometheus, 2008)

A Companion to Some Issues in Human Sexuality by Joanna Cox and Martin Davie (Church House Publishing, 2003)

A Companion to Ethics by Peter Singer (ed.) (Blackwell, 1993)

Glossary

a posteriori knowledge – knowledge gained by logical deductions made from observation and experience of the material world.

a priori – can be known without human experience.

a priori knowledge – knowledge that can be gained without human experience.

Act Utilitarianism – theory that individual actions must be determined by the amount they increase general utility or happiness, based on the principle of 'the greatest good of the greatest number'.

agape – one of the four words in Greek for love. Agape refers to communal love, which does not demand anything in return.

agapeism/agapeistic – the use of agape as the test for making moral decisions.

agent-centred – concerned with the moral agent, i.e. the person who makes an ethical decision or is primarily affected by one.

analytic statement – a statement that only requires the words within it to verify whether it is true or false. For example, 'all bachelors are single men' requires simply an understanding of the meaning of the word bachelor to verify the statement.

anthropocentrism – regarding humankind as the central or most important element in existence.

anthropomorphism – the attribution of human characteristics to an object, animal or God.

antinomianism – the idea that chosen Christians are freed, by God's grace or predestination, from the obligation to observe moral laws.

anti-realism – rejection of the idea that things have an intrinsic value independent of the human mind.

Arminianism – followers of Jacobus Arminius, a Dutch Protestant theologian. They rejected predestinationism and asserted the importance of human responsibility for moral actions.

autonomous individual – a person who is free to choose.

autonomous morality – morality determined by the self.

biodiversity – the variety of plant and animal life in the world or in a particular habitat

Categorical Imperative – something human beings are duty-bound to do, whatever the circumstances.

celibacy – abstaining from marriage and sexual relations.

Church Fathers – any of the great bishops, early philosophers and theologians and other eminent Christian teachers of the early centuries. They are divided into the Latin Fathers, such as St Augustine of Hippo (354–430), and the Greek Fathers, for example St Basil the Great (330–379).

cognitivism – the belief that moral truths exist and that ethical statements can be verified empirically.

consequentialism – the consequences of an action solely determine whether it is the right thing to do.

conservation – preservation, protection or restoration of the natural environment and wildlife.

constant union of objects – the inter-relationship of things, the causal link.

denomination – refers to the different branches of the Christian Church.

deontology – a moral system based on duty. What is moral is what you have a duty to do.

descriptive – describing how things are.

designer baby – a baby whose genetic make-up has been selected to ensure the presence or absence of particular genes or characteristics.

DNA – deoxyribonucleic acid, which carries the genetic information of living beings. DNA is the main constituent of chromosomes.

donor father – a man who donates his sperm for use in fertility treatment.

ecocentrism – the belief that the rights and needs of humans are not more important than those of other living things.

ecosystem – biological community of interacting organisms and their physical environment.

ego – the conscious sense of self as presented to the external world, mediating between the id and the superego.

Electra complex – the sexual desire of a daughter for her father and the sense of rivalry with the parent of the same sex.

embryo – unborn human, especially in the first eight weeks from conception, after implantation and before all organs are developed.

emotivism – the idea that moral judgements are expressions of the moral agent's feelings rather than statements of fact.

empirical – based on observation or experience rather than theory.

empiricism – the idea that knowledge can only be gained by analysing sensory experiences of the material world.

ensoulment – when the soul enters the foetus and it becomes a human being.

epistemology – the theory of knowledge, including the origin of knowledge, the roles of experience and reason in generating knowledge and the validity of knowledge.

eschatology – study of ideas about the end of life/time and the Day of Judgement and resurrection.

eschaton – the end of the world, the final event in the divine plan.

ethical naturalism – belief that moral laws can be verified through observation of the natural world.

eudaimonia – Greek for happiness, flourishing or a state of contentment.

eugenics – science of improving the population by controlled breeding to increase the occurrence of characteristics which are viewed as desirable.

extramarital sex – sexual act between a married person and someone other than their marriage partner.

the Fall – the story in Genesis 3 of Adam and Eve's fall from grace. Christian writers, from Paul onwards, saw the events of the Fall as the defining moment when human beings set themselves apart from God.

foetus – unborn human more than eight weeks after conception.

form – in Plato an ideal that exists independent of human life, such as beauty, truth or virtue.

free will – the ability to act as you choose, without constraint.

freedom of choice – the idea that human beings exercise free will.

fundamentalism – the belief in the strict literal interpretation of Scripture and sacred texts. In Christianity this is the belief in the literal interpretation of the Bible.

Gaia – the earth viewed as a vast self-regulating organism, as put forward by James Lovelock and Lynn Margulis.

genome – the complete set of genes or genetic material present in a cell or organism.

globalisation – the process by which businesses or other organizations develop international influence or start operating on an international scale.

globalism – viewing the world on a global basis rather than in terms of nations.

Golden Mean – the situation when something works efficiently by avoiding extremes of excess and deficiency.

Golden Rule – the Golden Rule of Jesus is 'do to others as you would have them do to you' (Matthew 7:12). It can also be expressed as 'love your neighbour as yourself' (Mark 12:31).

grace – a gift or favour of God.

Green lobby – pressure groups that campaign on ecological issues.

hard determinism – the idea that human beings are controlled by external forces and are not able to exercise free will.

Hedonic Calculus – system of calculating whether an action will maximize pleasure and minimize pain.

hedonism – the pursuit of pleasure.

heteronomous morality – morality determined by others, such as parents and society.

Hypothetical Imperative – something human beings ought to do, to achieve a certain end.

id – the unconscious part of the psyche which creates impulses and desires.

idealism – philosophical viewpoint that argues that ideas/ideals exist and are discovered by the mind.

immanence – idea that God is present in and sustains every part of the universe.

inference of the mind – the way the mind infers related ideas from empirical data.

insurgency – rebels or revolutionaries rising in active revolt.

intuitionism – belief that ethical propositions are true or false and known by intuition.

last resort – in Just War theory, the idea that war should only take place after every peaceful method of resolving conflict has been attempted.

legalism – excessive adherence to law or formula.

liberal Christians – Christians that believe in the centrality of the individual conscience in moral matters and in social justice.

libertarianism – the idea that human beings are able to exercise free will when making decisions.

liberty of spontaneity – the freedom to decide how to act in response to a determined event.

logical positivism – the belief that the only meaningful philosophical problems are those which can be solved by logical analysis.

magisterium – the teaching authority of the Roman Catholic Church.

Marxism – a philosophical, political and economic view of man and society developed by Karl Marx and Friedrich Engels. Marxists typically perceive the social world in terms of class and economic factors and are practically committed to a social revolution that will better the position of oppressed classes.

material substance – the physical object.

maxim – a moral principle, which demands practical application.

moral agent – the person who makes an ethical decision or is primarily affected by one.

moral law – in Kantian ethics a rule for how you should act, based on a maxim.

naturalistic fallacy – the idea that just because nature acts in a certain way it does not follow that this is how things ought to be.

negative autonomy – harmful effects of personal freedom, for example, ability to cause harm to the self through drug addiction or sexually transmitted infections.

non-cognitivism – the belief that moral truths are matters of personal choice and do not exist independent of human experiences.

objectivism – the notion that certain things, especially moral truths, are independent of personal or communal opinions or values. Moral objectivists assert that the validity of ethical statements cannot be a matter of subjective personal choice.

Oedipus complex – the sexual desire of a son for his mother and the sense of rivalry with the parent of the same sex.

optimific – the maximization of pleasure, happiness, welfare or whatever concept(s) a particular utilitarian thinks is essential for human fulfilment and well-being.

pacificism – belief that war and violence are only justifiable in defence of vulnerable and defenceless people.

pacifism – the belief that war and violence are unjustifiable and that all disputes should be settled peacefully.

paternalism – the idea that a person or group in authority is qualified to make decisions in the best interests of another person or group.

personhood – the attributes that make a human being an individual. This is partly the character of the individual and in part it is those things that give the human being freedom from others, for example, the right to make decisions.

phronesis – a Greek word that is best translated as practical wisdom. It is the ability to reflect on what ought to be done to achieve a virtuous end and what effects that action will have.

positive autonomy – positive effects of personal freedom, for example, ability to make personal decisions about marriage, partnership, love etc.

predestination – the doctrine that some people are born selected for salvation and others for damnation; how they act during their life cannot affect this.

premarital sex – sex before marriage.

prescriptive – instructing how to act.

primary precepts – general rules inbuilt into human beings as a consequence of being made by God.

principle of equal consideration of interests – idea in the work of Singer that individuals' preferences must be rooted in the notion that what I prefer must consider other people's interests and that what other people prefer must have regard to my interests. This is applicable to all sentient beings.

principle of justice – Sidgwick's idea that justice is as important as happiness in determining the utility of an action or moral rule.

property rights – idea that you have certain rights. One of these is that what you own is yours to use as you wish. This includes your body.

proposition – a statement or assertion that expresses a judgement or opinion.

qualitative Utilitarianism – an analysis of actions or moral rules that takes into account the quality of happiness or welfare produced.

Quality of Life – idea that for life to be considered worthwhile a human being has to possess certain attributes, for example sentience, ability to communicate, to reason, to work and enjoy leisure, etc.

quantitative Utilitarianism – an analysis of actions or moral rules that takes into account the quantity of happiness or welfare produced.

rational forms – concepts such as justice, truth or beauty.

realism – belief that concepts have a value in and of themselves, which is independent of the human mind, of opinions or of feelings.

reason – the ability to analyse an argument, to criticize it and to calculate logically its strengths and weaknesses.

relativism – the theory that there are no universal truths; truth is relative to the subject and can vary from person to person and society to society.

Rule Utilitarianism – theory that life is too short to judge every action on the basis of 'the greatest good of the greatest number'. Instead rules exist, which are based on the maximization of happiness principle, that make it easier to act.

salvation history – the idea that the Bible documents God revealing himself in history as Saviour.

Sanctity of Life – the sacredness of human life.

saviour sibling – a baby whose genetic make-up has been selected so their stem cells can be used in treatment of a sibling.

secondary precepts – any rule that is rationally deduced from one of the primary precepts. Thus suicide is morally wrong because human beings have a natural inclination to preserve life.

sentient – able to experience sense or feeling.

sentient-centred – concerned with all sentient animals and not just humans.

slippery slope argument – the theory that a course of action may lead by degrees to something bad happening or a situation getting progressively worse.

soft determinism – the idea that human beings' actions are to some extent controlled by external forces, but they are still held accountable for their choices.

soul – the spiritual, non-physical part of a human being or animal regarded as immortal.

spare embryo – during the in vitro fertilization process several embryos will be developed; of these the best will be implanted into the woman. The unused embryos can be frozen for later treatment, donated for research, training or to other patients or they may be destroyed.

stem cell – a cell at an early stage of development which has the potential to develop into any type of cell, for example a blood cell or a brain cell.

stewardship – the responsibility to manage or look after another's property. In Christianity, the God-given responsibility to care for the world.

summum bonum – the highest good, which is only achievable in the moral community.

superego – the moral conscience that advises the ego and regulates the id.

supervenience – the idea that the rights and wrongs of a practical moral issue are consequent on a concept or religious belief.

surrogate mother – a woman who bears a child on behalf of another woman. This can be from the implantation of a fertilized egg from the other woman or by using her own egg fertilized by the other woman's partner.

sustainability – conserving an ecological balance by avoiding depletion of natural resources.

synod – an assembly of the clergy and sometimes the laity in a particular Church.

synthetic statement – a statement that requires external information, usually empirical data, to verify whether it is true or false. For example, 'the Battle of Hastings took place in 1066' requires empirical information from contemporary documents and archaeological evidence to verify the statement.

tabula rasa – the mind as a blank slate before ideas are imprinted on it by sensory reactions to the external world.

teleology – designed for or directed towards a final end.

Torah – the Torah contains the first five books of the Old Testament, the so-called books of Moses. The books are Genesis, Exodus, Leviticus, Numbers and Deuteronomy. These books have within them the Mosaic Law, which is central to Jewish ethical tradition.

trade union – a group of trades or professions formed to protect their rights and interests.

transcendental idealism – Kant's theory that humans construct knowledge by imposing universal concepts onto sensory experiences.

universalizability – the principle that moral values are universal and therefore universally applicable.

verification principle – statements are only valid if they can be verified or deduced from empirical data.

Virtue Ethics – morality based on the good an action produces for the moral agent.

voluntarism – morality based on obedience to the will of God or a system of thought.

welfare cost–benefit analysis – a system of discovering whether the social and economic benefits of a decision are outweighed by its cost and disadvantages.

Index